NIKON D750

THE EXPANDED GUIDE

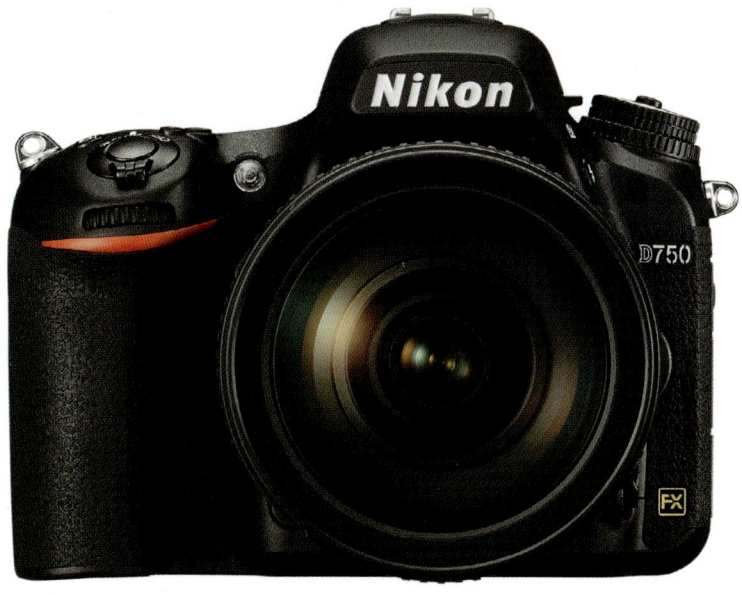

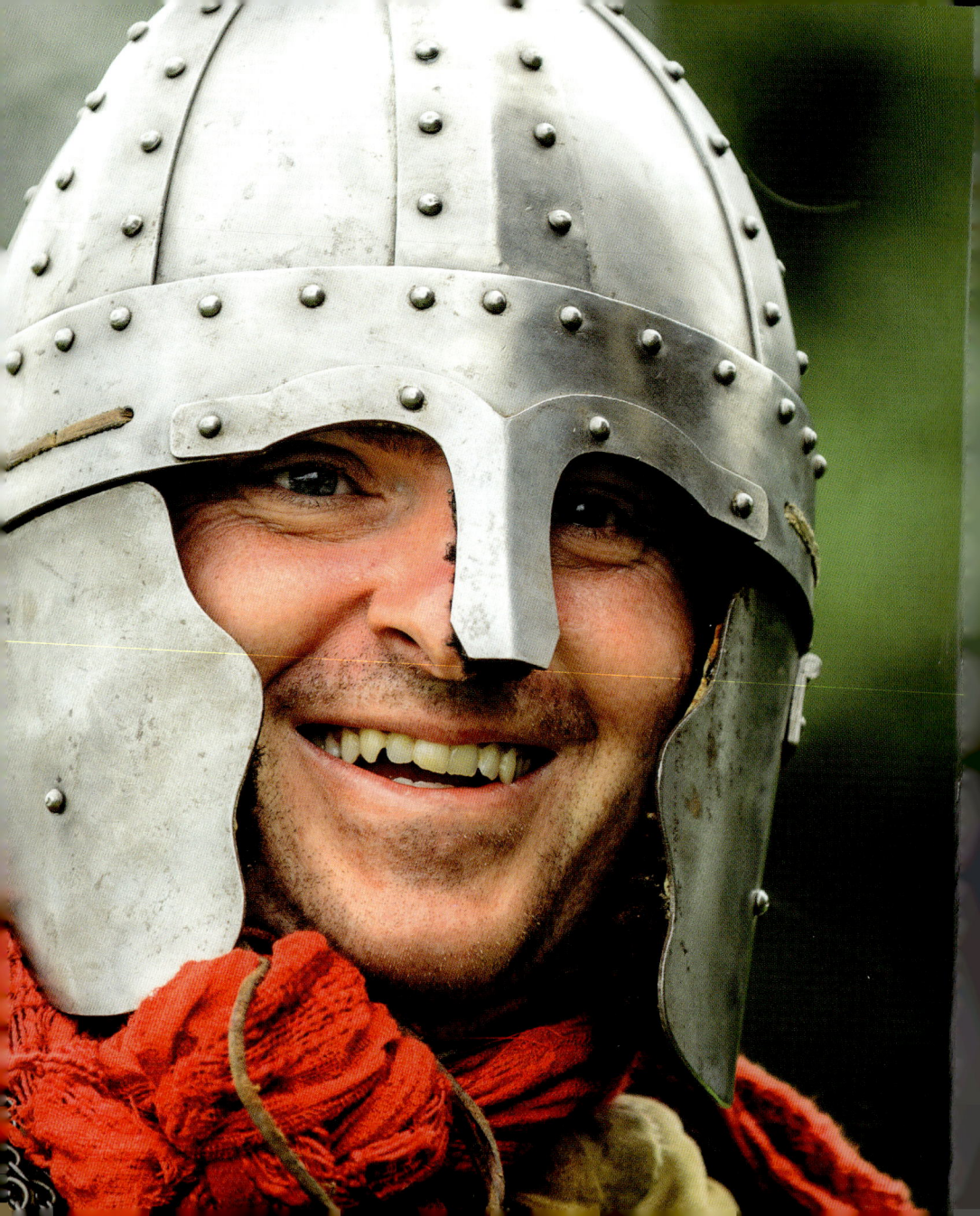

NIKON D750

THE EXPANDED GUIDE

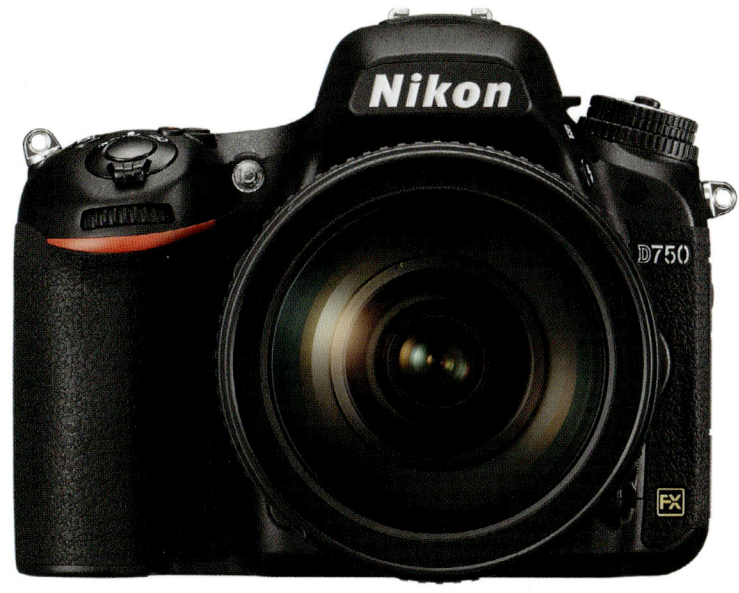

Jon Sparks

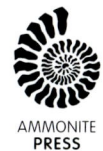

AMMONITE
PRESS

First published 2015 by
Ammonite Press
an imprint of AE Publications Ltd
166 High Street, Lewes, East Sussex, BN7 1XU, UK

Text © AE Publications Ltd, 2015
Images © Jon Sparks, 2015
Product photography © Nikon, 2015
Copyright © in the Work AE Publications Ltd, 2015

ISBN 978-1-78145-142-7

The rights of Jon Sparks to be identified as the author
of this work have been asserted in accordance with the
Copyright, Designs, and Patents Act 1988, Sections 77
and 78.

While every effort has been made to obtain permission from
the copyright holders for all material used in this book, the
publishers will be pleased to hear from anyone who has not
been appropriately acknowledged, and to make the correction
in future reprints.

The publishers and author can accept no legal responsibility for
any consequences arising from the application of information,
advice, or instructions given in this publication.

British Library Cataloging in Publication Data: A catalog record
of this book is available from the British Library.

Editor: Rob Yarham
Series Editor: Richard Wiles
Design: Richard Dewing Associates

Typefaces: Giacomo
Color reproduction by GMC Reprographics
Printed in China

PAGE 2 ‹‹
HISTORY MAN
The D750's autofocus is
as good as any current
DSLR. There was certainly
no hesitation with this
shot and the image is
absolutely pin-sharp.
300mm, 1/1000 sec.,
f/4.5, ISO 400.

» CONTENTS

1 OVERVIEW

The Nikon D750 is a new addition to the company's range of full-frame digital SLR (DSLR) cameras, taking its place between the D610 and D810, and borrowing features from both. For instance, its 24-megapixel sensor is similar, though not identical, to that in the D610, and its overall dimensions are closer to this camera too. On the other hand, its autofocus system is akin to the D810's (and to the top-of-the range D4s), although said to have been improved still further. Its maximum shooting speed is faster than either the D810 or D610. There are also a couple of standout features which distinguish it from any other full-frame Nikon, namely a semi-articulated screen (a boon for movie shooters in particular) and onboard WiFi connectivity.

READY TO SHOOT »
When you unpack a new camera, it's tempting to start shooting right away—and taking pictures is the best way to learn. However, it still makes sense to peruse this book sooner rather than later, to ensure you don't miss out on new features and functions.
85mm, 1/100 sec., f/8, ISO 100.

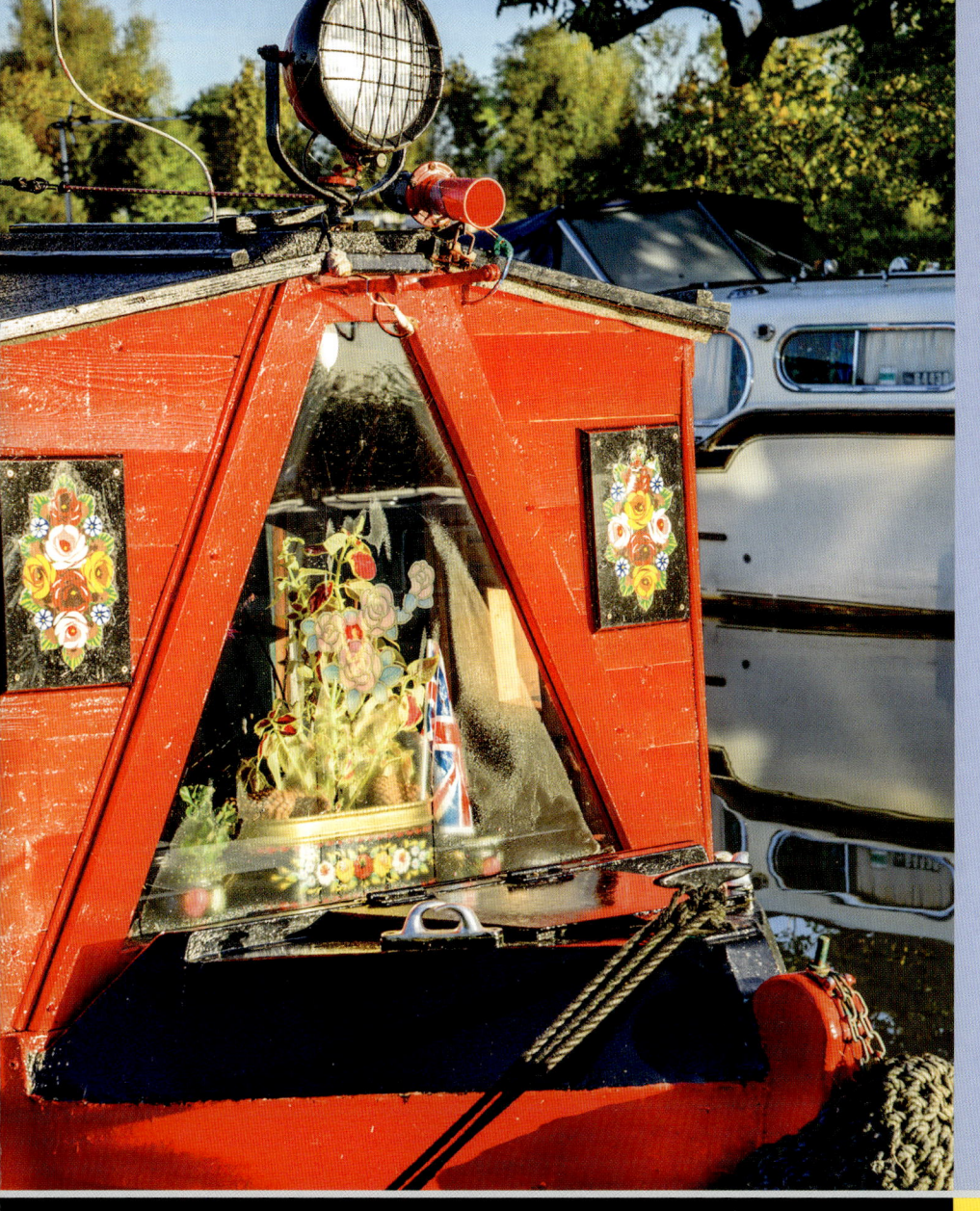

1

› Evolution of the Nikon D750

Among major camera makers, Nikon has always been noted for continuity as well as innovation. When the main manufacturers introduced their first viable autofocus 35mm cameras in the 1980s, most of them jettisoned their existing lens mounts, but Nikon stayed true to its tried and tested F-mount system. It's still possible to use the vast majority of classic Nikon lenses with the latest digital cameras like the D750, although some camera functions may be lost.

For this and other reasons, "evolution" accurately describes the development of Nikon's digital cameras. Nikon's first digital SLR was the E2s. Sporting a then-impressive 1.3-megapixel sensor, its body

design was based on the F801 35mm SLR. However, the true line of descent of the D750 begins with the 2.7-megapixel D1, in 1999. Its sensor adopted the DX format (see page 10), which remained in use with every Nikon DSLR prior to the D3.

Following the 2007 introduction of the D3 as Nikon's first full-frame DSLR, the D700 (2008) used the same sensor but in a smaller, lighter body. Physically and functionally, the D800/D800E (2012) appeared to be direct descendants of the D700, but internally there was a huge change—a jump from a 12-megapixel sensor to a 36-megapixel sensor. In the same year, Nikon also introduced the D600, a smaller and lighter full-frame DSLR; in fact its body dimensions and weight were remarkably similar to the DX-format D7000.

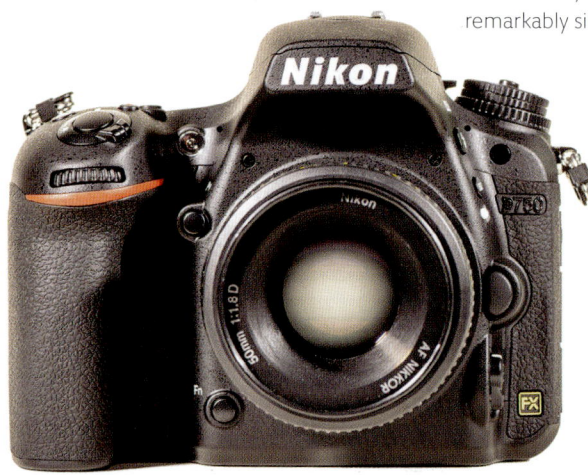

Nikon D1 (1999) ⌄

A truly ground-breaking camera, the Nikon D1 was arguably the first DSLR from any maker to offer a viable alternative to film—despite offering a mere 2.7 megapixels.

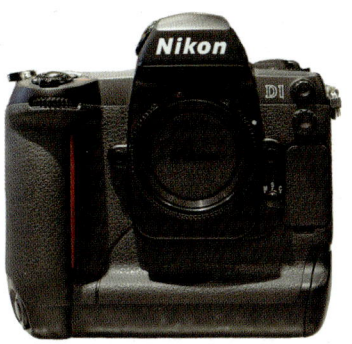

Nikon D3 (2003) ⌄

Nikon's first "full-frame" DSLR took the world by storm, its blistering speed, super-rugged build, and unprecedented low-light ability proving far more significant for many users than its conservative pixel count.

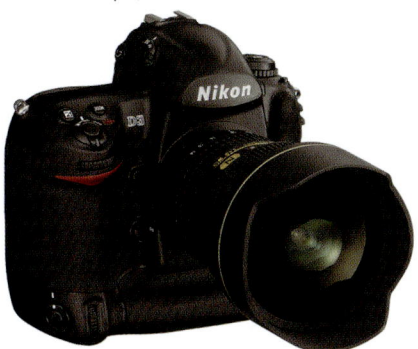

Nikon D700 (2008) ⌄

Nikon's second full-frame FX DSLR attracted many professionals and discerning amateurs, offering the same sensor and same superb image quality as the D3 in a lighter and more compact body.

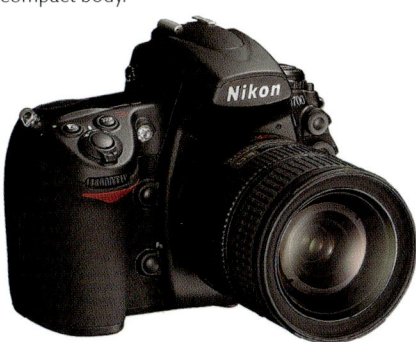

Nikon D610 (2010) ⌄

The D610 was in most respects identical to the D600, apart from a revamped shutter assembly introduced following problems with shutters in the D600 spraying tiny amounts of oil onto the low-pass filter over the sensor.

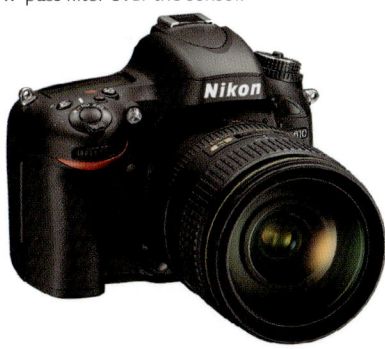

1

The 2014 launch of the D750 marked a further expansion of Nikon's full-frame DSLR lineup, which boasts five current models (D610, D750, D810, Df, and D4s). Nikon now offers a wider choice in FX format than in DX, where there are just three models (D3300, D5300, and D7100), although rumors continue to circulate about the possibility of a successor to the "pro DX" models (D300/D300s).

› Nikon FX-format sensor

The D750 is one of the lightest full-frame Nikon DSLRs to date, albeit a little heavier than the Df. It is also marginally lighter than the DX-format D7100. The body is a mix of polycarbonate and magnesium alloy, designed to reduce weight while remaining robust.

The D3 (2007) was the first Nikon DSLR to adopt a "full-frame" sensor, which Nikon designates FX. Measuring approximately 36 x 24mm, it's almost exactly the same size as a 35mm film frame. More than doubling the area of the DX sensor, the FX gathers more light and each individual photosite (pixel) is proportionately larger, an advantage of particular significance in the flagship D4s and the Df. Their "mere" 16.2 megapixels and consequently larger photosites give them the ability to capture extremely clean, low-noise images, even at very high ISO ratings: both allow ISO to be set all the way to an outlandish 204,800. The D810, on the other hand, boasts over 36 million pixels—this offers exceptional ability to capture fine detail, but only when using the very best lenses and impeccable technique. The D750 (like the D610), with 24 megapixels, adopts a middle way.

CMOS (Complementary Metal Oxide Semiconductor) sensors are now used across Nikon's DSLR range. The D750's CMOS sensor, with 24.3 million effective pixels, produces images at a native size of 6016 x 4016 pixels.

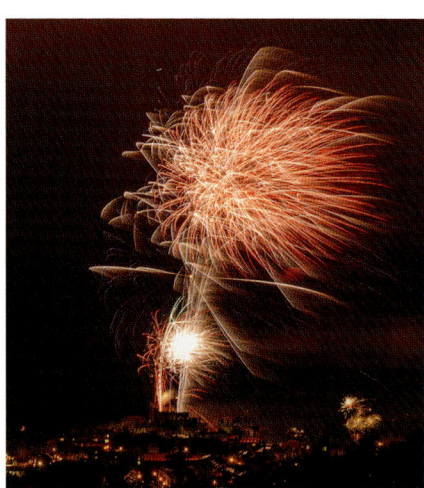

FIREWORKS 〈〈
The D750's sensor is very capable in many situations, including low light and long exposures.
62mm, 60 sec., f/16, ISO 100, tripod.

› About the Nikon D750

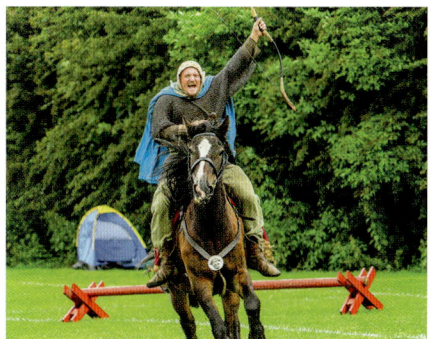

ACTION CAMERA   ⨠
The D750 has mostly been presented as
an action camera.
200mm, 1/1000 sec., f/4, ISO 1400.

The D750 is an extremely versatile camera,
but Nikon's marketing has mostly stressed
its capabilities as an action camera, both
for stills and movies. Key reasons for this
emphasis are its relatively light weight,
highly capable autofocus system,
respectable continuous shooting rate,
and its semi-articulated rear screen.

The D750 is the lightest full-frame
Nikon DSLR to date, albeit only a few
grams lighter than the D610 and Df. It is
also marginally lighter than the DX-format
D7100. The body is a mix of polycarbonate
and magnesium alloy, designed to reduce
weight while remaining robust.

In terms of speed, its autofocus system
is similar to that in the D810 and D4s, with

51 AF points, albeit covering a slightly
smaller area. While its maximum
continuous shooting rate of 6.5 frames per
second is substantially slower than the
11fps offered by the D4s, it does beat the
rest of the FX lineup.

For stills shooting, the semi-articulated
rear screen adds occasional flexibility but
doesn't aid speed, because focusing when
using the screen is considerably slower; its
main benefit is to improve handling when
shooting movies. The rear screen is a
bright, crisp 3.2-in. LCD panel; both the
screen and the pentaprism viewfinder give
100% image coverage.

Another feature which may speed up
operation for some users is the presence
of on-board WiFi, though its abilities here
are limited because (officially, at least) it
can only connect to mobile devices using
Nikon's own mobile app.

The 24-megapixel CMOS sensor offers
14-bit image conversion and self-cleaning
function. Images are processed using
Nikon's latest EXPEED 4 processing engine.
It also supports "Full HD" movie capture at
1920 x 1080 pixels.

Like all Nikon SLRs the D750 is part
of a vast system of lenses, accessories,
and software. This *Expanded Guide* to the
Nikon D750 will guide you through all
aspects of the camera's operation, and
its relation to the system as a whole.

1 » MAIN FEATURES OF THE NIKON D750

Sensor

24.3 effective megapixel FX-format RGB CMOS sensor, measuring 35.9 x 24mm, and producing a maximum image size of 6016 x 4016 pixels. Crop function allows capture in 1.2x and DX formats; self-cleaning function.

Image processor

EXPEED 4 image processing system featuring 14-bit analog-to-digital (A/D) conversion.

Focus

Multi-CAM 3500 FX II autofocus module with 51 AF points covering much of the image area, supported by Nikon Scene Recognition System, which tracks subjects by shape, position, and color. Three focus modes: (S) Single-servo AF; (C) Continuous-servo AF; and (M) Manual focus. Five AF-area modes: Single-area AF; Dynamic-area AF; 3D tracking; Group-area AF; and Auto-area AF. Rapid focus point selection and focus lock.

Exposure

Four metering modes: matrix metering; center-weighted metering; spot metering; highlight-weighted metering. 3D Color Matrix Metering III uses a 91,000-pixel color sensor to analyze data on brightness, color, contrast, and subject distance from all areas of the frame. With non-G/D type lenses, standard Color

Matrix Metering III is employed. Two fully auto modes: auto; auto (flash off). Four user-controlled modes: (P) Programmed auto with flexible program; (A) Aperture-priority auto; (S) Shutter-priority auto; (M) Manual. 16 Scene modes: portrait; landscape; child; sports; close-up; night portrait; night landscape; party/indoor; beach/snow; sunset; dusk/dawn; pet portrait; candlelight; blossom; autumn colors; food.

ISO

ISO range between 100 and 12,800, with extensions down to 50 (Lo) and up to 51,200 (Hi). Exposure compensation from −5 Ev to +5 Ev; exposure bracketing facility (up to nine-frame spread).

Shutter

Shutter speeds from 1/4000 sec. to 30 sec., plus B. Maximum frame advance 6.5fps.

Viewfinder and Live View

Pentaprism viewfinder with 100% coverage and 0.7x magnification. Live View available on rear LCD monitor.

Movie mode

Continuous feed in Live View mode allows movie capture in .MOV format (MPEG-4 compression) with image size (pixels) of: 1280 x 720, 1920 x 1080. Frame rates 60fps/30fps/25fps/24fps at large size; 60fps/50fps at smaller size.

Buffer

Buffer capacity allows up to 100 frames (JPEG fine, large) to be captured in a continuous burst at 6.5fps, up to 33 NEF (RAW) files (dependent on RAW settings).

Flash

Pop-up flash (manually activated) with Guide Number of 12 (m) or 39 (ft) at ISO 100 supports i-TTL balanced fill-flash for DSLR (when matrix or center-weighted metering is selected) or Standard i-TTL flash for DSLR (when spot metering is selected). Five flash-sync modes: Front-curtain sync; Red-eye reduction; Slow sync; Red-eye reduction with slow sync; Rear-curtain sync. Flash compensation from −3 to +1 Ev; FV lock.

LCD monitor

Semi-articulating 3.2-in., 1,229,000-pixel TFT LCD display with wide color gamut (close to sRGB) and 100% frame coverage.

Custom functions

Over 50 parameters and elements of the camera's operations can be customized through the Custom setting menu.

File formats

The D750 supports NEF (RAW) (14-bit and 12-bit) and JPEG (Fine/Normal/Basic) file formats.

System backup

Compatible with: more than 60 current and many more non-current Nikkor lenses (functionality varies with older lenses); SB-series flashguns; Multi-Power Battery Pack MB-D16; Wireless remote controller WR-1/WR-10; GPS unit GP-1; Stereo Microphone ME-1; and many other Nikon system accessories.

Connectivity

Onboard WiFi. Connectors for external microphone, USB, HDMI, and Nikon remote cords/wireless controllers.

Software

Supplied with Nikon View NX2 (incorporates Nikon Transfer 2); compatible with Nikon Capture NX-D and many third-party imaging applications.

1 » FULL FEATURES AND CAMERA LAYOUT

FRONT OF CAMERA

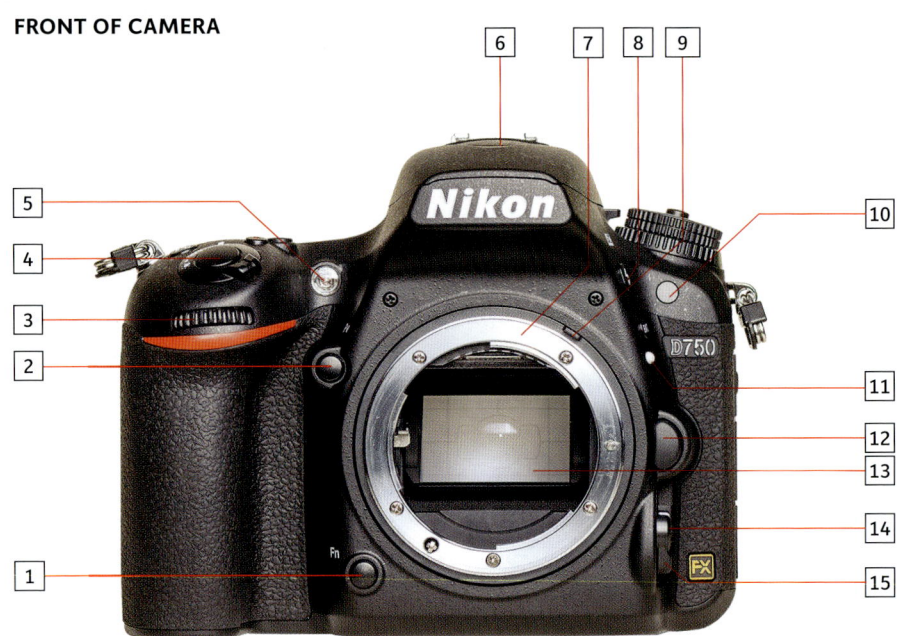

1	Fn button	10	Infrared receiver
2	Depth-of-field preview button	11	Mounting index
3	Sub-command dial	12	Lens-release button
4	Shutter-release button	13	Mirror
5	AF-assist illuminator/Self-timer/Red-eye reduction lamp	14	AF-mode button
		15	Focus mode selector
6	Built-in flash		
7	Lens mount		
8	Flash pop-up button		
9	Meter coupling lever		

BACK OF CAMERA

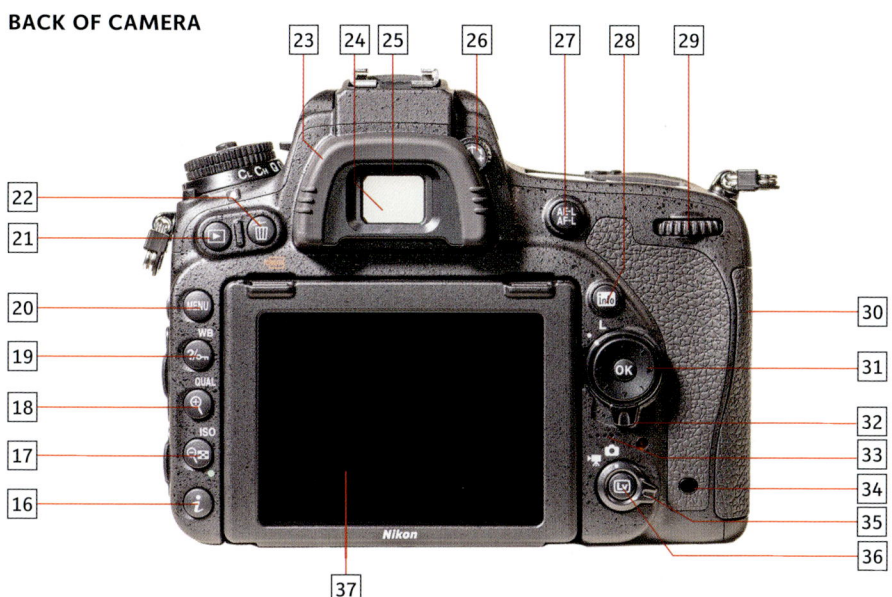

16	*i* button	27	AE-L/AF-L button
17	Thumbnail/playback zoom out/ ISO button	28	info button
		29	Main command dial
18	Playback zoom in/QUAL button	30	Memory card slot cover
19	Protect/Help button	31	Multi-selector
20	MENU button	32	Focus selector lock
21	Playback button	33	Speaker
22	Delete/Format button	34	Infrared receiver
23	Eyepiece	35	Live View selector
24	Viewfinder	36	Live View button
25	Rubber eye-cup	37	LCD monitor
26	Diopter adjustment dial		

1 » FULL FEATURES AND CAMERA LAYOUT

TOP OF CAMERA   **LEFT SIDE**

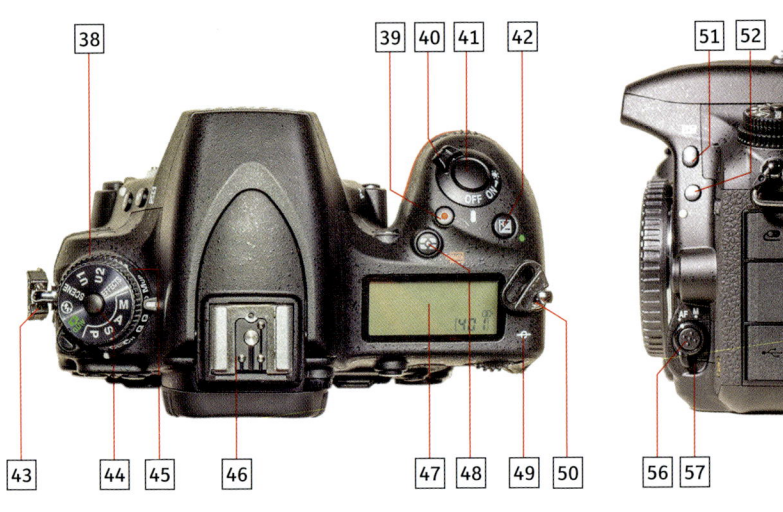

38 Mode dial	**47** LCD control panel	**51** Flash/Flash mode/Flash compensation button
39 Movie record button	**48** Metering/format button	**52** BKT button
40 Power switch	**49** Focal plane mark	**53** Accessory terminal
41 Shutter-release button	**50** Camera strap mount	**54** External microphone connector/headphone connector cover
42 Exposure compensation/ two-button reset button		**55** USB connector/HDMI mini-pin connector cover
43 Camera strap mount		**56** AF-mode button
44 Mode dial lock release		**57** Focus mode selector
45 Release mode dial		
46 Accessory hotshoe		

BOTTOM OF CAMERA

RIGHT SIDE

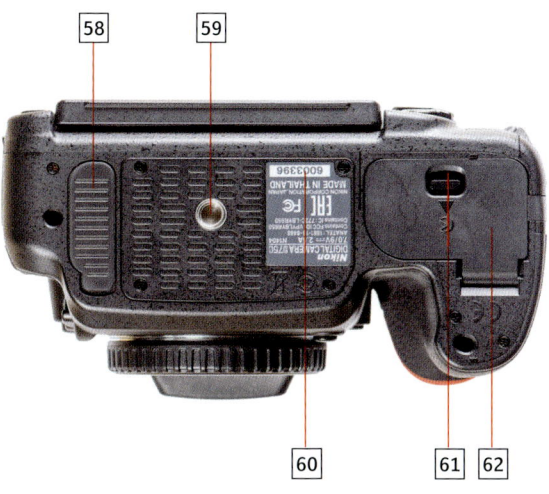

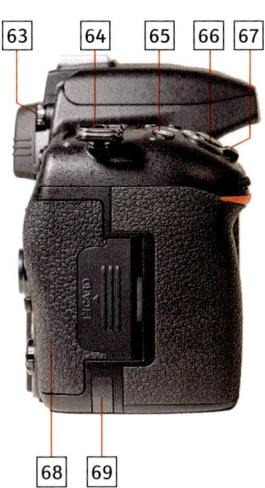

58	Contact cover for optional MB-D12 battery pack
59	Tripod socket (¼in)
60	Camera serial number
61	Battery compartment release lever
62	Battery compartment

63	Diopter adjustment dial
64	Camera strap mount
65	Exposure compensation/ two-button reset button
66	Shutter-release button
67	Power switch
68	Memory card slot cover
69	Power connector cover

1 » VIEWFINDER DISPLAY

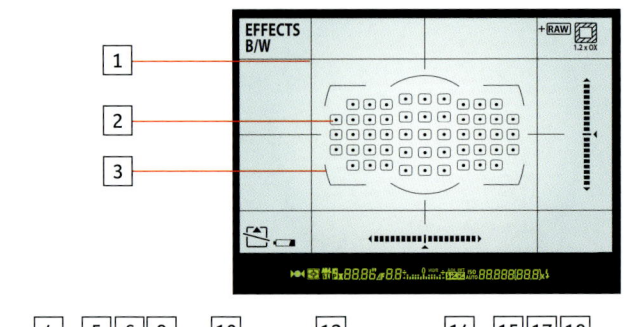

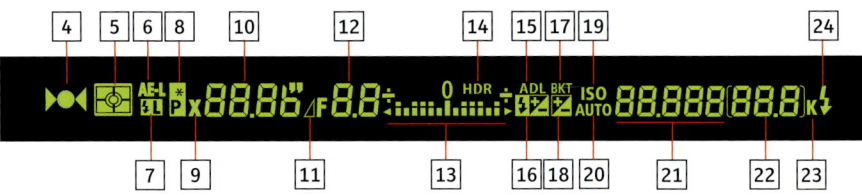

1	Framing grid	**14**	HDR indicator
2	Focus points AF-area mode	**15**	ADL indicator
3	AF-area brackets	**16**	Flash compensation indicator
4	Focus indicator	**17**	Exposure and flash, WB, or ADL bracketing indicator
5	Metering	**18**	Exposure compensation indicator
6	Autoexposure (AE) lock indicator	**19**	ISO sensitivity indicator
7	FV lock indicator	**20**	Auto ISO sensitivity indicator
8	Flexible program indicator	**21**	ISO sensitivity AF-area mode
9	Flash sync indicator	**22**	No. of exposures remaining in buffer Preset manual WB recording indicator Exposure or Flash compensation value
10	Shutter speed Autofocus (AF) mode	**23**	"K" (when over 1000 exposures remain)
11	Aperture stop indicator	**24**	Flash-ready indicator
12	Aperture (f-number or number of stops)		
13	Exposure indicator or Exposure compensation indicator		

» LCD CONTROL PANEL

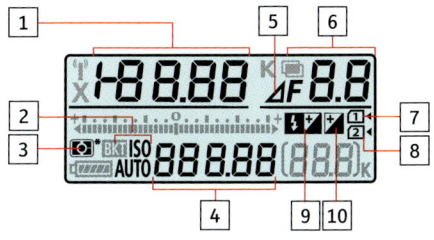

1 | Shutter speed
Exposure compensation value
Flash compensation value
White balance fine-tuning
Color temperature
White balance preset number
Number of shots in exposure and flash
 bracketing sequence
Number of shots in white balance
 bracketing sequence
Number of intervals for interval timer
 photography
Focal length (non-CPU lenses)

2 | ISO sensitivity indicator
Auto ISO sensitivity indicator

3 | Metering

4 | ISO sensitivity
Autofocus mode

5 | Aperture stop indicator

6 | Aperture (f-number)
Aperture (number of stops)
Bracketing increment
Number of shots in ADL bracketing
 sequence
Number of shots per interval
Maximum aperture (non CPU lenses)
PC mode indicator

7 | Memory card indicator (Slot 1)

8 | Memory card indicator (Slot 2)

9 | Flash compensation indicator

10 | Exposure compensation indicator

11 | WiFi indicator

12 | Flash sync indicator

13 | Exposure/bracketing indicator
Exposure
Exposure compensation
Exposure/flash bracketing
White balance bracketing
ADL bracketing

14 | Battery indicator

15 | Exposure/flash bracketing indicator
White balance bracketing indicator
ADL bracketing indicator

16 | Color temperature indicator

17 | Multiple exposure indicator

18 | Number of exposures remaining
Number of shots remaining before
 memory buffer fills
AF-area mode indicator
Preset manual white balance recording
 indicator
Time-lapse recording indicator
Manual lens number
Capture mode indicator

HDMI-CEC connection indicator

19 | "K" (appears when memory remains for
 over 1000 exposures)

The Nikon D750 has 18 separate buttons, half a dozen dials, and hundreds of items in its menus. If this plethora of controls seems overwhelming, it's important to realize that you don't have to master them all at once. The D750 can be used as simply as any "point-and-shoot" camera, but will still deliver far superior image quality.

The Nikon D750 arrives set to its simplest operating mode—AUTO Auto—and you can revert at any time by returning the mode dial to this position.

You can also quickly reset almost all other camera settings to the initial default by holding down the ⊕ and ⊠ buttons (marked with green dots) for at least 2 seconds; this is known as a two-button reset.

However, all those buttons and dials are a sign that the camera offers great versatility and imaging power. Leaving it at default settings misses out on much of this, but you don't need to dive in at the deep end either. The key is understanding which modes and which settings are suited to your photography. A great starting point is by exploring the Scene modes (see pages 36–43).

This chapter will cover the location and use of the main controls and explore the main shooting modes and other functions. The following chapter delves into the menus in more depth.

Tip

The camera also provides on-screen help during shooting and when using the menus. Press ?/O⊓ to bring up information relating to the item currently selected on the screen. During playback this button has a different function.

SEEING THE LIGHT   »
The D750 performs well in a wide range of situations, including low-light, and while its default settings will produce perfectly acceptable images, you will soon need to explore its functions more fully to achieve the best results. *85mm, 1/40 sec., f/10, ISO 800.*

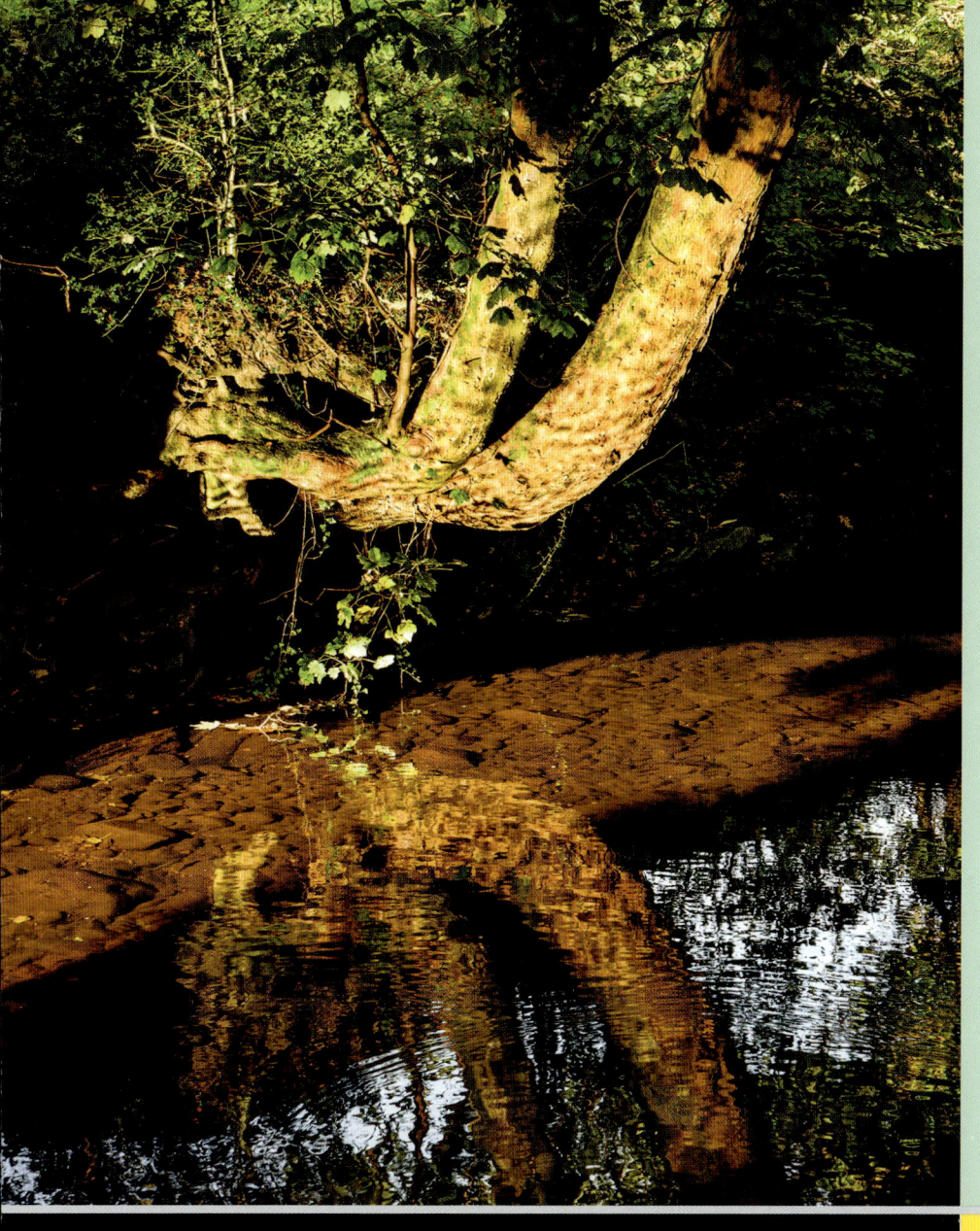

2 » CAMERA PREPARATION

Some basic operations, including charging the battery and inserting a memory card, are essential before the camera can be used. When first switched on, the camera will also prompt you to set language, time, date, and time zone (see under Setup menu, page 132).

› Attaching the strap

To attach the strap, ensure the padded side will face inwards (so the maker's name faces out). Attach one end to one of the

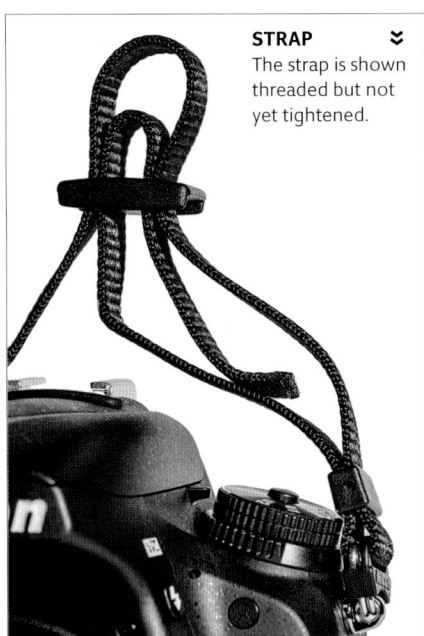

STRAP ⌄
The strap is shown threaded but not yet tightened.

eyelets located at top left and right sides of the camera. Release the strap from the buckle, then pass the free end through the eyelet. Bring the end back through the buckle, at the side further from the eyelet, then double back through the other side of the buckle. Adjust the length as required, but leave a decent "tail" for security. When satisfied with the length, tighten the strap firmly and slide up the sleeve to keep the "tail" neatly tucked away. Repeat the operation on the other side.

› Adjusting for eyesight

The D750 offers dioptric adjustment, between -3 and $+1m^{-1}$, to allow for individual variations in eyesight. Ensure this is optimized for your eyesight (wearing glasses or contact lenses if you normally do so) before using the camera. The diopter adjustment control is just to the right of the viewfinder. With the camera switched on, rotate this control until the viewfinder display (e.g. exposure readouts and other data) appears sharpest.

DIOPTER ADJUSTMENT DIAL ⌄

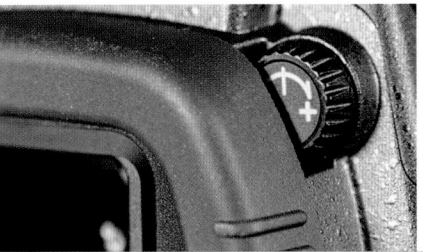

› Mounting lenses

Switch the camera off before changing lenses. Remove the rear lens cap and the camera body cap, or the lens, if already mounted. To remove a lens, press the lens-release button and turn the lens clockwise (as you face the front of the camera). Align the index mark on the lens with the one on the camera body (white dot), insert the lens gently into the camera, and turn it anti-clockwise until it clicks home. If the lens is correctly aligned it will mount smoothly; do not use force. Avoid touching electrical contacts on the lens and camera body. Dirty contacts can cause a malfunction. Replace the lens or body caps as soon as possible.

Most Nikon F-mount lenses can be used on the D750; see page 190 for more detail. When using lenses with an aperture ring, rotate this to minimum aperture before use on the D750.

LENS-RELEASE BUTTON   ❯❯

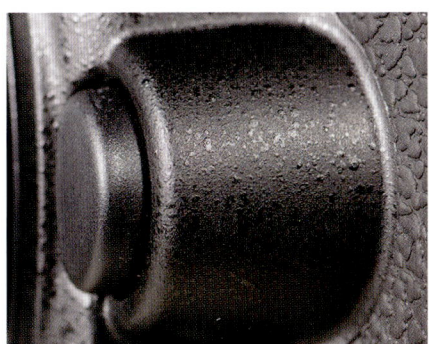

› Inserting and removing memory cards

The D750 has dual slots for Secure Digital (SD) cards, including high-capacity SDHC and SDXC cards. The upper slot is designated Slot 1; if you're only loading one card, use this slot. To manage the use of the two slots, see page 103.

1) Switch off the camera and check that the green access lamp (on the camera back below the Lv switch) is not lit.

DUAL MEMORY CARD SLOTS   ❯❯

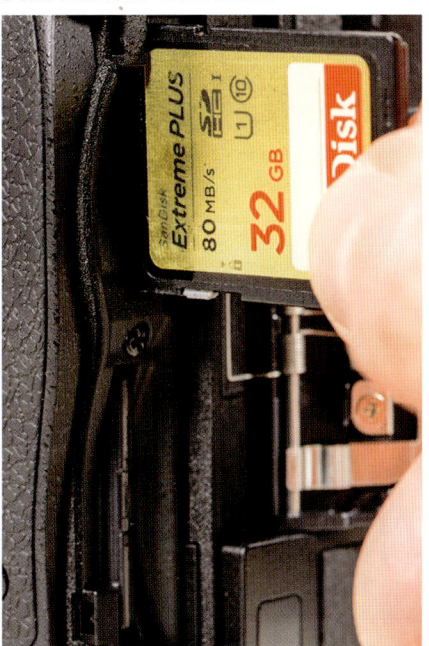

2

2) Slide the card slot cover on the right side of the camera gently to the rear, until it springs open.

3) To remove a memory card, press the card gently into the slot until it springs out slightly. Pull it gently from its slot.

4) Insert an SD card into the chosen slot, with its label side towards you and the "cut off" corner at top left. Slide the card into the slot until slight resistance is felt. Push more firmly (but without excessive force) and the card will click fully home. The green access lamp will light briefly.

5) Close the card slot cover.

Warning!

The card slot cover has no lock or latch and it is possible to open it accidentally, for instance when taking the camera from a bag or pouch. Take care at such times. The cover is secure enough in normal shooting.

Formatting a memory card

You'll need to format new memory cards, or ones that have been used in another camera, before using them with the D750. Formatting is also the most efficient way to erase images from a card so you can reuse it—but first make sure images have been saved elsewhere!

One way to format a card is to press and hold the two **FORMAT** buttons (m̄ and **MODE**) for a few seconds, until a blinking **FOR** appears in the viewfinder and control panel (and *Format* in the information display, if active). If both card slots are occupied, the icon for the card in Slot 1 (see page 23) will blink. Turn the main command dial to select Slot 2 instead. Release the buttons and press them again to format the selected card. Press any other button to exit without formatting it.

You can also format card(s) through the Setup menu (see page 130). I find this method quicker.

Either way, you must repeat the procedure to format the second card. You cannot format both cards simultaneously.

› Inserting the battery

The Nikon D750 is supplied with an EN-EL15 li-ion rechargeable battery, as used in other models like the D810 and D7100. The battery should be fully charged before first use.

Invert the camera and locate the battery compartment below the handgrip. Release the latch to open the compartment. Insert the battery, contacts first, with the flat face facing rearwards. Nudge the gold-colored latch aside, then slide the battery gently down until the latch clicks into position. Shut the battery compartment cover, ensuring it locks.

To remove the battery, switch off the camera, and open the compartment cover as above. Press the orange latch to release the battery and slide it gently from the compartment.

Battery charging

Use the supplied MH-25a charger to charge the battery (older MH-25 chargers are compatible). Connect the power cord to a mains outlet. Align the battery, terminals first, with the slot on the charger: the battery will only fit this when correctly orientated. Slide the battery into the slot until it snaps home.

The charge lamp blinks while the battery is charging, and shines steadily when charging is complete. A fully discharged battery will take around 2½ hours to recharge fully.

INSERTING THE BATTERY ⌄

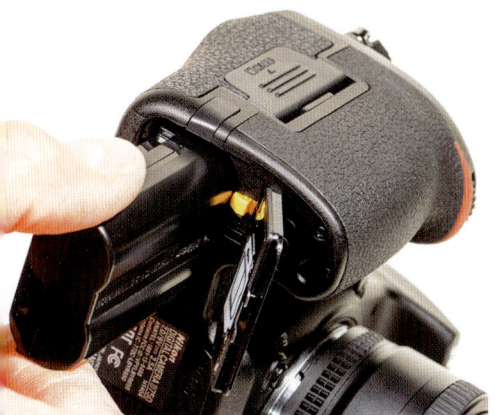

› Battery life

Battery life depends on various factors. Extreme cold can reduce battery life (see page 218). Other factors that increase battery drain include: heavy use of the LCD screen; use of the built-in flash; long auto meter-off delays; and continuous use of autofocus (as when tracking moving subjects). Extensive Live View/movie shooting is particularly draining.

Under stringent (CIPA) conditions, the D750 manages over 1200 shots from a fully charged EN-EL15 battery. In normal use, avoiding the draining factors noted above, you may do considerably better.

The control panel gives an approximate indication of remaining charge; for more detail see **Battery Info** in the Setup menu (see page 132).

A low battery icon appears in the viewfinder when the battery is approaching exhaustion. The control panel icon blinks when it is exhausted.

For information on alternative power sources, see page 213.

> ### Tip
>
> *The charger can be used abroad (100–240 V AC 50/60 Hz) with a suitable travel plug adapter. Do not use a voltage transformer.*

2 » BASIC OPERATION

With strap, lens, battery, and memory card on board, the D750 is ready to shoot. As soon as you want to change any settings, review or playback your shots, use Live View, or shoot movies, you'll need to refer to the rear screen—or, for many functions, you can use the control panel instead.

Many principal camera functions are accessed through the two command dials, mode dial, and release mode dial, alone or in conjunction with various buttons. Menu navigation is principally via the multi-selector. However, in Auto and Scene modes it is perfectly possible (although not necessarily recommended) to shoot with virtually no recourse to any of these.

Switching the camera on
The power switch has three positions:
OFF The camera will not operate.
ON The camera operates normally.
☀ Move the power switch beyond **ON** and release (it will not stay in this position). This illuminates the control panel for about 10 seconds. Custom setting d10 allows you to keep the panel illuminated whenever the camera is active.

Operating the shutter
The shutter-release button operates in two stages. Pressing it lightly, until you feel initial resistance, clears the information display, menus, or image playback (if active), and activates the metering and focus functions, making the D750 instantly ready to shoot. Press the button down fully to take the picture.

POWER SWITCH AND ⌄⌄
SHUTTER-RELEASE BUTTON

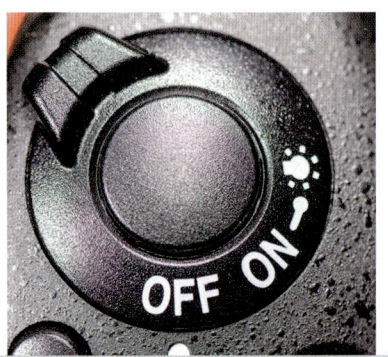

INFORMATION DISPLAY ON THE ⌄⌄
REAR LCD SCREEN

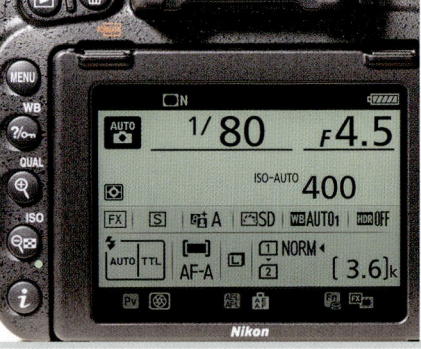

› Control panel and information display

Key shooting information is displayed in the small control panel on top of the camera. The same information, and more, can be viewed in a larger form—the information display—on the rear LCD screen by pressing `info`. As the D750 does not have a touchscreen, the information display is passive: you interact with it using buttons and dials. The D750 features a redesigned interface which makes this process easier.

⚙ button: quick settings
Pressing ⚙ brings up a list of key settings (other than those which have a dedicated button) to allow rapid access. Scroll through the list with the multi-selector and press ⓄⓀ to enter the corresponding item.
The following items are included:
Choose image area; **Set Picture Control**; **Active D-Lighting**; **HDR** (high dynamic range); **Remote control mode** (ML-L3);

PRESSING ⚙ ACCESSES KEY ITEMS ⯆ FROM THE CAMERA'S MENUS

Choose image area	FX
Set Picture Control	☐LS
Active D-Lighting	☐OFF
HDR (high dynamic range)	OFF
Remote control mode (ML-L3)	☐OFF
Assign Fn button	--
Assign preview button	--
Assign AE-L/AF-L button	--
	ⓘCancel

Assign Fn button; **Assign preview button**; **Assign AE-L/AF-L button**; **Long exposure NR**; **High ISO NR**.

Using the LCD screen
The screen can be tilted through a range of angles, enabling viewing when you can't use the camera at eye level. As it is more vulnerable to damage when opened out, make sure it's reset flush with the camera body when not needed.

> ### Tip
>
> *The screen can be hard to see clearly in bright sunlight. Screen shades are available which help to get around this problem (see page 213).*

A RANGE OF SCREEN POSITIONS ⯆

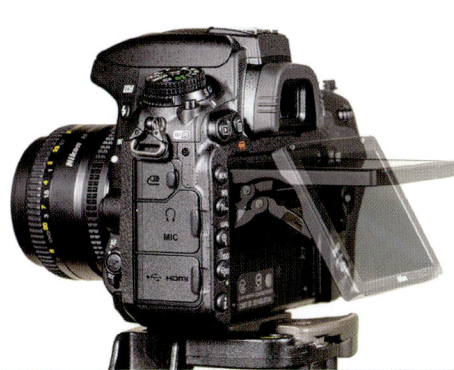

› Command dials

In the core "User-control" exposure modes (**P**, **S**, **A**, and **M**) (see page 44), the two command dials become fundamental to the operation of the D750. Additionally, they are used in conjunction with many of the control buttons to change key settings (see the table opposite): hold down the appropriate button and rotate the dial to make a selection. The plethora of different options may appear daunting but, in practice, operation is simple and soon becomes intuitive.

By default, when used on their own, the dials operate as follows.

Main command dial

In Shutter-priority or Manual mode, rotating the main command dial selects the shutter speed. In Program mode it will engage program shift, changing the combination of shutter speed and aperture. In Aperture-priority mode it has no effect.

Sub-command dial

In Aperture-priority or Manual mode, rotating the sub-command dial selects the aperture. In Shutter-priority or Program mode it has no effect.

MAIN COMMAND DIAL ⌄

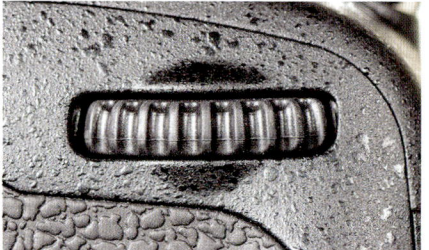

SUB-COMMAND DIAL ⌄

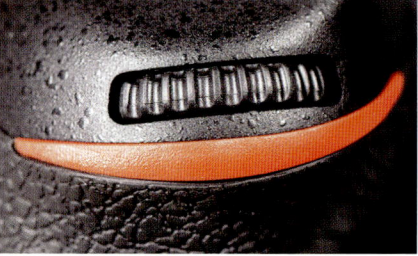

Using the command dials in conjunction with other buttons

COMMAND DIAL	OTHER BUTTON	FUNCTION
Main	⧾⧿	Select the level of exposure compensation (see page 54)
Main	**AF-A**	Select the flash mode (see page 158)
Sub	**AF-A**	Select the level of flash compensation (see page 160)
Main	**QUAL**	Select image quality (see page 74)
Sub	**QUAL**	Select image size (see page 76)
Main	**ISO**	Select ISO sensitivity (see page 58)
Sub	**ISO**	Select Auto-ISO sensitivity (see page 59)
Main	**WB**	Select white balance setting (see page 62)
Sub	**WB**	Select white balance preset (see page 62)
Main	▨	Select metering mode (see page 52)
Main	⊕	Select AF mode (see page 66)
Sub	⊕	Select AF-area mode (see page 70)

More functions can be added, as the command dials can also be used in conjunction with the Fn, Preview, and **AE-L/AF-L** buttons. You can choose which functions these perform through Custom Setting f2, f3, and f4 (see pages 122–124).

› Multi-selector

The multi-selector, on the camera back, is also an important part of the control system. Its primary use when shooting is in selecting the focus point (see page 70). It is also used to navigate through images in playback (see page 84) and navigating through the menus (see page 96).

The collar around the multi-selector has an **L** (Lock) position. When this is locked, the multi-selector can still be used for playback and menu navigation, but the focus point cannot be moved. To enable control of the focus point (see page 70), move the collar to the unlocked position (white dot).

The (OK) button at the center of the multi-selector is used to confirm settings.

MULTI-SELECTOR ⌄⌄

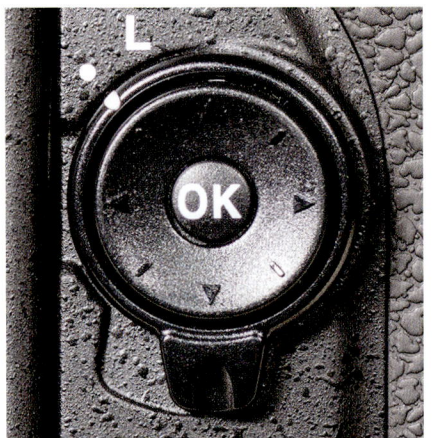

› Release mode

Release mode determines whether the camera takes a single picture or shoots continuously, and can also allow the shot to be delayed. The release mode dial has seven possible positions. To prevent accidental switching between release modes, the dial is provided with a lock button. Depress this to allow the dial to rotate to the desired position.

The maximum shooting rate for all file formats is around 6.5 frames per second (fps), although this is not always

> **Tip**
>
> *When the built-in flash is raised, C$_L$, C$_H$, and Q$_C$ release modes all function like Single Frame mode.*

RELEASE MODE DIAL, SET TO ⌄⌄
QUIET MODE

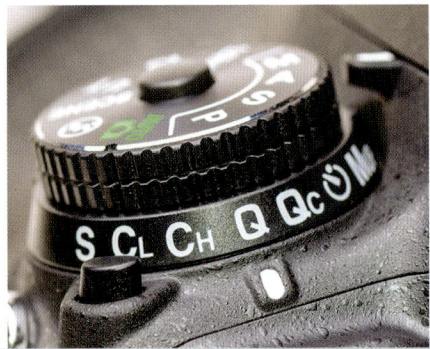

attainable—difficulty in focusing can slow
things down, as can the use of slower
shutter speeds. The speed of the memory
cards can also be a factor (see page 32).

Release mode options

SETTING	DESCRIPTION
S Single Frame	The camera takes a single shot each time the shutter release is fully depressed.
C$_L$ Continuous Low speed	The camera fires continuously as long as the shutter release is fully depressed. The default frame rate is 3fps but this can be varied between 1 and 6fps using Custom Setting d5.
C$_H$ Continuous High speed	The camera fires continuously at the maximum possible frame rate as long as the shutter release is fully depressed.
Q Quiet mode	The camera shoots as normal but there are no alert beeps and the mirror-return after each shot is damped to provide a quieter release.
Q$_C$ Quiet continuous	The camera fires continuously but there are no alert beeps and mirror-return is damped to provide a quieter release. May be marginally slower than C$_H$ under the same conditions.
↻ Self-timer	The shutter is released a set interval after the release button is depressed. The default interval is 10 sec., but 2 sec., 5 sec., or 20 sec. can be set via Custom Setting c3.
M$_{UP}$ Mirror-up	The mirror is raised when the shutter release is fully depressed; press again to take the picture. Useful to minimize vibration caused by "mirror slap". Best used with remote release.

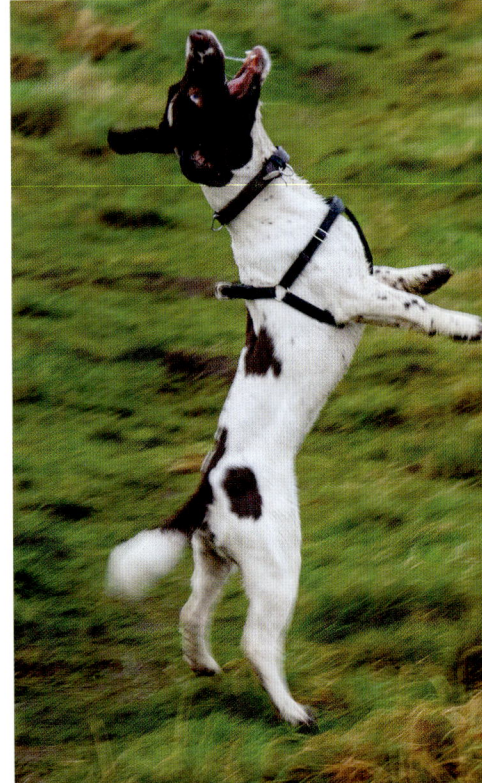

Buffer

Images are initially held in the camera's internal memory ("buffer") before being written to the memory card(s). The maximum number of images that can be recorded in a continuous burst depends upon file quality, drive mode, card speed (see page 216), and available buffer space. The figure for the number of burst frames possible at current settings is shown in the viewfinder at bottom right when the release button is half-pressed. (This figure assumes Continuous High speed shooting, but is displayed in all modes.)

If *(0)* appears, the buffer is full, and the shutter will be disabled until enough data has been transferred to the memory card to free up space in the buffer. This will

normally only be an issue when shooting long continuous bursts in Continuous High speed release mode. Even then it is more likely to be noticed as a slowdown to 1 or 2fps rather than a complete standstill, but on rare occasions you may have to lift your finger from the shutter-release button and re-press to resume shooting.

DOG DAYS »
Buffer capacity may be a consideration when shooting action sequences in continuous bursts.
85mm, 1/100 sec., f/6.3, ISO 1000.

» EXPOSURE MODES

Exposure modes, selected from the mode dial, are fundamental to the camera's operation. The choice of Exposure mode makes a significant difference to the amount of control you can—or can't—exercise. The mode dial is provided with a lock: press the button at the center of the dial to release the dial, then rotate it to the required position. Your chosen mode is indicated in the information display.

The D750 has a very wide choice of exposure modes, but they can be conveniently divided into three main groups: Full Auto modes, Scene modes, and User-control modes.

User-control modes give you complete freedom to control virtually everything on the camera. In Full Auto and Scene modes, by contrast, the majority of settings are determined automatically, including basic shooting settings, whether flash can be used, and how the camera processes the shot.

Full Auto modes use generalized settings that aim to cover most eventualities, while Scene mode settings are tailored to particular common shooting scenarios.

There is some scope to override the automatic choices—typically, you can change the ISO setting, and, in modes which automatically activate the flash, you can turn it off. Still, most settings are out of your hands.

The mode dial has three extra positions—**U1**, **U2**, and **EFFECTS**. **U1** and **U2** allow instant access to predetermined User settings (page 94). **EFFECTS** gives access to a range of stylized image effects (see page 42).

MODE DIAL ⌄

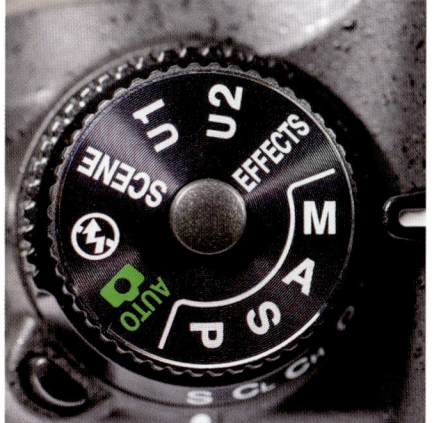

› Full Auto modes

In its manual, Nikon calls these "point-and-shoot" modes, which is probably a fair reflection of the way they're likely to be used. Left to itself like this, the camera is capable of getting acceptable shots under most conditions, but results may not always exactly match what you had in mind. This may be OK for snapshots, but kills creativity, and barely scratches the surface of the D750's potential.

There's only one difference between the two Full Auto modes. In AUTO Auto mode the built-in flash activates automatically if the camera determines light levels are too low (unless a separate accessory flashgun is attached and switched on, in which case this overrides the built-in unit). You can turn it off if you need to, but of course this just duplicates ⚡ Auto (flash off) mode.

In ⚡ the flash stays off, irrespective of light level. This is useful in situations where flash is banned or would be intrusive, or when you just want to begin to discover what the D750 can do in low light.

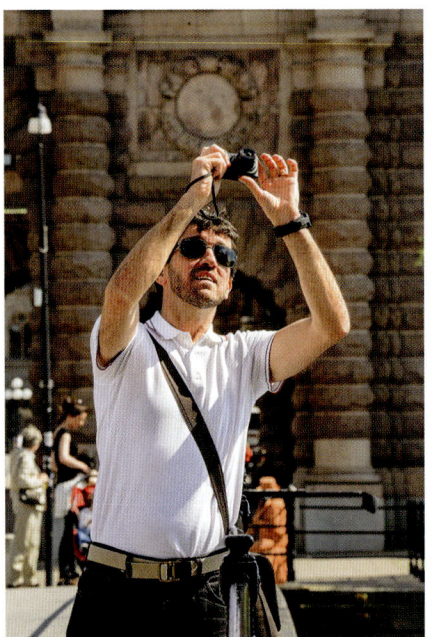

FULL AUTO MODE «

Full auto mode is ideal when shots need to be grabbed quickly, but can diminish the sense of control and creativity.
200mm, 1/160 sec., f/8, ISO 100.

› Taking the picture

Basic picture taking is essentially the same in all Full Auto and Scene modes.

1) Select the mode by rotating the mode dial to the appropriate position; for Scene modes, set it to SCENE and then use the information display and main command dial as described on page 36.

2) Frame the picture.

3) Half-depress the shutter-release button to activate focusing and exposure.

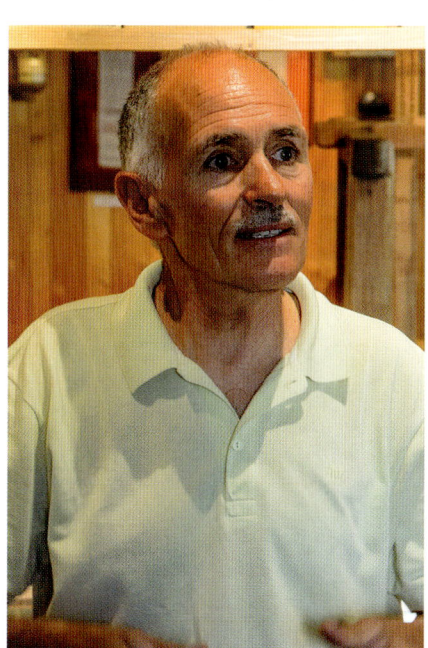

Focus point(s) are displayed in the viewfinder, and shutter speed and aperture settings appear at the bottom of the viewfinder.

4) Fully depress the shutter release to take the picture.

› Exposure warnings

In all modes except Manual, if the camera detects that light levels are too low or, more rarely, too high for an acceptable exposure, a warning (flashing exposure indicators) is displayed in the viewfinder and the control panel, and in the information display, if it's active.

The camera will still take pictures but they may be underexposed or subject to camera shake if it's too dark, or overexposed if it's too light. Possible solutions include using flash, adjusting the ISO sensitivity (see page 58), or changing the shutter speed or aperture setting in S or A modes respectively.

AUTO (FLASH OFF) «
Auto (flash off) mode is suitable when flash is banned or—as in this case—it could overwhelm pleasing ambient light.
85mm, 1/125 sec., f/5.6, ISO 3200.

2 › **Scene modes**

Scene modes are a quick way to set the camera for shooting in particular situations. They can also be a first step to exploring a wider range of options on the D750.

To select a Scene mode, set the mode dial to SCENE. Rotate the main command dial and the monitor scrolls through the available modes, with the current mode's icon highlighted. (If this screen does not appear, press **info** to activate the information display.) The mode's name also appears, with a thumbnail image illustrating an appropriate subject. This selection screen disappears after a few seconds, but the mode icon remains in the top left corner of the information display.

Scene modes determine basic shooting parameters like how the camera focuses and how it sets shutter speed and aperture.

They also dictate how the camera processes JPEG images (see page 74), as Nikon Picture Control settings (page 90) are predetermined.

Most Scene modes also employ Auto White Balance (see page 62), but in some cases the white balance setting is predetermined to suit specific subjects.

In some Scene modes, the built-in flash will automatically activate if the camera determines light levels are too low. In others, the built-in flash remains off regardless of the light level. However, if you attach a separate flashgun this will operate normally.

INFORMATION DISPLAY ON THE REAR LCD SCREEN ⌄

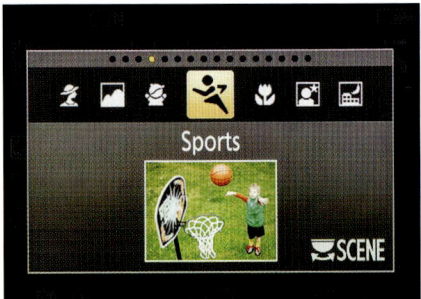

LANDSCAPE MODE »
Landscape mode is designed to deliver good depth of field and vibrant colors.
24mm, 1/160 sec., f/11, ISO 400.

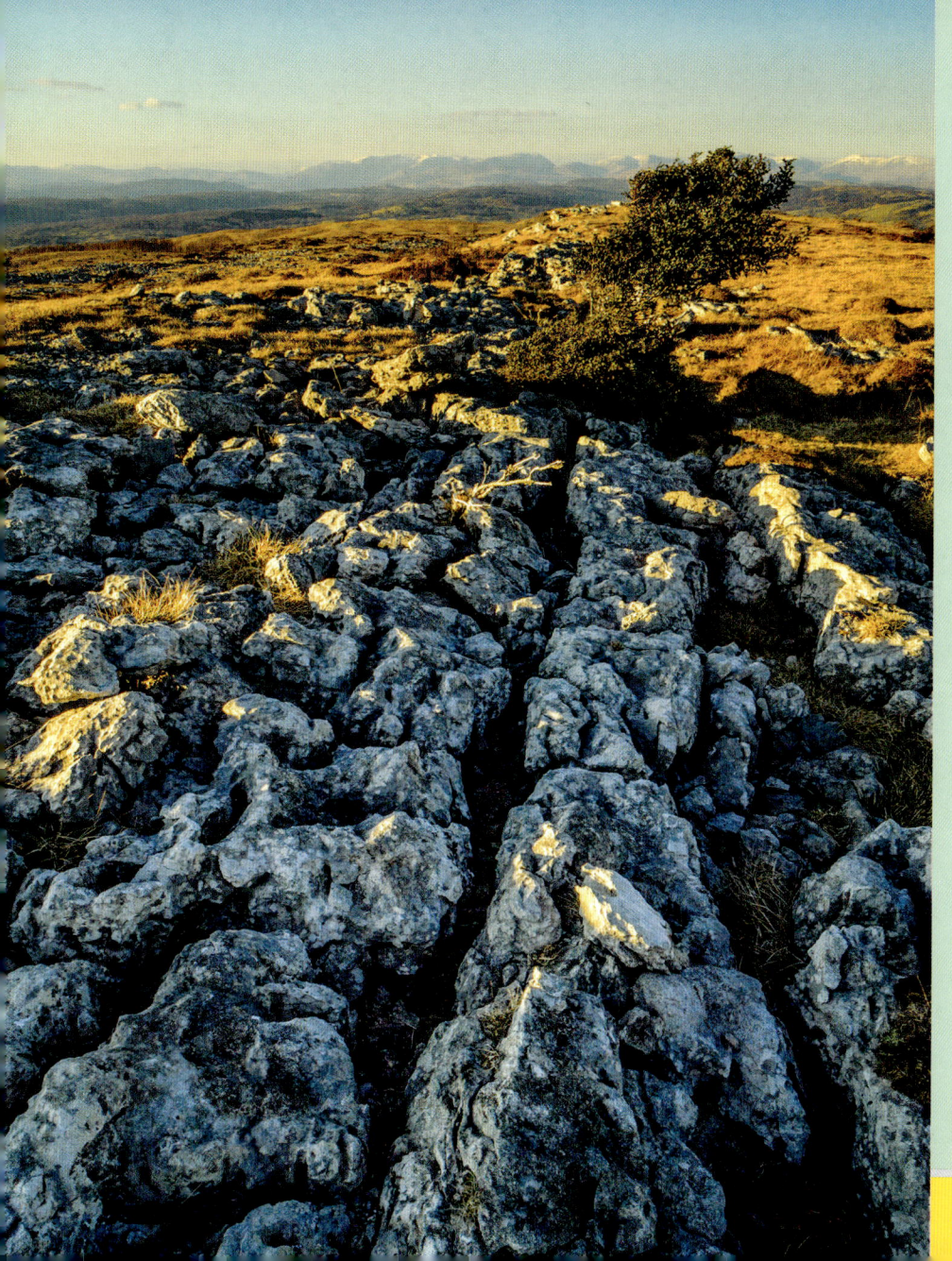

Default settings for Scene mode

Mode	AF mode	AF-Area mode	White Balance	Flash Mode	Picture Control	Notes
Portrait	AF-A	Auto-area AF	Auto1	Auto	Portrait	Camera sets wide aperture to reduce depth of field.
Landscape	AF-A	Auto-area AF	Auto1	Off	Landscape	Camera sets small aperture to increase depth of field. This can lead to slow shutter speeds—a tripod may be needed.
Child	AF-A	Auto-area AF	Auto1	Auto	Standard	Camera sets wide aperture to reduce depth of field, but uses higher shutter speeds than as subjects may be more active and likely to move.
Sports	AF-C	51-point dynamic area	Auto1	Off	Standard	Camera sets fast shutter speed to freeze movement, usually leading to wide aperture and therefore shallow depth of field.
Close up	AF-S	Auto-area AF	Auto1	Auto	Standard	Camera sets medium–small aperture to improve depth of field, often leading to slow shutter speeds—a tripod may be needed.
Night portrait	AF-A	Auto-area AF	Auto2	Auto slow sync	Portrait	In low ambient light, camera sets long shutter speed to record an image of the background. Tripod often needed.
Night landscape	AF-A	Auto-area AF	Auto2	Off	Standard	Allows long exposures (up to 30 sec.). Tripod usually required. Long Exposure noise reduction (page 105) often applies, leading to delay before another shot can be taken.

Default settings for Scene mode

Mode	AF mode	AF-Area mode	White Balance	Flash Mode	Picture Control	Notes
🎉 Party/indoor	AF-A	Auto-area AF	Auto2	Auto with red-eye reduction	Standard	Gives shorter exposure times than 📷 , so more suitable for handheld shooting. Red-eye reduction flash creates noticeable shutter delay (see page 158).
🏖 Beach/snow	AF-A	Auto-area AF	Auto1	Off	Landscape	Exposure compensation may be applied automatically to preserve bright tones.
🌅 Sunset	AF-A	Auto-area AF	Direct sunlight	Off	Landscape	Long exposures are common. Tripod often required.
🌆 Dusk/dawn	AF-A	Auto-area AF	Preset	Off	Landscape	Long exposures very common. Tripod usually required.
🐾 Pet portrait	AF-A	51-point dynamic area	Auto1	Auto	Standard	Generally very similar to 🧒 Child, but AF-assist illuminator turns off.
🕯 Candlelight	AF-A	Single-point	Preset	Off	Standard	Long exposures very common. Tripod usually required. Portrait subjects need to keep still.
🌸 Blossom	AF-A	Auto-area AF	Auto1	Off	Landscape	Employs Active D-Lighting (see page 88) to retain detail in highlight areas.
🍂 Autumn colors	AF-A	Auto-area AF	Auto1	Off	Vivid	Tripod sometimes needed.
🍴 Food	AF-A	Single-point	Auto1	Manual	Standard	Built-in flash can be used but not recommended as it produces ugly shadows at close range.

Using Scene modes

Some experienced photographers may be dismissive of Scene modes, but there's no doubt that they have real value both as part of the learning process and as a very quick way to set the camera appropriately when time is at a premium.

Scene modes also allow you to override the automatic settings in several ways. This makes them more versatile and can offer another step along the learning curve. The more you use these overrides, the closer you approach the experience offered by the User-control modes.

There are some things you can't override, notably the White Balance (page 62) and Picture Control (page 90) settings. However, if you shoot RAW, even these aren't locked in to the final image. You also can't access Active D-Lighting or HDR (high dynamic range) options.

Overrides

In all Scene modes you can access the full range of image quality, area, and size options, notably the ability to shoot RAW (page 74).

In all Scene modes, ISO (page 58) is controlled automatically by default, but you can always override it by pressing **ISO** and rotating the main command dial.

In all Scene modes you can override the default focusing settings by pressing ⊕ and rotating the main command dial (to set AF mode) or the sub-command dial (to set AF-area mode).

SPORTS MODE ⯆

Sports mode can be used for all kinds of rapid action, including wildlife.

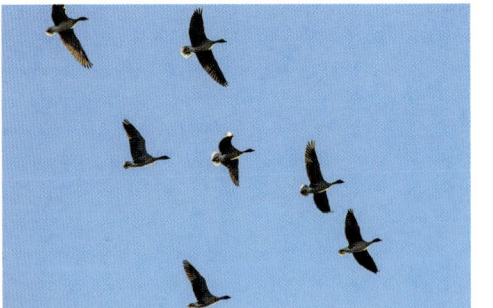

NIGHT LANDSCAPE MODE ⯆

Night landscape mode allows long exposures, such as in this nighttime urban scene.

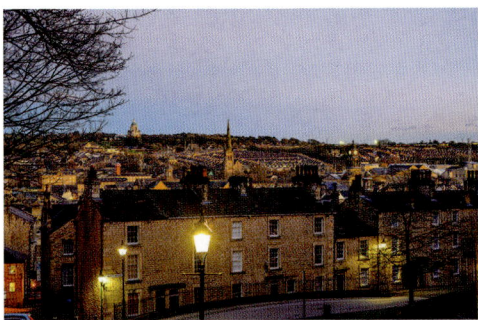

Flash options

In some Scene modes (see table on pages 38 and 39), the built-in flash activates automatically if the camera deems light levels are too low. You can turn it off, if necessary, by pressing ⚡ and rotating the main command dial until the 🚫⚡ icon appears in the information display. Alternatively, attaching a separate flashgun will override the built-in unit, and often improves results dramatically (see page 162). You can also select other flash modes, or set flash compensation (pages 158 and 160).

In other Scene modes, the built-in flash remains off regardless of the light level. Here you can't change settings to override this, but if you attach a separate flashgun it will operate normally.

There's one anomaly: in 🍴 Food, the built-in flash does not operate automatically but can be activated manually with ⚡. (However, think twice about using flash in a restaurant, as you'll probably irritate other diners.)

Exposure options

You can't directly set aperture or shutter speed, and you can't bracket exposures (page 56), but you can use exposure compensation (page 54) and exposure lock (page 55).

BEACH/SNOW MODE ≫
Beach/snow mode preserves a light, bright feel, also useful when the ground is pale.

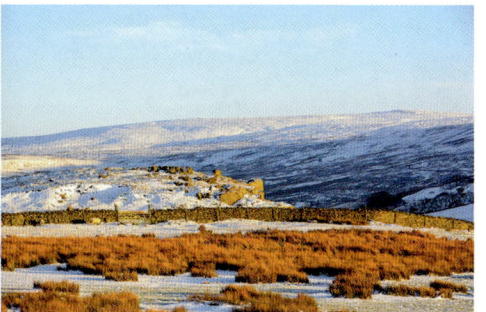

AUTUMN COLORS MODE ≫
Autumn colors mode favors the red and golden hues of fall.

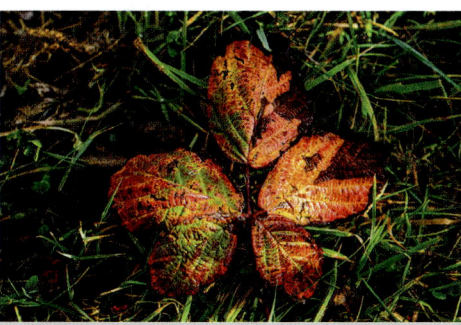

› Special Effects modes

Special Effects modes are Scene modes taken to extremes, producing various striking effects through a combination of shooting settings and image processing. They always produce JPEG images: if Image Quality is set to RAW, the camera will create a Fine JPEG image instead. Some of these effects can also be applied to existing images through the Retouch menu (page 138).

In most Effects modes, the built-in flash does not operate; a separate flash can be used but will often undermine the effect. The built-in flash is available only in 🖌 Color Sketch.

Effects modes can be used in Live View or Movie mode. In some cases, movies may play back jerkily.

Live View gives a preview of the effect, which is often helpful and for some modes, such as 🖋 Selective Color, essential. In 🖌 Color Sketch and 🏠 Miniature Effect, shooting in Live View/movie allows you to adjust the strength of the effect (press ⓞⓚ to see options).

Selecting Special Effects modes is just like selecting Scene modes (page 36), except of course that you start by setting the mode dial to EFFECTS.

The following modes are available:

🌃 Night Vision Uses extreme high ISO settings (maximum Hi 4 or ISO 102,400); produces monochrome images. Autofocus is available only in Live View/movie shooting, and not always then: manual focus may be required. No options (except exposure compensation).

Night Vision allows handheld shooting in remarkably low light—but it's mono-only, and quality is compromised. Using a tripod or flash is usually a better bet.

🖌 Color Sketch Turns a photo into something resembling a colored pencil drawing. There are Live View options for Vividness and Outlines.

🏠 Miniature Effect Mimics the recent fad for shooting images with extremely small and localized depth of field (see page 49), making real landscapes or city views look like miniature models. Movie clips play back at high speed.

Live View options: Use multi-selector to reposition the in-focus zone.

Selective Color Select particular color(s); other hues are rendered in monochrome. Colors can only be selected in Live View (select the color under the focus point by pressing ▲). This selection remains active if you exit Live View and shoot using the viewfinder, but you lose the preview of the effect.

Silhouette The camera's metering favors bright backgrounds such as vivid skies; foreground subjects record as silhouettes. Most effective for subjects with interesting outlines.

High key Produces images filled with light tones, usually with no blacks or deep tones at all.

Low key Low key is basically the opposite, creating a deep, low-toned image.

COLOR SKETCH ⌄

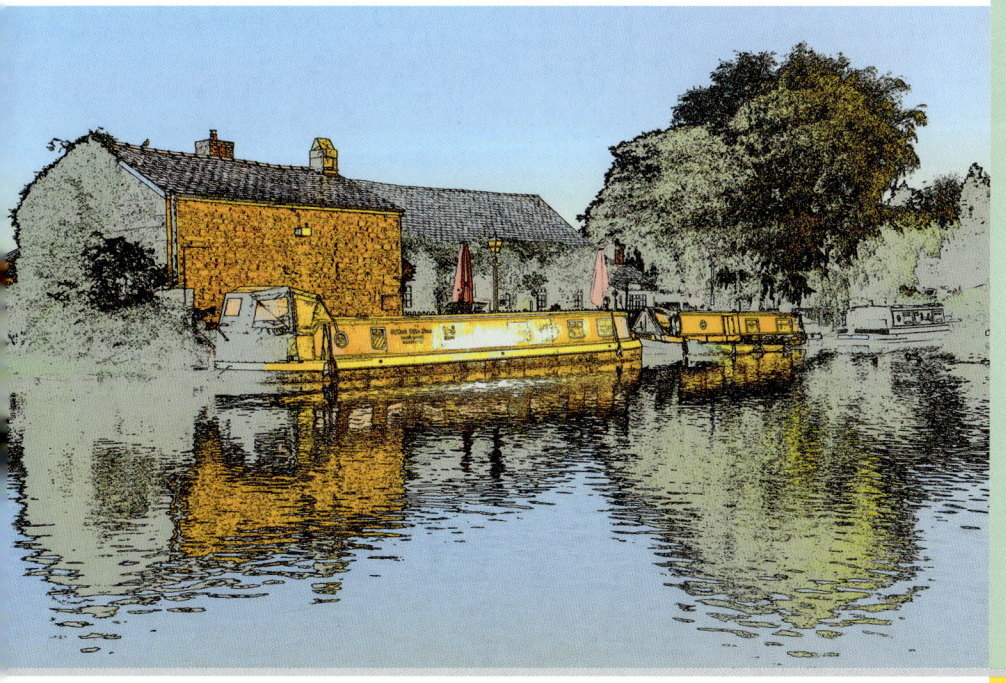

› User-control modes

The remaining four modes are traditional standards, which will be familiar to any experienced photographer. It's these modes which really allow you to harness the full power of the D750.

As well as allowing direct control over the basic settings of aperture and shutter speed (even in P mode through flexible program), these modes give you free rein to employ controls like White Balance (page 62), Active D-Lighting (page 88), and Nikon Picture Controls (page 90). These give you lots of influence over the look and feel of the image. You can also select different metering modes (page 52) for finer control over exposure. You can exploit HDR (high dynamic range) imaging, shoot multiple exposures, and, at least in manual mode, use shutter speeds longer than 30 seconds.

Note:
Programmed auto mode is not available with older lenses lacking a CPU. If a non-CPU lens is attached, the camera will switch to Aperture-priority mode.

› (P) Programmed auto

In **P** mode the camera sets a combination of shutter speed and aperture that will give correctly exposed results in most situations. This is ideal for snapshots and when time is of the essence, but many people feel it reduces creative control. However, you still have considerable room for maneuver through options like flexible program (see below), exposure lock (page 55), and exposure compensation (page 54).

Flexible program

Without leaving **P** mode you can vary the combination of shutter speed and aperture by rotating the main command dial to engage flexible program (also known as program shift). This is a very quick way to achieve practically the same direct control over aperture and shutter speed that you get in (**S**) Shutter-priority or (**A**) Aperture-priority modes.

When flexible program is in effect the **P** indication in the control panel and information display (but not the viewfinder) changes to **P***.

PROGRAMMED AUTO MODE ⌄

Programmed auto mode allows a quick response but also lets you tailor camera settings to suit your own creative ideas.
200mm, 1/160 sec., f/8, ISO 400.

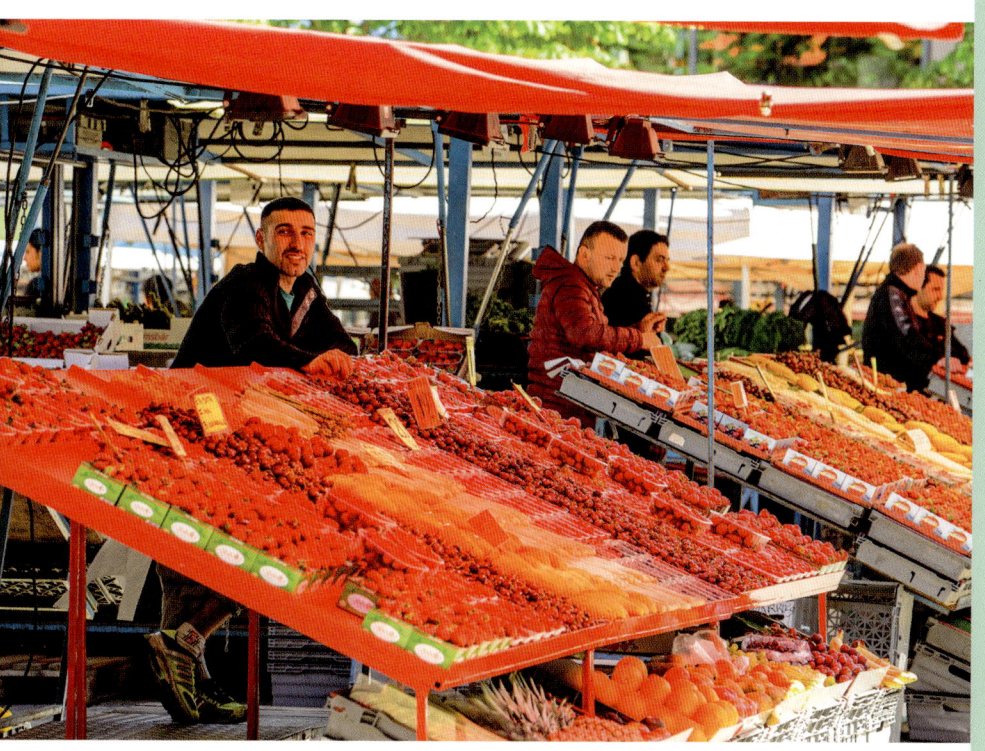

2

› (S) Shutter-priority auto

In Shutter-priority (**S**) mode, you control the shutter speed using the main command dial, and the camera sets an appropriate aperture for correctly exposed results. You can set shutter speeds between 30 sec. and 1/4000 sec. You can fine-tune exposure through exposure lock, exposure compensation, or exposure bracketing.

Significance of shutter speed

Shutter speed is significant mainly in relation to the way motion is recorded. Basically, high shutter speeds tend to freeze motion, while slower ones are more likely to record it with a degree of blur. This is relevant both to movement of your subject and to movement of the camera itself. Intentional camera movement and/or use of controlled blur, as in panning shots, can create very effective results (and is something that Sports mode does not cater for).

> **Note:**
> Shutter-priority auto is not available with older lenses lacking a CPU. If a non-CPU lens is attached, the camera will switch to Aperture-priority mode. The S indicator in the control panel will blink and A will be displayed in the viewfinder.

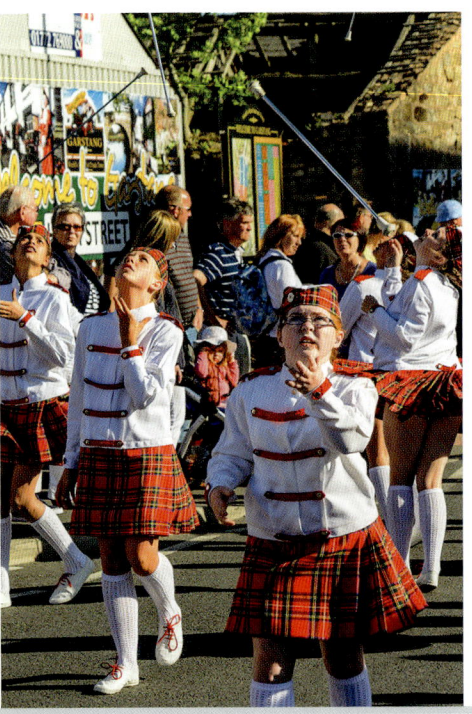

ACTION STATIONS «
Fast shutter speeds are an obvious choice when shooting action.
200mm, 1/50 sec., f/11, ISO 100.

On the other hand, unintentional movement, usually termed camera shake, can ruin a shot. Fast shutter speeds are just one way in which we can avoid or minimize the effects of camera shake.

Movement is not just a concern for sports and wildlife specialists. For example, it can be an issue in portraits (especially of children and animals).

Even in "static" landscape photography, movement is often present, whether it's scudding clouds, running water, or foliage swaying in the breeze.

FAST TRAIN ⌄
Sometimes a less obvious choice works better. With a fast shutter speed this train would have appeared stationary, but a panning shot gives a good impression of speed.
200mm, 1/1000 sec., f/5.6, ISO 1000.

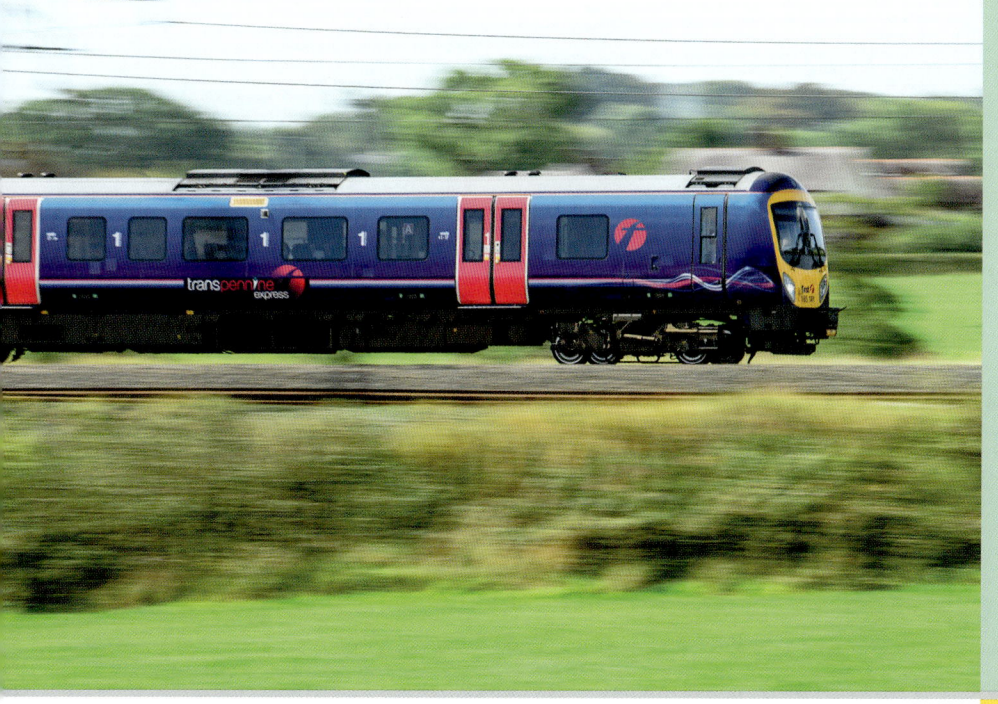

› (A) Aperture-priority auto

In Aperture-priority (**A**) mode, you control the aperture using the sub-command dial, and the camera sets an appropriate shutter speed to give correctly exposed results. The range of apertures you can set is determined by the lens that's fitted. You can fine-tune exposure through exposure lock, exposure compensation, or exposure bracketing.

Note:
Aperture-priority auto is available with older lenses lacking a CPU. For best results with such lenses, specify the maximum aperture of the lens via **Non CPU lens data** in the Setup menu (page 136).

SHALLOW GRAVESTONES ⌄
Aperture-priority mode is ideal for control over depth of field; here I used a wide aperture to keep the background soft.
200mm, 1/1000 sec., f/5.6, ISO 1000.

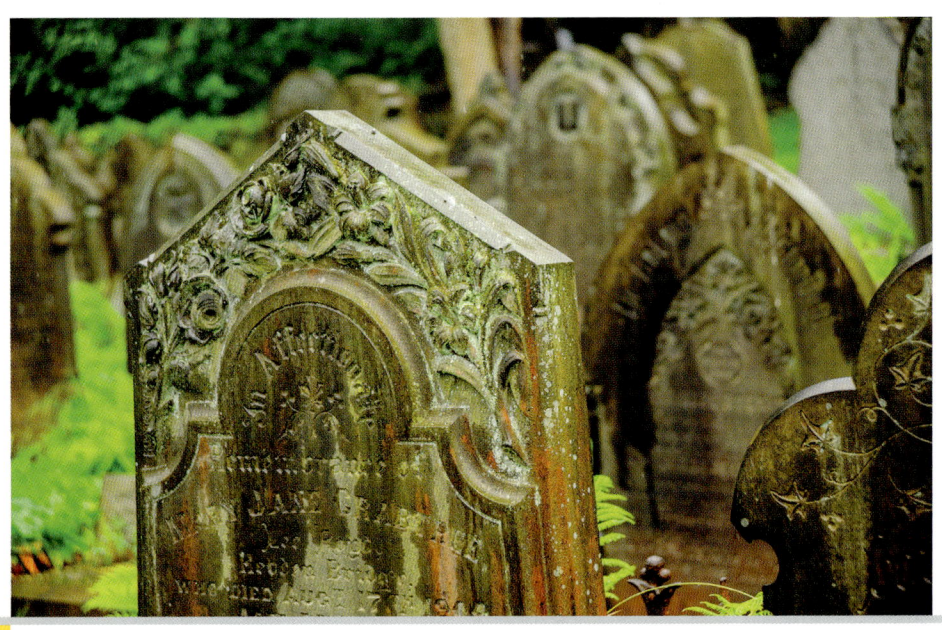

Significance of aperture

Aperture is principally significant as one of the key factors influencing depth of field. Depth of field describes the zone, in front of and behind the actual point of focus, in which objects appear to be sharp in the final image.

Sometimes a shallow depth of field is exactly what you want, as it makes the subject stand out against a soft background. For other images you may want to try to have everything sharp from front to back—this is the traditional approach in landscape photography, for instance.

Along with aperture, the other main factors determining depth of field are the focal length of the lens and the distance to the subject. With long lenses and/or nearby subjects, depth of field may remain shallow even at small apertures. This is very evident in macro photography (see page 168).

(see page 168)

DEEP THINKING ⌄

Here the intention was to ensure that depth of field covered everything in the image. Along with use of a fairly small aperture, careful placement of the focus point was key to achieving this: it was just beyond the large rocks in the foreground.
42mm, 1/100 sec., f/11, ISO 1000.

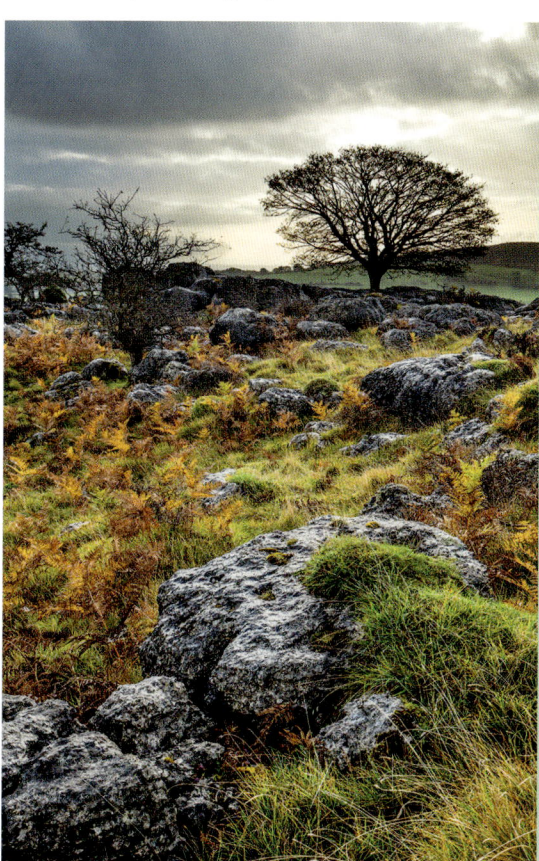

› (M) Manual mode

In **M** mode, you control both shutter speed (with the main command dial) and aperture (with the sub-command dial). Manual mode suits a considered approach, especially when time is not too pressing. Many photographers use it habitually to retain complete control.

The range of apertures that you can set is determined by the lens that's fitted. Shutter speeds can be set between 30 sec. and 1/4000 sec., as in Shutter-priority, but Manual mode offers two additional options, B and T (see below). These are the only ways to achieve exposures longer than 30 sec., which are desirable, and often essential, for many subjects, including fireworks displays, moonlit landscapes, star trails in the night sky, and more. You'll need a tripod or other solid camera support.

The exposure meter gives no reading when B or T are set. Sometimes the only way to get the exposure right is by trial and error—which can be a long-winded process. Check there is plenty of juice in the battery before any really long exposures.

B (Bulb)

Rotate the main command dial until *Bulb* appears in the viewfinder, control panel, and information display. In Bulb mode, the shutter remains open as long as the shutter-release button is held down. However, holding it down with your finger can cause camera shake and soon becomes tedious and uncomfortable. It makes much more sense to use a remote cord (see Accessories, page 213). Exposures longer than 30 minutes are only possible in B.

T (Time)

Rotate the main command dial until *Time* appears in the information display. The viewfinder and control panel show two dashes instead. Press and release the shutter button; the shutter remains open, either until you press the button again or until 30 minutes have elapsed.

Using the Analog exposure displays

In Manual mode, an analog exposure display appears in the center of the viewfinder readouts and in the information display. This shows whether the photograph would be under- or overexposed at current settings. Adjust shutter speed and/or aperture until the indicator is aligned with the **0** in the center of the display; exposure now matches the camera's recommendations. If necessary, make further adjustments for creative effect or to achieve a specific result.

LONG EXPOSURE   »

If there's no cable release to hand, the T setting is a good bet to minimize vibration when exposures longer than 30 sec. are required.
34mm, 40 sec., f/25, ISO 50, tripod.

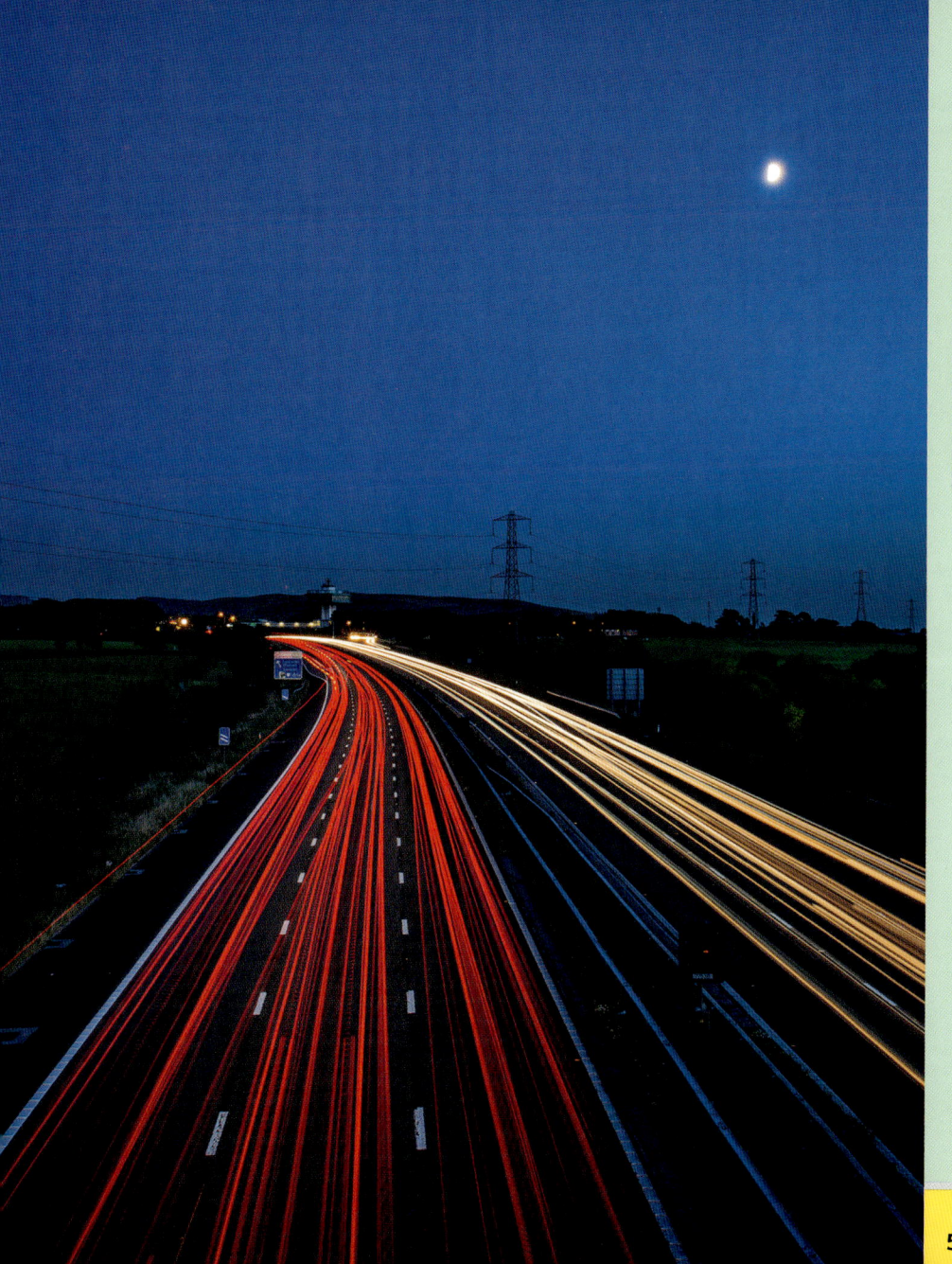

» METERING MODES

Metering—measuring light levels—is crucial in producing good images. The Nikon D750 provides four different metering modes; switch between them using [metering button icon] and the main command dial. The viewfinder, control panel, and information display all show which metering mode is in use.

› [matrix icon] Matrix (3D Color Matrix Metering III)

Using the D750's 91,000-pixel color sensor, 3D Color Matrix Metering III analyzes brightness, color, and contrast. With Type G or D Nikkor lenses, the system also uses information about the distance to the subject to further refine its reading. With other CPU lenses, this range information is not used (Color Matrix Metering III). With non-CPU lenses, Color Matrix Metering can still be employed if the focal length and maximum aperture are specified **using Non-CPU lens** data in the Setup menu.

Matrix metering is recommended for the vast majority of shooting and generally produces excellent results. In Full Auto and Scene modes, matrix metering is always used.

METERING MODE BUTTON »

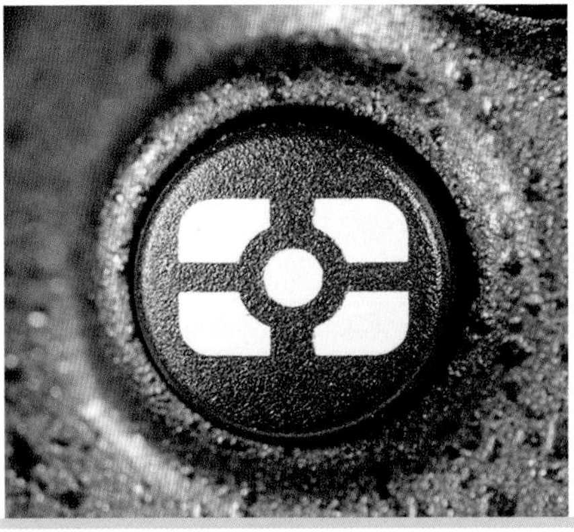

› [center-weighted icon] Center-weighted metering

In this very traditional form of metering, the camera meters the entire frame, but gives greater importance to the central area. At default setting this area is a circle 12mm in diameter. Provided a CPU lens is attached, this can be changed to 8, 15, or 20mm using Custom Setting b6; you can also choose **Average** metering, which meters the whole frame equally.

Center-weighted metering is sometimes used in portraiture, where the key subject occupies the central portion of the frame.

› ⦿ Spot metering

Here the camera meters from a circle 4mm in diameter (just 1.5% of the frame). If a CPU lens is fitted, this circle is centered on the current focus point. With a non-CPU lens, or if ▭ Auto-area AF is in use, the metering point will be the center of the frame.

Effective use of spot metering requires some experience, but in critical conditions it offers unrivalled accuracy. Spot metering attempts to reproduce the subject area as a mid-tone and this must be allowed for (e.g. by using exposure compensation) if the subject is significantly darker or lighter than a mid-tone.

› ⦿* Highlight-weighted metering

This mode is related to matrix metering, analyzing the entire frame, but with adjustment to retain maximum detail in the highlights. It's ideal for brightly lit subjects against dark backgrounds, like a spotlit performer on a darkened stage. Wedding photographers may find it helpful when dealing with white dresses. In landscape photography it tends to work well with scenes with white clouds or snow.

HEATHER ⌄
The bulk of this image is dark, but the heather flowers were the important element, so it seemed a good moment to give highlight-weighted metering a try.
100mm macro, 1/100 sec., f/5.6, ISO 400, tripod.

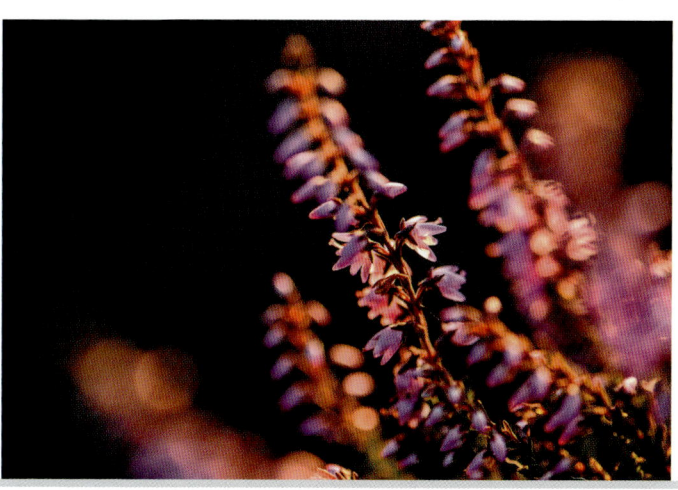

The D750 delivers accurate exposures under most conditions, but no camera is infallible. Nor can it read your mind or anticipate your creative ideas. Sometimes it needs a little help to get the exposure spot-on. Ways you can do this include exposure compensation, exposure lock (page 55), and exposure bracketing (page 56).

Exposure compensation is available in most modes, but not in Full Auto modes or Effects modes (other than 🎨). In these modes, exposure lock is the only way to fine-tune the exposure. Exposure bracketing is only available in **P**, **S**, **A**, and **M** modes.

› Using Exposure compensation

The basic principle is simple: to make the image lighter (to keep light tones looking light), increase the exposure—in other words, use positive compensation. Conversely, to make the image darker, use negative compensation.

In **P** mode, exposure compensation will vary both aperture and shutter speed. In **A** mode, only the shutter speed varies, and in **S** mode, only the aperture. (The same applies to exposure bracketing.)

1) Exposure compensation can be set between −5 Ev and +5 Ev, in steps of ⅓ Ev (default), ½ Ev, or 1 Ev. Use Custom setting b2 to change the increment.

2) Press 🔲 and rotate the main command dial to set negative or positive compensation as required; the compensation value is shown in the viewfinder, information display, and control panel.

3) Release 🔲. 🔲 appears in all displays, and—in modes other than **M**—the Analog Exposure Display appears, indicating the compensation level and with the central **0**

EXPOSURE COMPENSATION BUTTON ⌄

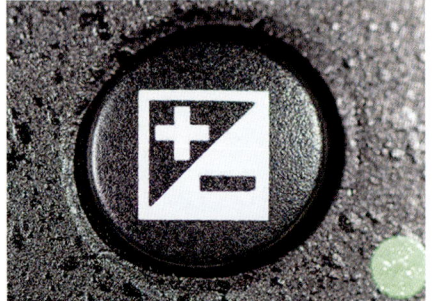

> ### Tip
>
> *Avoid exposure compensation in Manual mode. It doesn't change the shutter speed or aperture values but can skew the exposure readouts.*

blinking. The exposure compensation value is shown in the information display.

4) Take the picture as normal. If time allows, check that the results are satisfactory.

5) To restore normal exposure settings, press ⚡ and rotate the main command dial until the value returns to **0.0**. If you omit this step, exposure compensation will apply to later shots which don't need it.

› Exposure lock

For many people, exposure lock is the quickest and most intuitive way to fine-tune the camera's exposure setting. It's also the only method available in Full Auto and Scene modes.

It's mainly useful in cases where very dark or light areas (especially light sources) within the frame can over-influence exposure. Exposure lock allows you to meter from a more average area, by pointing the camera in a different direction or stepping closer to the subject, then hold that exposure while reframing the shot you want.

Using Exposure lock

There's more than one way to implement exposure lock, but they all start by aiming the camera in a different direction, or zooming the lens, to avoid potentially problematic dark or light areas (e.g. very bright skies behind a shady subject). If you're using center-weighted or spot metering, look for areas of middling tone, but still receiving the same sort of light as the main subject.

The recommended method is then to half-press the shutter-release button to take a meter reading. Keeping it pressed, you then press **AE-L/AF-L** to lock the exposure. Keep **AE-L/AF-L** pressed as you reframe the image and shoot in the normal way.

By default, **AE-L/AF-L** locks focus as well as exposure. You can change this using Custom Setting f6 **Assign AE-L/AF-L button** (see page 125). The most relevant option for using exposure lock is **AE Lock only**. You can also opt for **AE Lock (hold)**. In this case you can release **AE-L/AF-L**, and exposure will remain locked until you press **AE-L/AF-L** again, or the meters turn off.

You can also lock exposure simply by maintaining half-pressure on the shutter-release button. However, this limits your autofocus options; you can't refocus (in AF-S) or choose your initial focus point (in AF-C). If you're using manual focus, there's no such problem.

You can also separate the functions of the **AE-L/AF-L** and shutter-release buttons by enabling back-button autofocus (see page 69). In this case, you can use the shutter-release button for exposure lock without any limitations on autofocus.

› Exposure bracketing

Another quick and convenient way to secure a correctly exposed image is to shoot several frames at varying exposures, and select the best one later. The D750's bracketing facility allows this to be done very quickly, especially when using a continuous release mode.

1) Select the type of bracketing required using Custom setting e5. Select **AE only** to ensure that only exposure values are varied. (If flash is not active, **AE & flash** has the same effect.)

2) While pressing **BKT**, rotate the main command dial to select the number of shots required for the bracketing burst. You can choose between **2**, **3**, **5**, **7**, and **9** shots; the selected number is displayed in the control panel.

3) Still holding **BKT**, rotate the sub-command dial to select the exposure increment between each shot in the series. Possible values are: **0.3 Ev**, **0.7 Ev**, **1 Ev**, **2 Ev** and **3 Ev**.

4) Frame, focus, and shoot normally. The camera varies the exposure with each frame until the series is completed. In Cʜ or Cʟ release mode, the camera will pause at the end of the series, even if you keep the shutter release depressed.

5) To cancel bracketing and return to normal shooting, press **BKT** and rotate the main command dial until *OF* appears in the control panel and information display. The exposure increment that you chose using the sub-command dial will remain in effect next time you initiate bracketing.

BKT BUTTON ≫

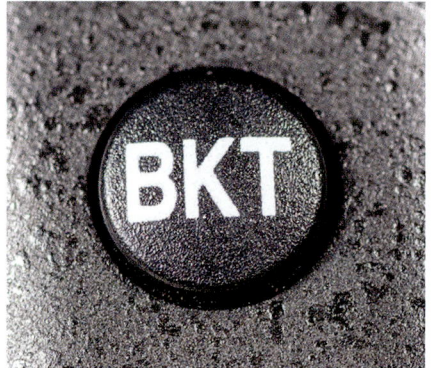

Tip

Using exposure bracketing while shooting moving subjects is a lottery: the frame with the best exposure may not coincide with the subject being in the best position. Ideally, use another method to optimize exposure settings before shooting action sequences.

Tip

In Manual mode, it's often just as easy to vary the shutter speed or aperture yourself. If metered exposure is 1/125 sec. at f/11, shooting extra frames at 1/60 sec. and 1/250 sec. will give the same result as a three-shot bracket with 1 Ev interval.

The D750 offers various forms of bracketing: choose between them using Custom Setting e6. The options are **AE & flash**, **AE only**, **Flash only**, **WB bracketing**, and **ADL bracketing**. **AE & flash** varies both the exposure and the flash level. **Flash only** varies the flash level without changing the base exposure. **WB bracketing** varies the white balance setting. **ADL bracketing** varies the level of Active D-Lighting applied (see page 88).

EXPOSURE BRACKETING ⌄

Exposure bracketing has been used here (from left to right):
−1 Ev; 0 Ev; +1 Ev
24mm, 1/200 sec.; 1/100 sec.; 1/50 sec., f/8, ISO 400.

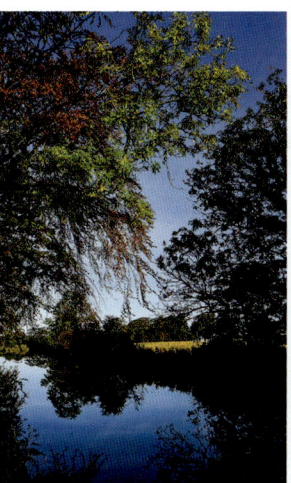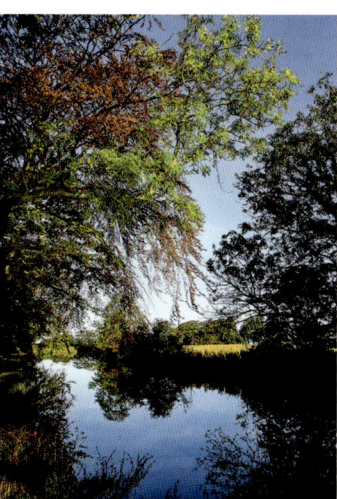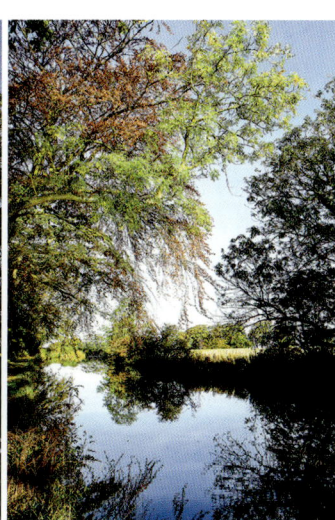

2 » ISO SENSITIVITY SETTINGS

The ISO sensitivity setting governs the sensor's response to greater or lesser amounts of light. The wide ISO ranges of digital cameras—especially those with larger sensors like DSLRs—are among their greatest features. The ability to pick a different ISO for every single shot, if you need to, is truly liberating.

At higher ISO settings, less light is needed to capture an acceptable image. Higher ISO settings are also useful when you need a small aperture for increased depth of field (see page 49) or a fast shutter speed to freeze rapid movement (see page 46). Conversely, lower ISO settings are useful in brighter conditions, and/or when you require wide apertures or slow shutter speeds.

The D750 offers ISO settings from 100 to 12,800, plus additional "extension" settings. **Lo0.3** is equivalent to 80 ISO, **Lo0.7** to 64 ISO, and **Lo1.0** to 50 ISO. The **Hi** settings are **Hi0.3** (equivalent to 16,000 ISO), **Hi0.7** (20,800 ISO), **Hi1.0** (25,600 ISO), and **Hi2.0** (51,200 ISO). Noise does become much more obvious, but it is possible to produce usable images and they can represent a real alternative to using flash under most conditions.

Tip

Viewed at 100%, high-ISO images may appear intolerably noisy. Remember that 100% "pixel peeping" is not normal viewing and images may still be perfectly acceptable for full-screen viewing and modest-sized prints. Experiment with a range of settings to see what level of image noise is acceptable for your needs.

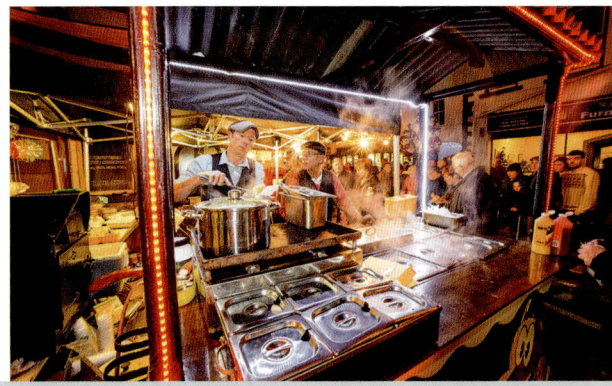

HIGH ISO «
Flash was used, but this shot still needed a high ISO setting to allow the background to register.
14mm, 1/15 sec., f/7.1, ISO 3200.

› Setting the ISO

The normal way to set the ISO is by pressing **ISO** and rotating the main command dial until the desired setting is shown in the information display, control panel, and viewfinder. Alternatively, use **ISO sensitivity settings** in the Photo Shooting menu.

Easy **ISO** is another option. Enabled via Custom setting d8, this allows ISO to be set simply by rotating the main command dial (in Aperture-priority mode) or sub-command dial (in Shutter-priority or Program mode). It does not apply in other modes.

ISO DIALOG IN THE INFORMATION DISPLAY ✲

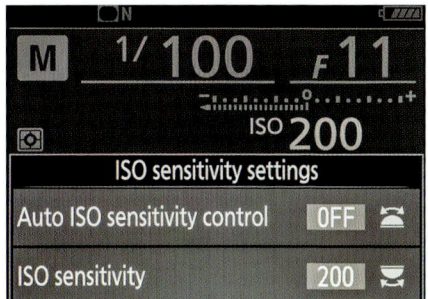

› Auto ISO

It's important to understand that the D750 offers two varieties of Auto ISO. In Full Auto, Scene, and Effects modes, ISO setting is normally fully automatic. (However, in almost all these modes, except 🌄, you can change to a manual setting simply by pressing **ISO** and rotating the main command dial.)

In P, S, A, and M modes, Auto ISO—the full name is now **Auto ISO sensitivity control**—means something different; it's more of a failsafe. You still set the ISO manually, but Auto ISO sensitivity control allows the D750 to deviate from the selected ISO if this becomes necessary to maintain correct exposure. For example, if you are using Shutter-priority with a shutter speed of 1/1000 sec. and an ISO setting of 100, prevailing light levels may not allow correct exposure within the aperture range available on the lens. The camera will then adjust the ISO until it can achieve acceptable exposure at an available aperture.

Auto ISO sensitivity control is off by default and must be enabled through the **ISO sensitivity settings** item in the Photo Shooting menu, using the **Auto ISO sensitivity control** submenu. This has further options as follows.

Maximum sensitivity allows you to limit the maximum ISO which the camera can employ when applying Auto ISO sensitivity control. For instance, if you feel that image noise is unacceptable above a setting of ISO 3200, you can set this as the upper limit.

Minimum shutter speed allows you to set a shutter speed limit below which the camera will not go. This only applies in P and A modes; in S and M modes the camera will continue to use the shutter speed you set. This submenu includes an **Auto** option; within this you can make a choice along a scale from **Slower** to **Faster**. If you err towards Faster, the camera will increase the ISO more quickly to maintain higher shutter speeds. The camera takes focal length into account; longer lenses require higher shutter speeds to avoid camera shake. If you use a range of focal lengths, the flexibility offered by the Auto option is appealing.

BLURRING WATER ⌄

For this image, I used the lowest available ISO setting and a small aperture to get the longest possible shutter speed to blur the water. *24mm, 4 sec., f/16, ISO 100, tripod.*

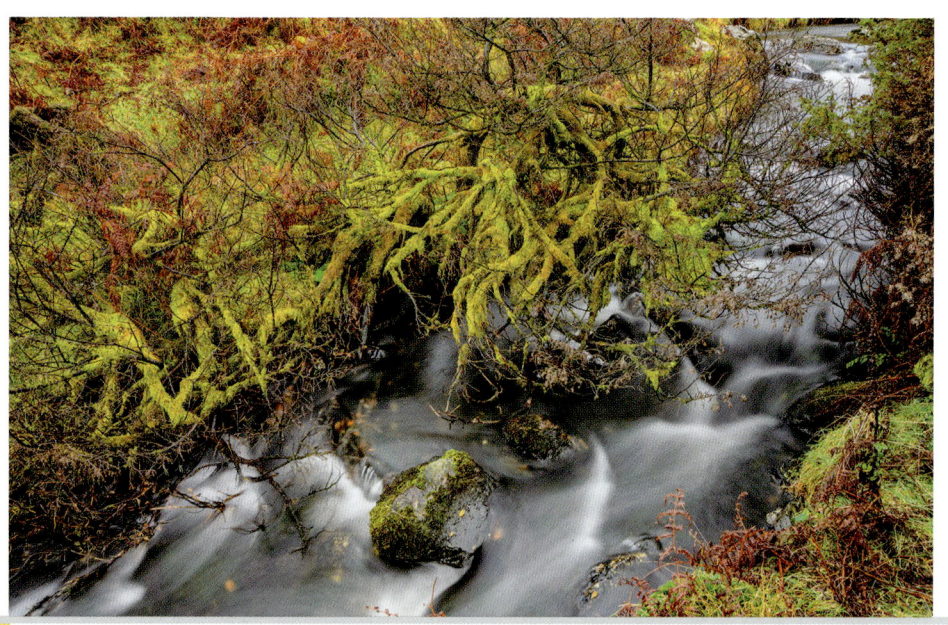

» COLOR SPACE

Color spaces define the range (or gamut) of colors which are recorded. To select the color space, use Color space in the Photo Shooting menu (page 104).

sRGB (the default setting) has a narrower gamut but images often appear initially brighter and more punchy. It's the usual color space on the Internet and in most photo printing stores, for example, and is generally appropriate for images that will be used or printed straight off, with little or no post-processing. Most mobile devices and many computer screens have a narrower gamut even than

sRGB. The D750's monitor screen gets pretty close to it.

Adobe RGB has a wider gamut and is commonly used in professional printing and reproduction. It's a better choice for for professional applications, especially in print, or where significant post-processing is anticipated. High-end computer screens generally have a wider gamut than sRGB but only a few can equal or exceed Adobe RGB; these are generally very expensive.

PEAK PERFORMANCE ≫
Low ISO settings give maximum dynamic range. Here, careful processing of the RAW file means there is good detail throughout the image. *14mm, 1/100 sec., f/11, ISO 100, tripod.*

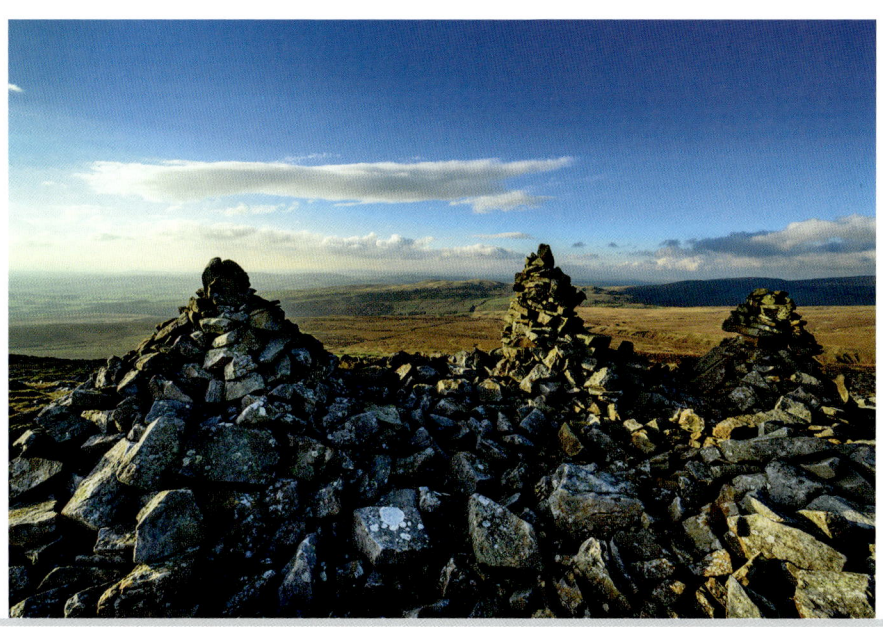

›› WHITE BALANCE

Light sources, natural and artificial, vary enormously in color. The human eye and brain are generally very good at compensating for this and seeing things in their "true" colors—we nearly always see grass as green, and so on. Digital cameras also have a capacity to compensate for the varying colors of light and, used correctly, the D750 can produce natural-looking colors under almost any conditions.

Automatic white balance produces very good results most of the time. For finer control, or for creative effect, a wide range of user-controlled settings are available.

When shooting RAW, the camera white balance setting is not crucial, as it can be adjusted in post-processing. However, it's still helpful to get it right as it does affect how images look on playback and review.

When shooting movies, where there's no RAW option, the right white balance setting can be vital, though using a Flat Picture Control (page 92) gives more room for maneuver.

WHITE BALANCE ››
These images were shot with different white balance settings to show the changes in color cast: **1**) Incandescent; **2**) Cool-white fluorescent; **3**) Direct sunlight; **4**) Flash; **5**) Cloudy; **6**) Shade.

› Setting the white balance

There are two ways to set the white balance:

1) Hold down **WB** and rotate the main command dial until the required icon is displayed in the control panel. This is quicker, but the second method offers extra options.

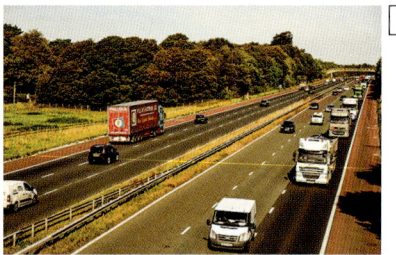

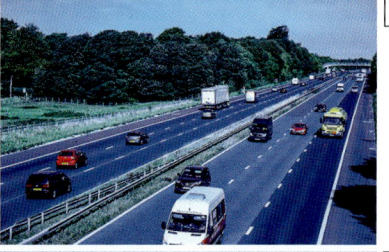

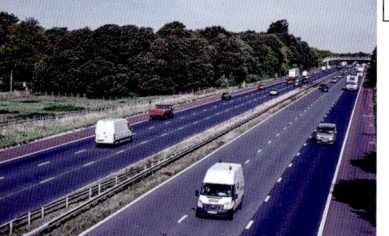

2) In the Photo Shooting menu, select **White balance**, then highlight and select the required setting. In most cases, a graphical display appears, with which you can fine-tune the setting (see below). Or just press (OK) to accept the standard value.

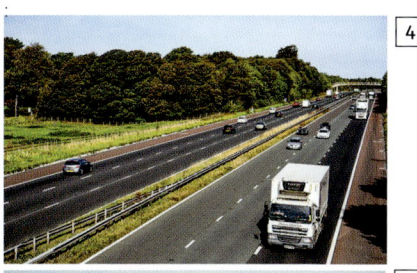

4

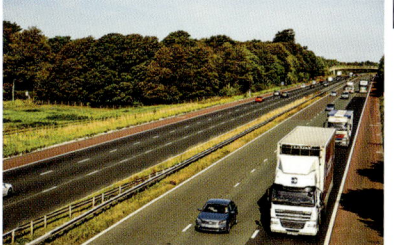

5

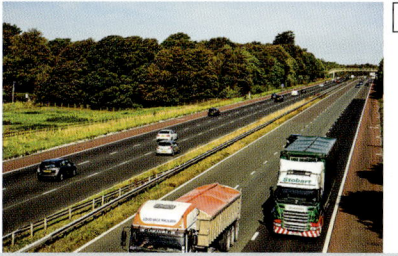

6

› Fine-tuning white balance

The basic options offered by **WB** and the Main Command Dial, or the top level of the Shooting menu item, are just the start.

Fine-tuning with the sub-command dial

For most of the standard WB settings, if you hold **WB** and turn the sub-command dial, you'll see a letter and number in the information display, alongside a graphical "spectrum". Turn the dial to the left to shift the image towards amber (**a1**–**a6**), to the right to shift towards blue (**b1**–**b6**).

Fine-tuning in the Photo Shooting menu

Auto has two sub-options: **Normal** (**AUTO1**), which keeps colors correct as far as possible, and **Keep warm lighting colors** (**AUTO2**), which does not fully correct warm hues such as those generated by incandescent lighting. This can work quite well for sunrise/sunset shots as well.

If you select **Incandescent**, **Direct sunlight**, **Flash**, **Cloudy**, or **Shade**, then press ▶ , a graphical display appears and you can fine-tune the setting using the multi-selector. When done, press (OK) to accept the new value.

When you select **Fluorescent**, a submenu appears from which you can

2

Icon	Menu option	Color temp.	Description
AUTO	Normal	3500–8000°K	Camera sets white balance automatically, based on information from imaging and metering sensors. Most accurate with Type G and D lenses.
	Keep warm lighting colors		
☀	**Incandescent**	3000°K	Use in incandescent (tungsten) lighting, e.g. traditional household bulbs.
	Fluorescent: *Submenu offers seven options*:		
	1) Sodium-vapor lamps	2700°K	Use in sodium-vapor lighting, often used in sports venues.
	2) Warm-white fluorescent	3000°K	Use in warm-white fluorescent lighting.
	3) White fluorescent	3700°K	Use in white fluorescent lighting.
☼	4) Cool-white fluorescent	4200°K	Use in cool-white fluorescent lighting.
	5) Day-white fluorescent	5000°K	Use in daylight white fluorescent lighting.
	6) Daylight fluorescent	6500°K	Use in daylight fluorescent lighting.
	7) High temp. mercury-vapor	7200°K	Use in high color temperature lighting, e.g. mercury vapor lamps.
☀	**Direct sunlight**	5200°K	Use for subjects in direct sunlight.
⚡	**Flash**	5400°K	Use with flash. Value may require fine-tuning with large-scale studio flash.
☁	**Cloudy**	6000°K	Use in daylight, under cloudy/overcast skies.
⌂	**Shade**	8000°K	Use for subjects in shade on sunny days.
K	**Choose color temp.**	2500–10,000°K	Select color temperature from list of values.
PRE	**Preset Manual**	n/a	Derive white balance direct from subject or light source, or from an existing photo.

select the appropriate variety of fluorescent lamp. (The default is 4: **Cool-white fluorescent**.) If required, you can then press ▶ to do some further fine-tuning, as above.

Domestic energy-saving bulbs are compact fluorescent units. Their color temperature varies widely so take test shots if possible, or shoot RAW.

> **Note:**
> When you use method 1 (on page 62) to select Fluorescent, the precise value will be whatever was last selected via the submenu in the Photo Shooting menu. If you've never done this, the default will apply.

› Choose color temp.

This option allows you to dial in a specific color temperature. If you select it using the main command dial, you adjust the numerical value using the sub-command dial. In the Photo Shooting menu, you gain an extra option to adjust the balance on a green–magenta scale alongside the color temperature scale.

› Preset Manual White Balance

You can set the white balance to precisely match any lighting conditions, by taking a reference photo of a neutral white object, or by copying white balance data from an existing image on the memory card. This is extremely useful when absolute color accuracy is required (for instance, for professional images of fabrics or artwork) but it is, quite frankly, a complicated procedure that few of us will ever employ. If you do need to do this for JPEG images, see the Nikon manual for details. It's normally much easier to shoot RAW and tweak the white balance later; a reference photo is still helpful when high precision is required.

> **Tip**
>
> *The endpapers of this book are designed to serve as "gray cards", ideal for reference photos for setting a preset white balance or for precise post-processing of RAW images.*

2 » FOCUS

The D750 has a wide range of focus options, but they all boil down to how the camera focuses, determined by the focus modes, and where it focuses, determined by the AF-area modes.

› Focus modes

To switch between manual focus and autofocus use the focus selector switch on the front of the camera by the lens mount. To choose the AF mode, press ⊕, in the center of this switch, and rotate the main command dial. As you do this, the settings are shown in the viewfinder, control panel, and information display. The information display continues to indicate the chosen focus mode.

FOCUS SELECTOR SWITCH ❮❮

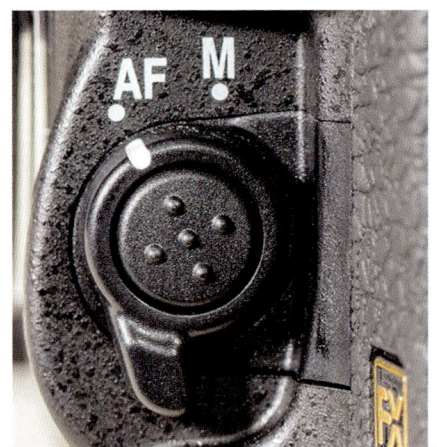

AF-A Auto-servo AF
AF-A means that the camera automatically switches between two autofocus modes—single-servo AF and continuous-servo AF (see below). Initially the camera is set to AF-A in all exposure modes. You can change this in all modes except Effects modes.

AF-S Single-servo AF
The camera focuses when the shutter release is pressed halfway. If you keep it half-pressed, focus remains locked on this point. The shutter cannot release to take a picture unless focus has been acquired (*focus priority*). AF-S is recommended for accurate focusing on static subjects.

AF-C Continuous-servo AF
In this mode, recommended for moving subjects, the camera continues to seek focus as long as you keep the shutter release depressed—if the subject moves, the camera will refocus. The camera is able to take a picture even if it hasn't acquired perfect focus (release priority).

The D750 employs predictive focus tracking; if the subject moves while AF-C is active, the camera analyzes the movement and attempts to predict where the subject will be when the shutter is released.

MOVING TARGET ⌄

AF-C mode tracks moving subjects.
180mm, 1/400 sec., f/4, ISO 800.

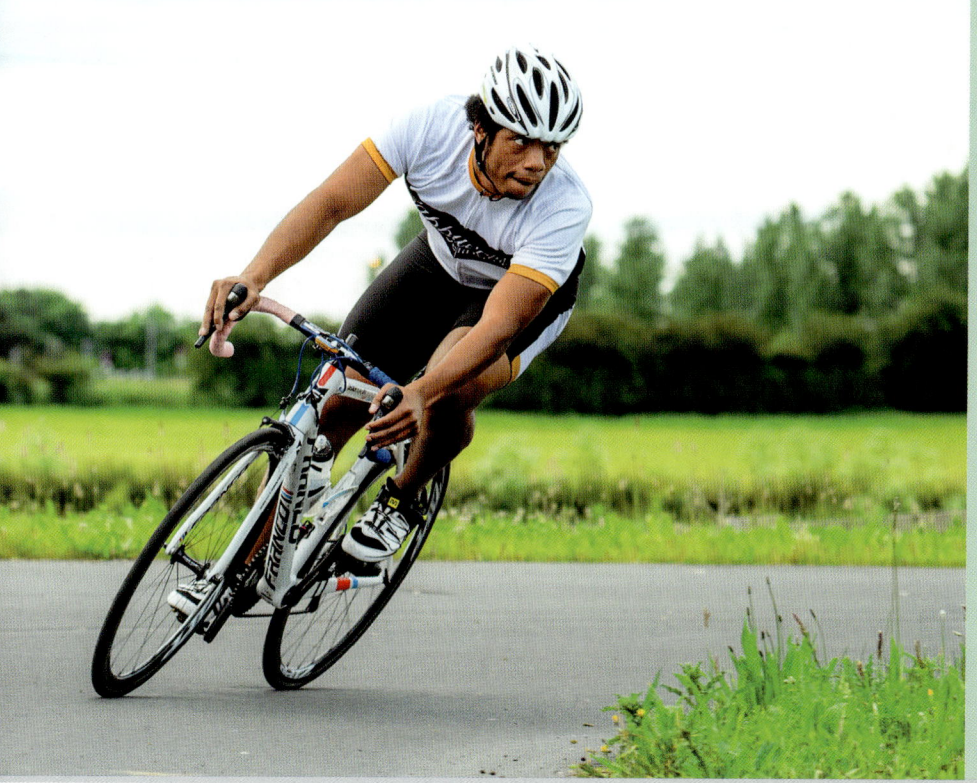

2 › Manual focus

When a camera has sophisticated AF capabilities, manual focus might appear redundant, but many photographers still value the extra control and involvement. There are also certain subjects and circumstances which can bamboozle even the best AF systems. Manual focusing is a straightforward process, which hardly requires description: set the focus mode selector to **M** and use the focusing ring on the lens to bring the subject into focus.

MANUAL FOCUS ⌄
I focused manually on one of the nearby clumps of moss (though using AF and focus lock would have been equally easy).
85mm, 1/40 sec., f/10, ISO 200.

Focus confirmation
When focusing manually, you can still take advantage of the camera's focusing technology, thanks to focus confirmation. It requires you to select an appropriate focus point, as if you were using autofocus. When the subject at that point is in focus, a white dot appears at far left of the viewfinder data display. When it's not in focus, triangles suggest which way to turn the focus ring to bring it into focus.

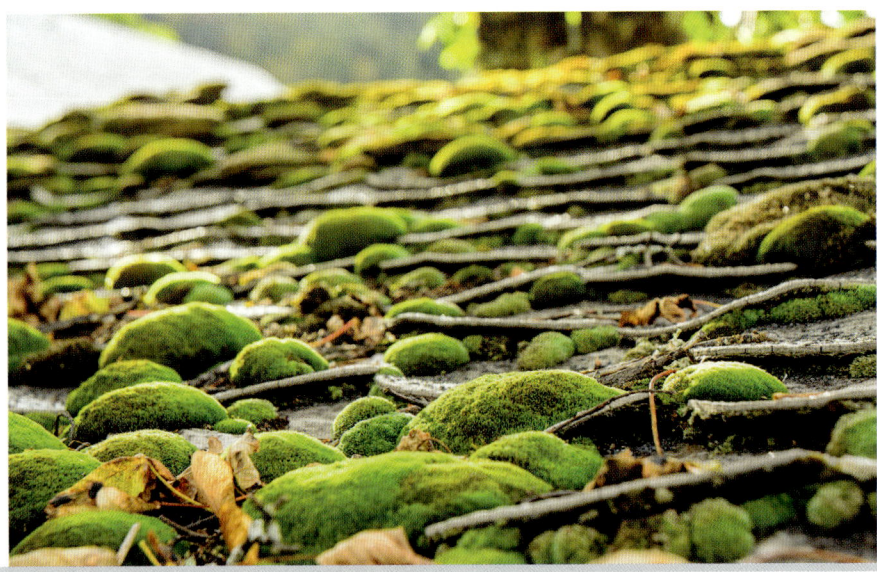

› AF-assist illuminator

The AF-assist illuminator—a long name for a small lamp—can help the camera focus in dim light. It requires the camera to be in AF-S, and either the central focus point must be selected or Auto-area AF must be engaged. If these conditions are met, it illuminates automatically when required. For effective operation, the lens should be in the range 24–200mm. The AF-assist illuminator can be turned off using Custom setting a7.

› Back-button autofocus

At standard settings, **AE-L/AF-L** is used to lock both exposure and focus. You can use Custom setting f4 to change its behavior

AF-ASSIST ILLUMINATOR   ⌄⌄

to lock only focus, or only exposure. And there's another option: **AF-ON only**. When this is enabled, the shutter-release button no longer controls autofocus; you can initiate AF only by pressing **AE-L/AF-L**. Many pros choose to use this approach, often called "back-button AF".

The logic is that this allows you to get the best of both worlds (AF-C and AF-S). To do so, you must set the camera to Continuous-servo AF. Then, if you press **AE-L/AF-L** and release it, the camera focuses once. It does not refocus if you press the shutter-release button. This effectively duplicates AF-S even though the camera is set to AF-C. On the other hand, if you keep pressure on **AE-L/AF-L**, the camera focuses continuously.

This effectively lets you switch seamlessly between AF-C and AF-S, without any pause in shooting, merely by using **AE-L/AF-L**. It also means that the camera only refocuses when you tell it to, by deliberately pressing **AE-L/AF-L**. And it also means that you can use the shutter-release button for exposure lock, simply by maintaining half-pressure on it.

The D750 has 51 focus points covering the central portion of the frame (indicated by a faint outline in the viewfinder). To focus on the desired subject, the camera must use appropriate focus point(s); this is the function of AF-area modes. To choose the AF-area mode, press and hold ⊕ and rotate the sub-command dial.

VIEWFINDER DISPLAY ⏷

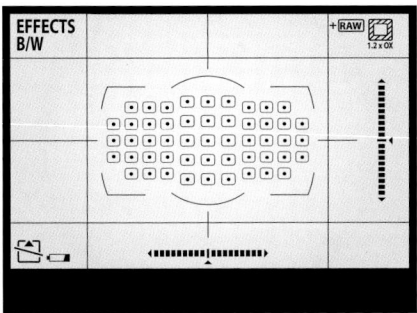

The viewfinder displays the available focus areas as well as an in-focus indicator at the left of the menu bar.

Single-area AF

In this mode, you select the focus area manually, using the multi-selector to move quickly through the 51 focus points. The chosen focus point is illuminated in the viewfinder. This mode is best suited to relatively static subjects.

Dynamic-area AF

Dynamic-area AF has several sub-modes. These can only be selected when the AF mode is AF-C (page 66).

In all sub-modes, you still select the initial focus point, as in Single-area AF; if the subject moves, the camera will then employ other focus points to maintain focus, but it's still trying to track the subject you selected, and will default back to the original focus point if possible.

The sub-mode options determine the number of focus points that will be employed for this: 9, 21, or the full 51 points.

⬛ 3D tracking

This uses a wide range of information, including subject colors, to track subjects that may be moving erratically. It's the obvious choice for action shooting, unless the subject is moving directly towards or away from the camera (when Group-area AF is very effective).

⬕ Group-area AF

In this mode, you select a group of five focus points (though only the outer four appear in the viewfinder). You can position the group, using the multi-selector, as you normally do with a single focus point. When you focus, the camera takes data from all five points and focuses on the closest subject that coincides with one of them. This can improve focus acquisition and performance on fast-moving subjects. Group-area AF is available in both AF-S and AF-C. In AF-S, if a face or faces are detected, the camera will prioritize them for focusing.

Auto-area AF

This mode makes focus point selection fully automatic; in other words, the camera decides what the intended subject is. The camera employs face-detection technology, and if a human face is detected it will prioritize it for focusing—which may or may not be what you want.

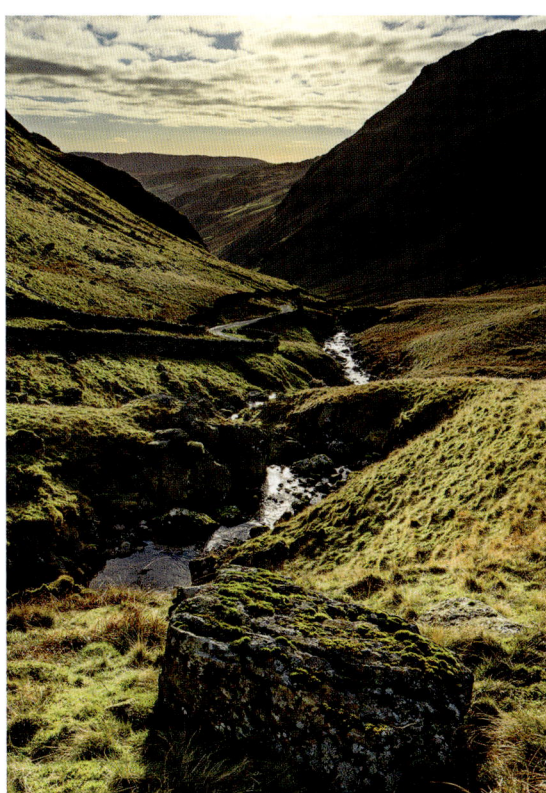

SINGLE-AREA AF **«**
Single-area AF was used for this landscape shot, selecting a point near the foreground to keep as much in focus as possible.
85mm, 1/640 sec., f/8, ISO 800.

The D750's 51 focus points cover the central part of the frame, almost equal to the DX-crop area. This allows quick and accurate selection to cover most subjects, whether it's a static focus point in AF-S or the initial focus point in AF-C. Understandably, you can't manually select the focus point when ▣ Auto-area AF is engaged.

If the focus point doesn't move when you operate the multi-selector, it's probably because the selector lock (around the multi-selector) is locked (position **L**). Pressing the center of the multi-selector selects the central focus point, or centers the group (unless you change the options in Custom setting f1).

The 11 focus points closest to the center of the frame are the most sensitive and the most likely to keep on working when light levels drop really low.

> **Note:**
> Custom setting a7 lets you opt for **focus point wrap-around**, meaning that if you move the focus point to the edge of the available area, a further press on the multi-selector in the same direction takes it to the opposite edge of the area.

Focus lock

The D750's focus points cover a wide area—close to the full DX-crop area—but do not extend to the edges of the frame.

To focus on a subject outside this area, you can use focus lock. It's very similar in principle to exposure lock (page 55). You shift the camera until the subject is within the area covered by the focus points, then select a focus point and focus on the subject in the normal way.

You then lock the focus, reframe the image as desired, and take the shot. In Single-Servo AF mode, you can lock focus by keeping half-pressure on the shutter-release button, or press and hold **AE-L/AF-L**. In Continuous-Servo AF, *only* **AE-L/AF-L** can be used to lock focus. Keep pressing the appropriate button to maintain focus lock for further shots.

> ### *Tip*
> *Back-button AF (see page 69) makes focus lock even simpler: a single press on **AE-L/AF-L** sets focus and it remains set until you press **AE-L/AF-L** again.*

LOW LIGHT »

The camera had no trouble focusing in the relatively low light of Ripon Cathedral—I used a higher ISO setting.
300mm, 1/40 sec., f/5.6, ISO 3200.

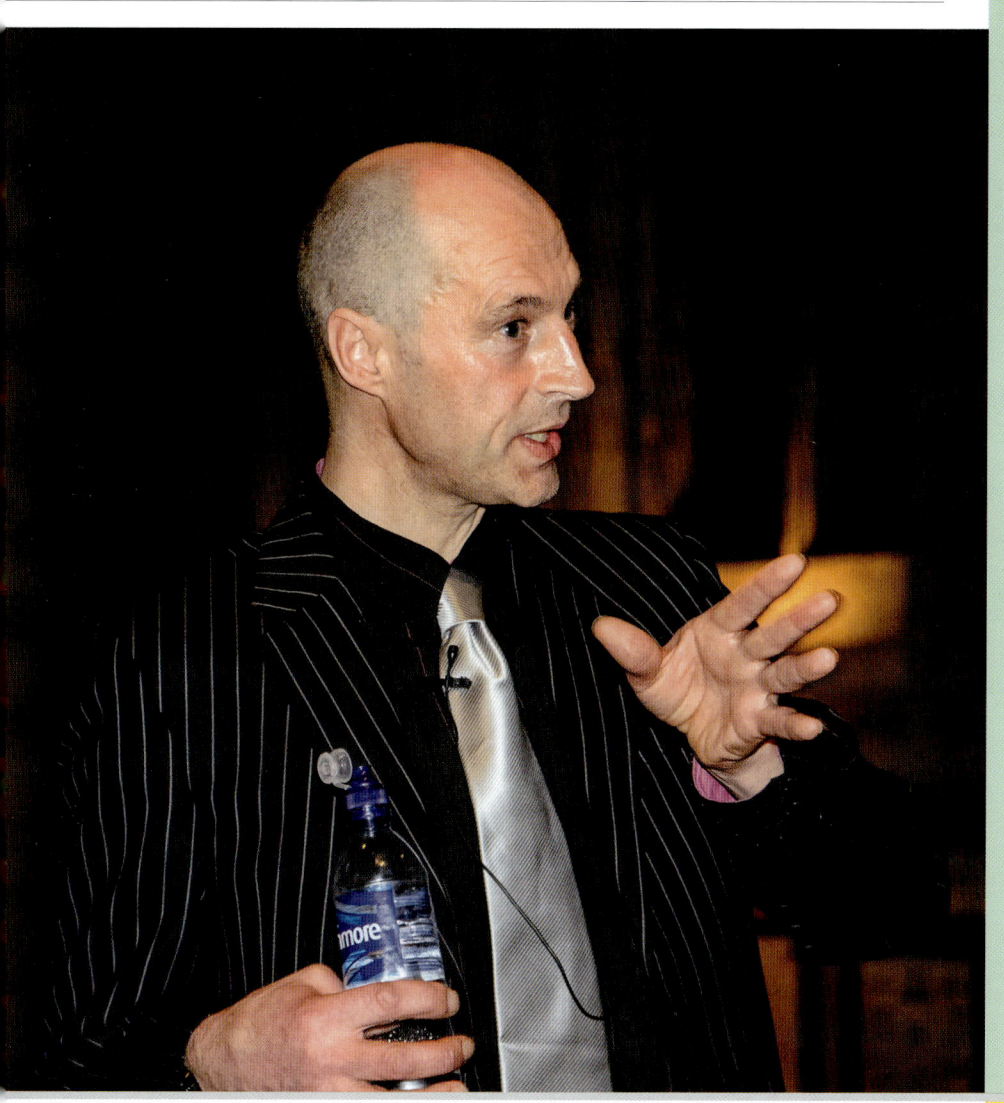

2 » IMAGE QUALITY

"Image quality" refers to the file format, or the way in which image data is recorded. The D750 can record two file types: NEF (RAW) and JPEG. JPEG files undergo significant processing in-camera to produce files that should be usable right away (for instance, for immediate printing), without further processing on a computer. However, this in-camera processing discards much of the information originally captured by the sensor.

NEF (RAW) files record this data "as is", giving much greater scope for further processing to achieve exactly the desired result. This requires suitable software such as Nikon Capture NX-D or Adobe Lightroom (see pages 227, 229). RAW or Camera RAW is a generic term for this kind of file; NEF is Nikon's RAW file format.

RAW files can be recorded at either 12-bit or 14-bit depth. 14-bit files capture four times more color information, but produce larger file sizes and (possibly) longer write-times.

The D750 can simultaneously record two versions of the same image, one JPEG for immediate needs and one RAW to be processed later for the ultimate result. You can opt for the two versions to be saved to separate memory cards (see **Role played by card in Slot 2** in the Photo Shooting menu, page 103).

Note:
In fact, every RAW file includes an embedded JPEG image. This is used for image review and playback, and is the basis of the histogram and highlights displays (page 86). It isn't accessible for standalone use.

› Setting image quality

There are two ways to set image quality:

1) Hold down ⊕ and rotate the main command dial until the required setting is displayed in the information display.

2) In the Photo Shooting menu, select **Image quality** using the multi-selector, and then highlight and select the required setting.

IMAGE QUALITY DIALOG ⤸

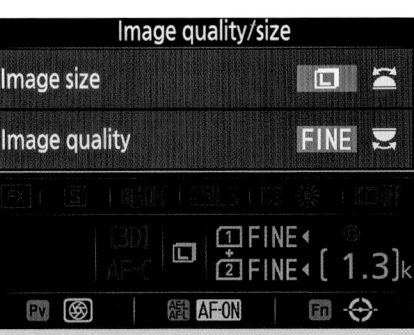

Image quality options

NEF (RAW)	12- or 14-bit NEF (RAW) files are recorded for the ultimate quality and creative flexibility. For NEF (RAW), there are three further options: compressed, lossless compressed, or uncompressed. Select options with **NEF (RAW) recording** in the Shooting menu.
JPEG fine	8-bit JPEG files are recorded with a compression ratio of approximately 1:4, suitable for demanding applications.
JPEG normal	8-bit JPEG files are recorded with a compression ratio of approximately 1:8, suitable for many less critical uses.
JPEG basic	8-bit JPEG files are recorded with a compression ratio of approximately 1:16, suitable for online use but not recommended for printing.
NEF (RAW) + JPEG fine **NEF (RAW) + JPEG normal** **NEF (RAW) + JPEG basic**	Two copies of the same image are recorded simultaneously, one NEF (RAW) and one JPEG.

There is occasional confusion between Image area and Image size. Image area refers to the portion of the sensor used to capture the image. Image size refers to the pixel count of the final image file.

› Image area

The D750 normally captures images using the whole of its 35.9 x 24mm FX-format sensor (labeled **36 x 24** for brevity). Other settings can be chosen through the Photo Shooting menu: select **Image area**, then **Choose image area**. Alternatively, press ◄�► as a shortcut: **Choose image area** is the first item in the list that appears.

DX (24 x 16) uses the central 24 x 16mm area of the sensor, equivalent to a DX-format camera. DX-crop enables the

use of DX lenses (see below), and may also allow a higher frame rate. It boosts the effective focal length of your lenses by 50% (see page 192), and it means that the focus sensors cover most of the frame.

1.2x (30x20) crops the image moderately while maintaining the standard aspect ratio. It has a 1.2x "teleconverter" effect (see page 193).

The viewfinder display adapts to image area selection by showing a heavy outline around the chosen area. The area excluded can also be shown grayed out, which can make framing easier, but only when **AF point illumination** (Custom setting a6) is **Off**.

Using DX lenses

DX lenses are designed for optimum performance with smaller DX-format sensors, as used in cameras like the D7100. They do not cover the full area of the FX-format sensor, so the corners of the frame are blacked out—an extreme case of vignetting (see page 197).

By default, the D750 automatically detects when DX lenses are fitted and sets a DX-format crop. This option can be turned off via **Auto DX crop** under **Image area** in the Photo Shooting menu—and there can be good reasons to do so (see page 103).

IN THE FRAME ⌄
1.2x and DX image areas, superimposed on the full FX frame.

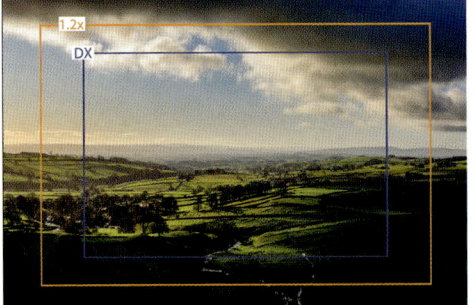

› Image size

When shooting JPEG, the D750 offers three options for image size. Final image dimensions also depend on the chosen Image area (see the table below).

When Image area is FX, Medium is roughly equivalent to a 13-megapixel camera and Small to a 6-megapixel camera. Even Small size images exceed the maximum resolution of almost all computer monitors and are far beyond the (approximately) 2 megapixels of an HD TV.

Image size options and dimensions

Image area	Large	Medium	Small
FX (36 x 24)	6016 x 4016	4512 x 3008	3008 x 2008
1.2x (30x20)	5008 x 3336	3752 x 2504	2504 x 1664
DX	3936 x 2624	2944 x 1968	1968 x 1312

Setting image size

There are two ways to set image size:

1) Hold down ⊕▦ and rotate the sub-command dial until the required setting is displayed in the control panel/information display. This is usually quicker.

2) In the Photo Shooting menu, select **Image size** using the multi-selector, then highlight and select the required setting.

DSLRs like the D750 are essentially designed around the viewfinder and it still has many advantages for the majority of picture taking. It's more intuitive and offers the sense of a direct connection to the subject. There's also much less risk of camera shake, and viewfinder-based autofocus is faster.

However, to fully realize the high image quality of today's cameras, discerning shooters use tripods regularly—this dilutes the handling advantages of the viewfinder. Also, Live View focusing, although much slower than viewfinder-based AF, is extremely accurate. The D750's tilting screen can be used with Live View to allow shooting from very high or low positions where you can't use the viewfinder.

LIVE VIEW ACTIVATION SWITCH ⏬

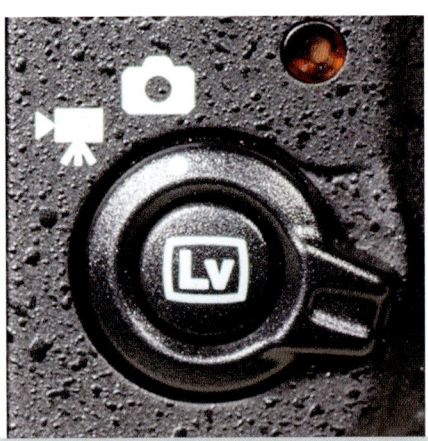

Live View is also the jumping-off point for shooting movies (see page 184), so familiarity with Live View is an advantage if you're new to movie shooting.

› Using Live View

Check the **Lv** switch on the rear of the camera is set to the still photography position **[camera icon]**. Press its center button to activate Live View. The mirror flips up, the viewfinder blacks out, and the monitor displays a continuous preview of the scene.

In continuous release modes, the mirror stays up between shots, making it hard to follow moving subjects. To exit Live View press the center button again.

› Live View display options

A range of shooting information is displayed at top and bottom of the screen, partly overlaying the image. Pressing **info** changes this information display, cycling through a series of screens— see the table opposite.

Exposure Preview
Normally, the Live View display shows the scene at a standardized brightness. However, the D750 can give you a live preview of the final image, based on current exposure settings. To activate this preview, press **[icon]** in

Live View info	Details
Information ON	Information bars superimposed at top and bottom of screen.
Information OFF	Top information bar disappears, key shooting information still shown at bottom.
Framing guides	Grid lines appear, useful for critical framing.
Histogram	(Available in Exposure Preview only.)
Virtual horizon	Displays a horizon indicator on the monitor to assist in leveling the camera.

Live View and select **Exposure Preview>On** from the options on the right of the screen. If the results look under- or overexposed, you can use exposure compensation (page 54) to rectify matters (in Manual, adjust aperture, shutter speed, or ISO). The screen also shows an analog exposure display at

the right side, and can display a histogram (see the table above).

There are some limitations: the preview can't show what the results will be if you're planning to use flash for the actual shot, or if bracketing is in effect. It may be less accurate if Active D-Lighting or HDR are being used. And, as ever, the screen can be hard to see properly in bright sunlight.

VIRTUAL HORIZON   ⌄⌄

Live View display options include a virtual horizon.

1/8   F22   ISO200   [547]

Tip

Whether you engage Exposure Preview or not, the Live View image does reflect the selected Picture Control (page 90), including Monochrome.

› Live View quick settings

Key settings (see the table below) can be quickly adjusted in Live View. Press ◂**ℹ**▸ to reveal these items at the right side of the screen.

   Scroll up or down using ▲/▼; press ▶ or **OK** to access the highlighted item.

LIVE VIEW QUICK SETTINGS ⌄

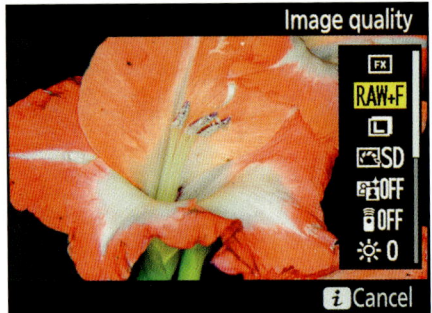

Live View quick adjustments	Details
Image area	See page 76.
Image quality	See page 74.
Image size	See page 74.
Picture Control	See page 90.
Active D-Lighting	See page 88.
Remote control mode	See page 196.
Monitor brightness	Adjust screen brightness with ▲/▼. This only affects the screen image and has no effect on the exposure level of actual images. Not available if Exposure preview is On. Settings changed here do not apply in normal shooting.
Exposure preview	See page 78.

› Focusing in Live View

Focusing in Live View operates differently from normal shooting. The usual focusing sensors are unavailable and the camera takes focus information directly from the main image sensor instead. This is significantly slower than normal AF operation, but very accurate. You can zoom in for a critical focus check: this is extremely handy for ultra-precise focusing, such as in macro work.

Live View has its own set of autofocus options. There are two AF modes and four AF-area modes.

Select Live View AF mode/AF-area mode when Live View is active. Press ⊕ and use the main command dial to select AF mode. Use ⊕ and the sub-command dial to select the AF-area mode.

Live View AF modes

The AF-mode options are Single-servo AF (AF-S) and Full-time servo AF (AF-F). AF-S corresponds to AF-S in normal shooting: the camera focuses when the shutter release is pressed halfway, and focus remains locked as long as the shutter release remains depressed.

AF-F corresponds roughly to AF-C in normal shooting, but responds differently to the shutter-release button. The camera seeks focus as long as Live View remains

FOCUSING IN LIVE VIEW ❯❯
The focus area (a red rectangle, which turns green when focus is acquired) can be positioned anywhere on screen.

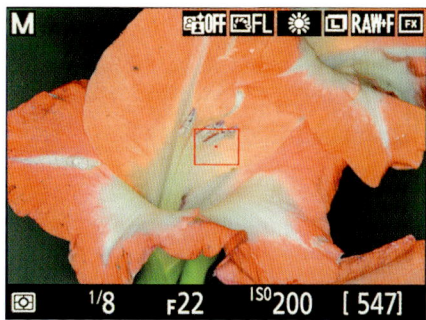

active. When you half-press the shutter release, the focus locks and remains locked until you release the button, or take a shot.

Live View AF-area mode Live View AF-area modes do not correspond to the ones used in viewfinder shooting.

WIDE *Wide-area AF and* NORM *Normal area AF* In both these modes, the focus area (outlined in red) can be moved anywhere on the screen, using the multi-selector. The difference is simply that in NORM the area is much smaller. Pressing ⊕ ▦ zooms the screen view, centered on the focus point. Press repeatedly to zoom closer. By selecting **Zoom on/off** in **Custom setting**

2

f1>Live view, you can jump to 50%, 100%, or 200% magnification by pressing (OK).

> ### Tip
>
> *The ability to place the focus point anywhere on screen is useful for off-center subjects, especially when using a tripod. In handheld shooting it's generally quicker and easier to use the viewfinder and employ focus lock (page 72).*

[📷] *Face-priority AF* In this mode, the camera automatically detects up to 35 faces and selects the closest, outlining it with a double yellow border. You can override to focus on a different person by shifting the focus point with the multi-selector. To focus on the selected face, press the shutter-release button halfway.

[⊡] *Subject tracking* When Subject tracking is selected, a white rectangle appears at the center of the screen. Align this with the desired subject using the multi-selector, then press (OK). The camera "memorizes" the subject and the focus target then turns yellow. It will now track the subject as it moves, and can even reacquire the subject if it temporarily leaves the frame. To focus, press the

shutter-release button halfway; the target rectangle blinks green as the camera focuses and then becomes solid green. If the camera fails to focus the rectangle blinks red instead: pictures can still be taken but focus may not be correct. To end focus tracking press [☀] again.

> ### Warning!
>
> *Subject tracking can't keep up with rapidly moving subjects. Viewfinder shooting is more effective for these.*

Manual focus

Manual focus operates much as in viewfinder shooting. However the Live View display still reflects the selected Live View AF mode. If this is Wide-area AF or Normal-area AF, the display still shows a red rectangle. If you zoom in to focus more precisely, the zoom centers on this rectangle. You can move it around using the multi-selector.

› Aperture in Live View

Unlike viewfinder photography, where the aperture remains wide open until the shot is taken, in Live View the lens is stopped down. This effectively offers a continuous depth of field preview (page 49). To take full advantage of precise focusing in Live View, it helps to have the aperture at its widest, as minimal depth of field makes subjects snap in and out of focus more clearly. By pressing the Preview (Pv) button, you can temporarily open the aperture for this purpose—we could call this "reverse depth of field preview". Press Pv again, or take a shot, to revert aperture to the selected setting.

CRITICAL FOCUSING ⌄
Normal area AF is the best choice for precision and accuracy—invaluable when depth of field is minimal.
100mm macro, 1/30 sec., f/11, ISO 100, tripod.

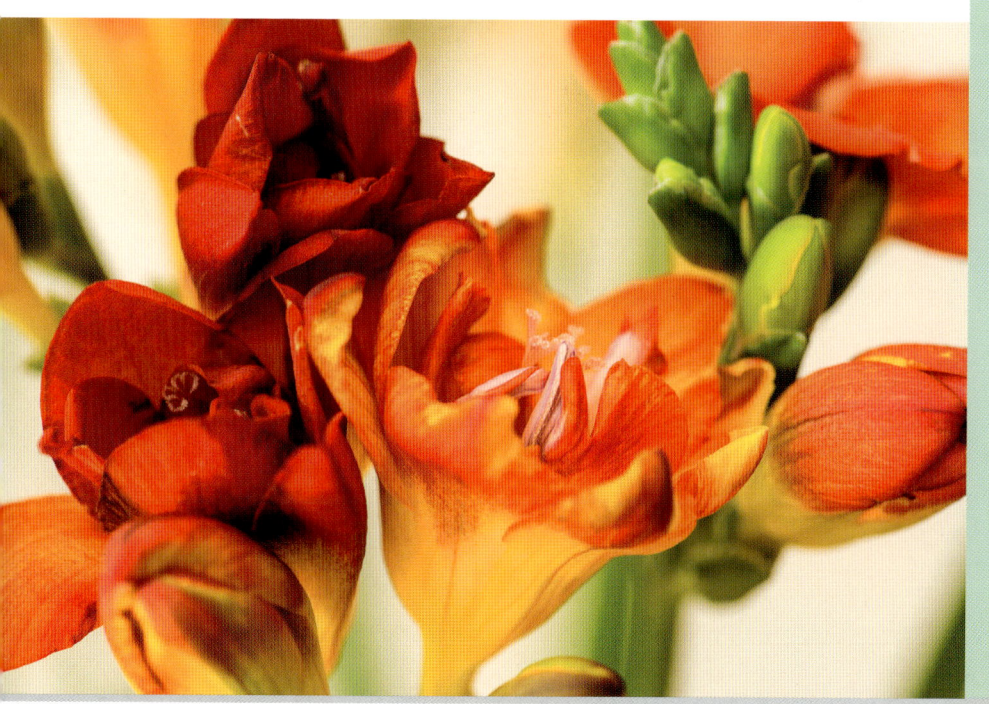

2 » IMAGE PLAYBACK

The D750's generous high-resolution LCD screen makes image playback both pleasurable and highly informative. Its wide color gamut gives an excellent indication of how images will look on a computer screen, if not in print.

To display the most recent image, press ▶ ; if **Image Review** (see page 100) is **On**, images are also displayed automatically after shooting. In continuous release modes, Image review begins after the last image in a burst is captured; images appear in sequence.

> **Note:**
> To conserve the battery, the monitor turns off after a period of inactivity. The default is 10 seconds but intervals between 4 sec. and 10 min. can be set using Custom Setting c4.

Playback pages	Selection	Details
Basic file info	Always available.	Large image, basic information at bottom of screen. Focus point used can also be shown: select using **Playback display options>Focus point**.
None (image only)	Enable from Playback menu.	Large image, no other data.
Overview	On by default; disable from Playback menu.	Small image, simple histogram, summary information.
Location data		Only appears when a GPS device was attached during shooting (see page 230).
Shooting data	Enable from Playback menu.	Pages 1–3 are always available. Page 4 only appears when Copyright Information is recorded (see page 133).
RGB histogram	Enable from Playback menu.	See page 86.
Highlights	Enable from Playback menu.	See page 87.

› Viewing photo information

The D750 records masses of information (metadata) about each image taken, and this can also be viewed on playback, using ▲/▼ to scroll through up to nine pages of information (see the table opposite). To determine which pages are visible, visit Playback display options in the Playback menu (page 100). Enable/disable options with ▶; press (OK) to confirm and exit.

› Viewing other images

To view other images on the memory card, use ▶ to view images in the order of capture, ◀ to view them in reverse order.

› Viewing images as thumbnails

To view multiple images, from the Image only or Overview pages, press 🔍🔳 repeatedly to display 4, 9, or 72 images. Use ▲/▼ to bring other images into view. The currently selected image is outlined in yellow. To return to full-frame view, press (OK).

› Calendar View

Calendar View displays images grouped by the date on which they were taken. With 72 images displayed, press 🔍🔳 again to

reach the first calendar page (Date View), with the most recent date highlighted, and pictures from that date in a strip on the right (the thumbnail list). Use the multi-selector to select other dates. Press 🔍🔳 again to enter the thumbnail list and scroll through pictures from the selected date; press ▶ for a larger preview of the selected image.

CALENDAR VIEW ⌄

› Memory card selection

A small icon at bottom left on the playback screen shows which memory card slot is being used for playback. To switch between card slots, press 🔍🔳 , select **Playback slot and folder**, highlight the desired slot and press (OK). If there are multiple folders on the card(s) you can choose between them.

2

› Deleting images

To delete the current image, or the selected image in thumbnail view, press 🗑. A confirmation dialog appears. To proceed, press 🗑 again; to cancel, press ▶ .
In Calendar View you can also delete all images taken on a selected date. Highlight that date in Date View, then press 🗑. A confirmation dialog appears: press 🗑 again to delete or ▶ to cancel.

› Protecting images

To protect the selected image, press ?/🔒.
To remove protection, press again.
Protected images can't be deleted by the above methods, but will be deleted when you format the memory card.

› Playback zoom

To examine details or assess sharpness, you can zoom in on an image by pressing 🔍📼 .
To return to full-frame view, press OK.
    You can use the multi-selector to view other areas of the image. Rotate the main command dial to view corresponding areas of other images at the same magnification.
    Maximum magnification is reached after 10 presses. This actually gives a magnification of 200%, making the image pixelated and of debatable value. Eight presses gives 100% magnification. You can enable a shortcut, so that a single press on

OK takes you direct to this point. To do this, use Custom setting f1 **OK button**: select **Playback mode**, then **Zoom on/off**. Choose between **Low**, **1:1**, and **High** magnification. 1:1 equates to eight presses/100%. The zoom centers on the focus point which was active when the picture was taken.

› Histogram displays

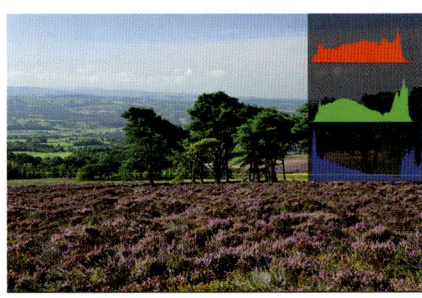

RGB HISTOGRAM DISPLAY   ⌃
A fairly typical histogram. This screenshot is from Nikon View NX2, but the camera-back histogram works the same way. The secondary peak on the right-hand side represents the light tones of the sky.

The histogram is a kind of graph showing the distribution of dark and light tones in an image. For assessing whether images are correctly exposed it's much more objective than examining the playback image itself, both for judging overall exposure and for assessing shadow and/or highlight clipping (see pages 87, 92).

The overview playback page shows a single histogram; checking **RGB histogram** under **Playback display options** (see page 84) enables a display showing individual histograms for the three color channels: red, green, and blue.

When shooting RAW, the Histogram (and Highlights) displays are based on the JPEG preview embedded with each RAW file. They are not, therefore, a foolproof guide to the potential for recovering highlight or shadow detail in that RAW file. This is particularly true when using "punchy" Picture Controls such as Vivid or Landscape, where JPEG processing discards more of the RAW data.

› Highlights

The D750 can also display a flashing warning for areas of the image with "clipped" highlights, i.e. completely white with no detail recorded. This gives another indication of whether an image is correctly exposed.

HIGHS AND LOWS ⌄
Washed-out highlights could have weakened the impact of this shot, so I checked the Highlights display.
28mm, 1/400 sec., f/13, ISO 250.

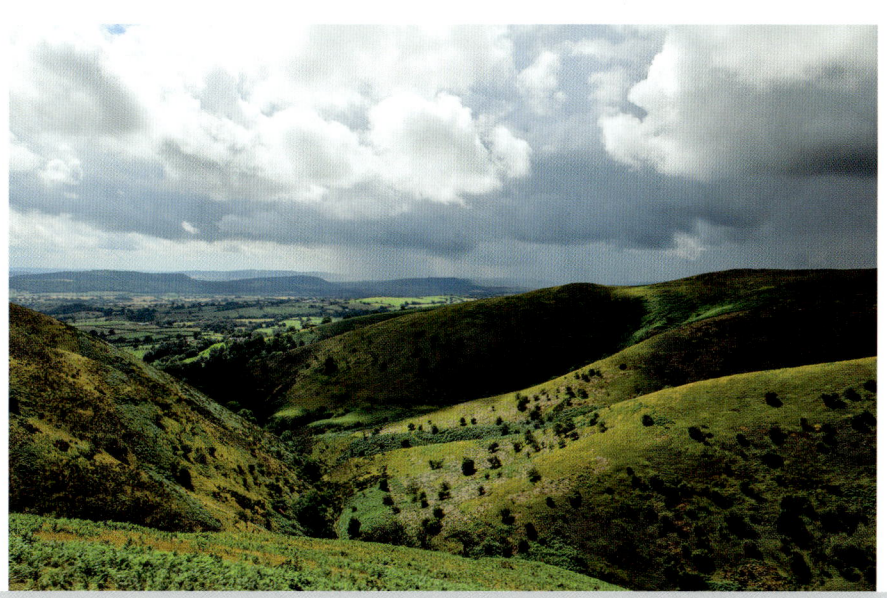

2 » IMAGE ENHANCEMENT

The D750 offers two main kinds of in-camera image adjustment and enhancement. First, certain settings can be applied before shooting an image—these are covered in this section. Second, you can create retouched copies of existing images on the memory card; this is done via the Retouch menu (see page 138).

Many of the controls that we've already considered have obvious and direct effects in the final image: aperture, shutter speed, ISO, white balance, and many more. The D750 provides other important ways to control the qualities of the image, notably Nikon Picture Controls and Active D-Lighting. These settings are directly relevant to JPEG images, but shouldn't be ignored when shooting RAW, as we'll see.

› Active D-Lighting

Active D-Lighting enhances the D750's ability to cope with scenes that show a wide range of brightness (dynamic range). In simple terms, it reduces the overall exposure to improve highlight capture, while mid-tones and shadows are boosted as the camera processes the image. Don't confuse it with the similarly named D-Lighting, which is a Retouch menu option.

Active D-Lighting can be accessed from the Photo Shooting menu, or by pressing

⊞ to reveal the Quick settings screen (see page 27). From the list of options, select **Off**, **Low**, **Normal**, **High**, **Extra high**, or **Auto** to determine the strength of the effect and press **OK**. This setting applies to all images until you reset Active D-Lighting.

> ### *Tip*
>
> *Because Active D-Lighting alters the overall exposure, it's advisable to turn it off when shooting RAW.*

ACTIVE D-LIGHTING   **»**
ADL Off (top) and High (bottom).
28mm, 1/25 and 1/50 sec., f/11, ISO 100, tripod.

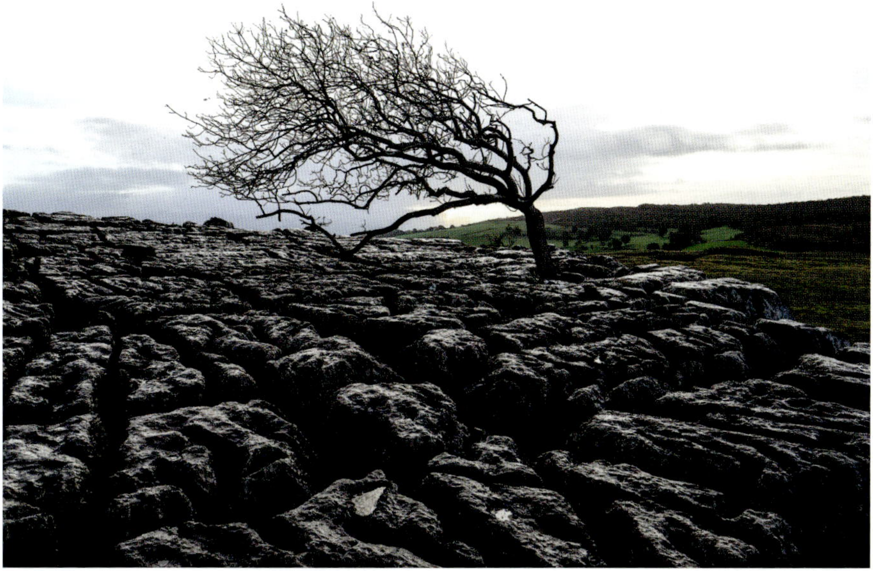

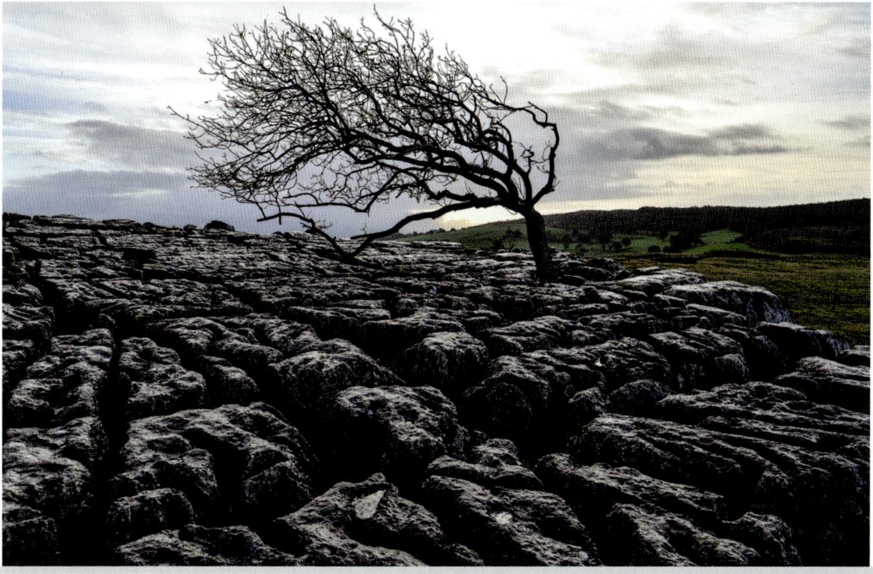

Picture Controls determine how the camera processes JPEG images. They also affect the preview image associated with each RAW file, on which Histogram and Highlights displays are based. Picture Controls also affect the appearance of the Live View preview image.

You can select Picture Controls from the Photo Shooting menu, or by pressing ◀**H**▶ to reveal the Quick settings screen (see page 27).

The D750 has seven pre-loaded Picture Controls: **Standard**, **Neutral**, **Vivid**, **Monochrome**, **Portrait**, **Landscape**, and **Flat**. These are mostly fairly self-explanatory. Portrait, for example, uses moderate settings for contrast, sharpening, and saturation, aiming to deliver natural colors and flattering skin tones. The Flat Picture Control deserves additional explanation (see page 92).

Each Picture Control has preset values for **Sharpening**, **Clarity**, **Contrast**, and **Brightness**. For color images, there are also settings for **Saturation** and **Hue**; the Monochrome Picture Control has **Filter effects** and **Toning** instead.

You can fine-tune these settings for each Picture Control. You can also create and save your own custom Picture Controls. Further ready-made Picture Controls are available online.

Modifying Picture Controls

From the Photo Shooting menu or Quick settings screen, select **Set Picture Control**, highlight the required Picture Control, then press ▶. Select **Quick Adjust** or one of the specific parameters. Use ▶ or ◀ to change the values. When all parameters are as required, press **(OK)**. Modified values are retained until you modify that Picture Control again.

Custom Picture Controls

You can create up to nine additional Picture Controls, either in-camera or using the Picture Control Utility included with Nikon View NX2. For further details see Picture Control Utility's Help pages.

To create Custom Picture Controls in-camera, select **Manage Picture Control** from the Photo Shooting menu. Select **Save/edit** and press ▶. Highlight an existing Picture Control and press ▶ again. Edit the Picture Control as described under Modifying Picture Controls above. When satisfied, press **(OK)**.

PICTURE CONTROLS COMPARISON »
The same subject shot using Flat (top) and Vivid (bottom) Picture Controls.
24mm, 1/30 sec., f/11, ISO 200, tripod.

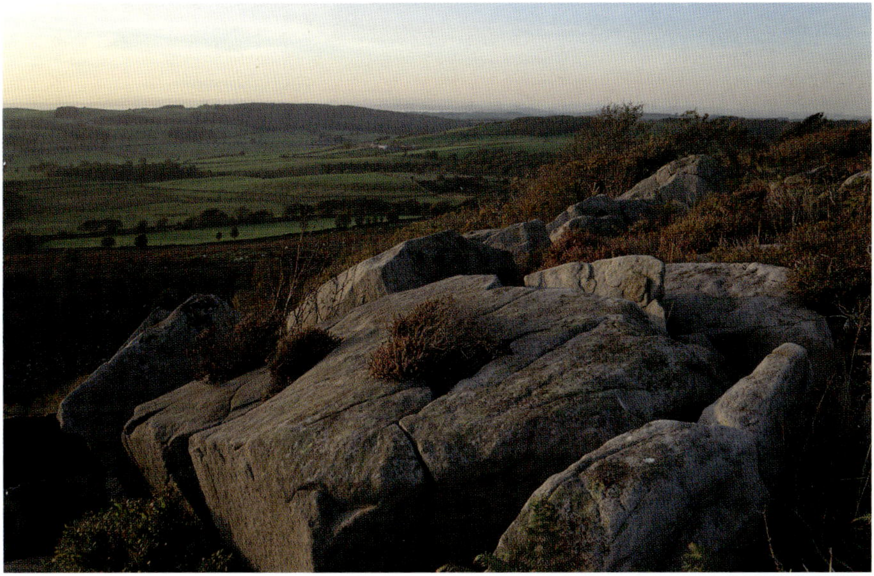

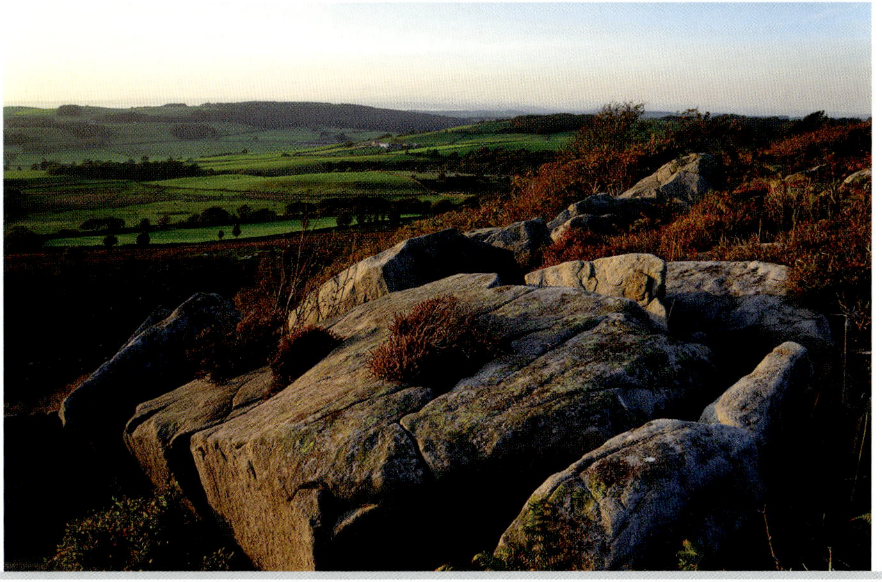

By default, the new version takes its name from the existing Picture Control on which it is based, plus a two-digit number (e.g. VIVID-02). You can give it a new name (up to 19 characters long) using the multi-selector to enter text. Finally, press (OK) to store the new Picture Control.

Flat Picture Control

The Flat Picture Control produces images which appear very subdued, with low contrast and saturation, and no in-camera sharpening. It is aimed mainly at movie-makers who intend to work on the color, contrast, and so on, of their footage in post-production. It's designed to preserve as much data as possible, giving maximum headroom for later adjustments and allowing movie shooters some of the flexibility and control that stills photographers gain by shooting RAW.

It can have value for stills photographers too, at least when shooting RAW. As mentioned above, the Histogram and Highlights displays are based on the JPEG preview embedded with each RAW file. As such, they will give a more accurate guide to the potential of the RAW file when you use a Flat Picture Control.

"Contrast", "dynamic range", and "tonal range" all refer to the range of brightness between the brightest and darkest areas of a scene. Our eyes adjust continuously, allowing us to see detail in both bright areas and deep shade. By comparison, even the best cameras can fall short, losing detail ("clipping") in shadows, highlights, or even both.

Possible remedies include shooting RAW, using Active D-Lighting for JPEG images, or fill-in flash (page 152). Even so, sometimes it's impossible to capture the entire brightness range of a scene in a single exposure. The histogram (page 86) and highlights (page 87) displays help identify such cases.

One solution is to shoot several exposures and then combine the results. The D750 can automate this, creating a high-dynamic range (HDR) JPEG image by merging two separate shots, with one exposure biased towards the shadows and one towards the highlights. HDR can be combined with Active D-Lighting for even greater range.

Because HDR needs two exposures, it can give odd results with moving subjects. HDR is unavailable if Image quality is set to **RAW** or **RAW+JPEG**.

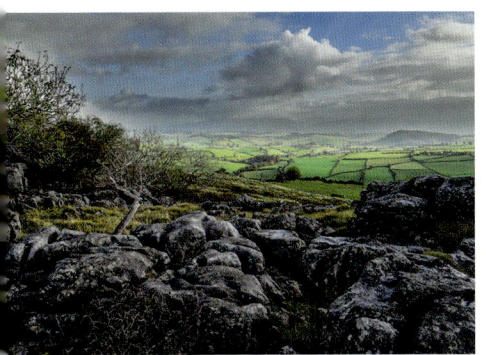
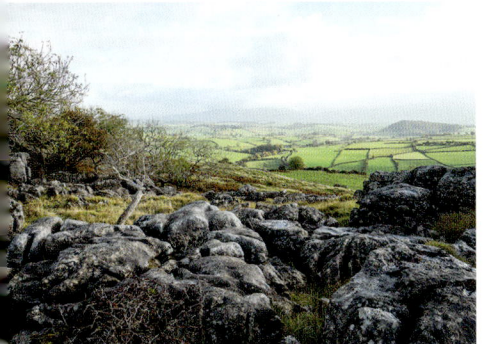
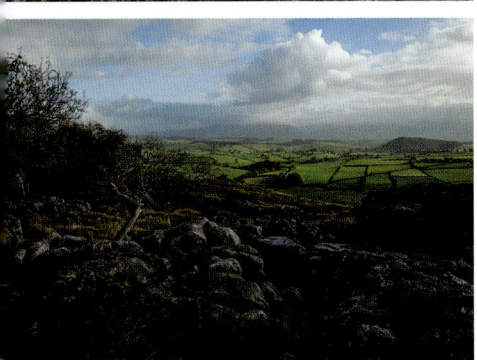

To set HDR

1) Select **HDR (high dynamic range)** in the Photo Shooting menu. Select **HDR mode** and press ▶.

2) Select **On (series)** to take a series of HDR images. Select **On (single photo)** to take just one. **HDR** appears in the control panel.

3) Select **HDR strength** to choose the differential in exposure between source images. **Auto** lets the camera determine this automatically, or you can select **Low**, **Normal**, **High**, or **Extra High**.

4) Shoot as normal. The camera takes two images in quick succession. It then takes a few seconds to merge them and display the result. During this time **Job Hdr** appears in the viewfinder and you can't take further shots.

5) If you selected **On (single photo)** at step 2, HDR shooting is automatically canceled. To shoot more HDR images, repeat the process from step 1.

COMPOSITE HDR IMAGE   **«**
An HDR image (top) and two (simulated) source frames (center and bottom).
24mm, 1/25 and 1/100 sec., f/11, ISO 200, tripod.

2 » USER SETTINGS

The U1 and U2 positions on the mode dial allow instant access to predetermined combinations of a wide range of settings. In essence they let you take a "snapshot" of the way the camera is set up at a particular moment—everything from Exposure mode to menu settings. You can then return it to that state at any time simply by rotating the mode dial to U1 or U2.

One obvious use for User settings is when the camera is shared between two people. For example, you may like a high level of manual control, but may sometimes hand the camera to a partner or child who likes things much simpler. U1 could be your setting, with the camera perhaps in Manual mode, and with preferred settings for things like white balance and AF mode already dialed in. U2 could take you directly to a preferred Scene mode for the secondary user. (There's little point in linking it to 📷 or 🌙 as these are directly accessible from the mode dial anyway.)

User settings can also be valuable if you regularly shoot at a particular location or under clearly defined conditions. If you're a sports photographer who regularly operates in a particular stadium, you could establish ISO, white balance, and all the other settings which produce the best results. If you use Manual, the camera will even recall the precise shutter speed and

aperture. If you save a User setting, on your next visit to the venue you can restore the settings with a single turn of the mode dial.

Each time you turn the dial to U1 or U2, the saved combination of settings is just a starting point; you can adjust all settings as normal, except that you can't change the Exposure mode because that would need the Mode dial to be moved from U1/U2.

To store User settings

1) Ensure the camera is set up, in all respects, as you require. Even in Auto or Scene modes, many options remain open (see page 36). In **P**, **S**, **A**, or **M** mode you can work through the whole gamut of settings if need be.
2) Go to Save user settings in the Setup menu and press ▶.
3) Highlight **U1** or **U2** and press ▶.
4) Highlight **Save settings** and press (OK).

To reset User settings

To create a new set of User settings for either dial position, replacing an earlier set, simply repeat the procedure above. Don't use **Reset user settings** in the Setup menu unless you really want to restore all settings at U1 or U2 to the camera's default values (e.g. exposure mode=Auto, Image quality=JPEG Normal, White Balance=Auto1).

SPEED DIAL »

User settings let you store and recall settings suitable for a specific venue.
70mm, 1/1250 sec., f/3.2, ISO 3200.

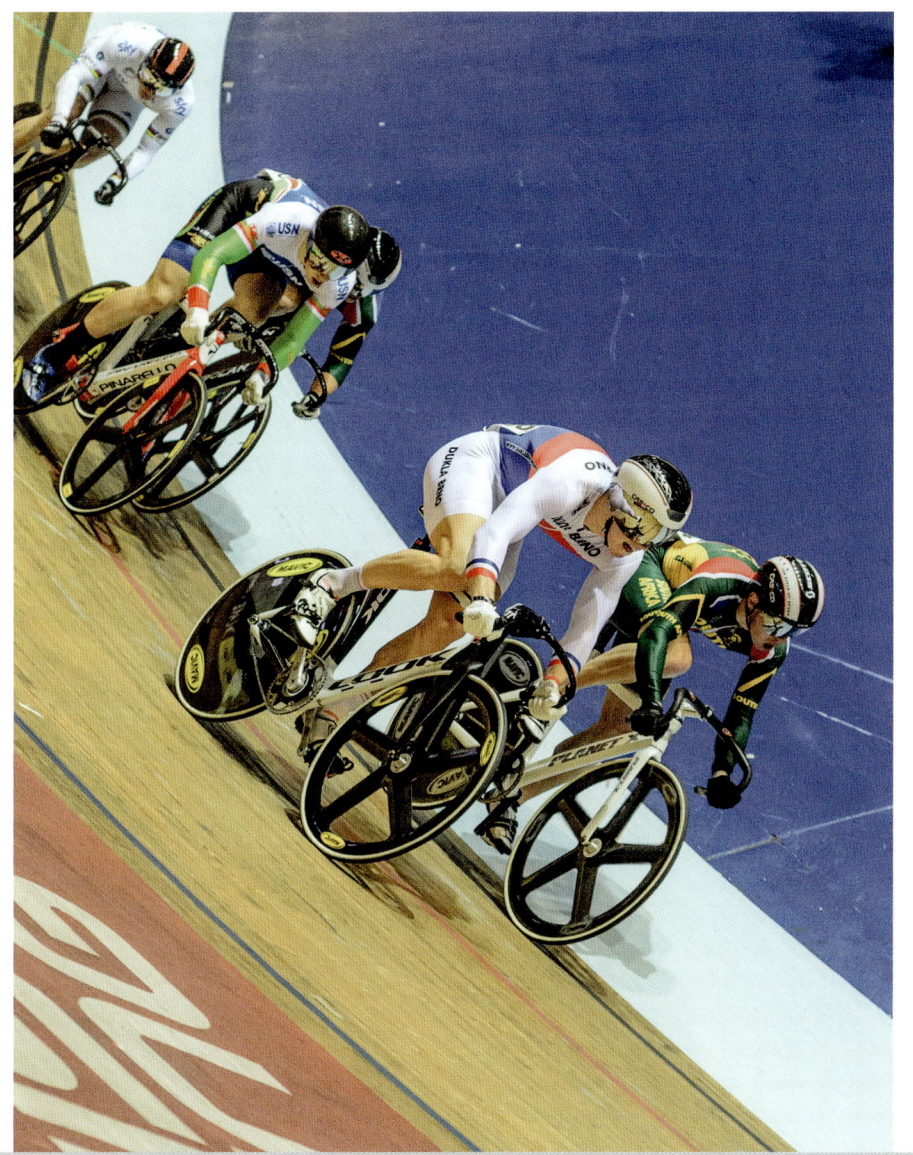

3 MENUS

The options that you access through dials and buttons are just the beginning. The menus offer many more ways to customize the D750 to suit your needs. There are seven main menus: **Playback**, **Photo Shooting**, **Movie Shooting**, **Custom Setting**, **Setup**, **Retouch**, and **My Menu/Recent Settings**.

The **Playback menu**, outlined in blue, covers functions related to playback, including viewing and deleting images. The **Photo Shooting menu**, outlined in green, is used to control shooting settings, such as ISO, white balance, or Active D-Lighting. Many of these, as we've already seen, can be accessed by other means. The **Movie Shooting menu**, outlined in yellow, serves a similar role for movie options. The **Custom Setting menu**, outlined in red, lets you fine-tune and personalize many aspects of the camera's operation. The **Setup menu**, outlined in orange, governs a range of functions such as LCD brightness, plus others that you may need to change only rarely, such as language and time settings. The **Retouch menu**, outlined in purple, lets you create modified copies of images on the memory card. Finally **My Menu** is outlined in gray; it is a handy place to store items from the other menus that you find yourself using regularly. Alternatively, it can become a **Recent Settings menu**.

Navigating the menus

The general procedure for navigating and selecting items from the menus is the same throughout:

1) To display the main menu screen, press **MENU**.

2) Use ▲ / ▼ to highlight the different menus. To enter the desired menu, press ▶.

3) Use ▲ / ▼ to highlight specific menu items. To select an item, press ▶. In most cases this will take you to a further set of options.

4) Use ▲ / ▼ to choose the desired setting. To select, press ▶ or (OK). In some cases you may need to scroll up to Done and then press (OK) to make changes effective.

MONOCHROME MILL »
Menus give access to an enormous range of options—including monochrome shooting.
110mm, 1/200 sec., f/11, ISO 250..

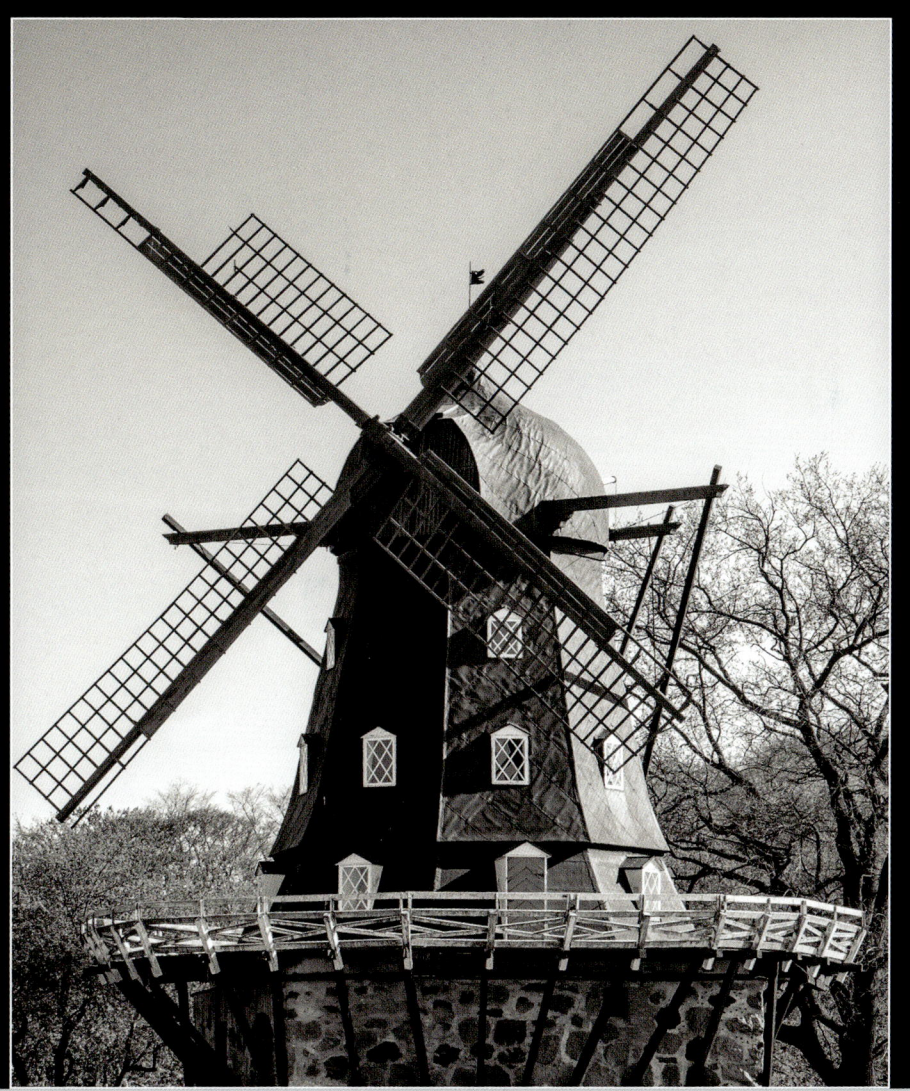

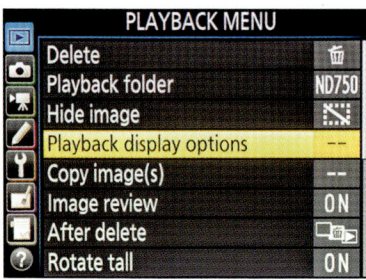

The Playback menu contains options affecting how images are viewed, stored, deleted and printed. Some items are only accessible when a memory card—with image(s) on it—is present.

› Delete

This function allows images stored on the memory card to be deleted, either singly or in batches. Individual images can also be deleted in normal playback, and this is usually more convenient (see page 86).

1) In the Playback menu, highlight Delete and press ▶.

2) In the menu options screen, choose **Selected**, **Date**, or **ALL**.

3) If you choose **Selected**, images in the active playback folder or folders (see next page) are displayed as thumbnail images. Scroll through them with the multi-selector. Press and hold ⊕ to view the highlighted image full-screen. Press ⊖ to mark the highlighted shot for deletion. It will be tagged with a 🗑 icon. If you change your mind, highlight a tagged image and press (OK) again to remove the tag.

Repeat to select further images. Press (OK) to see a confirmation screen. Select **YES** and press (OK) to delete the selected image(s).

4) If you choose **Date**, you'll see a list of dates on which images on the memory card were taken. Use the multi-selector to scroll through the list. Press ▶ to mark the highlighted date for deletion; a checkmark appears beside it. If you change your mind, highlight the date and press ▶ again to remove the tag.

Repeat to select further dates. Press (OK) to see a confirmation screen. Select **YES** and press (OK) to delete all image(s) taken on the selected date(s).

DUNES »

"Instant replay" was useful on this windy day for determining the right shutter speed for neither too much nor too little blur in the grasses. *24mm, 1/40 sec., f/10, ISO 200.*

› Playback folder

By default, the D750's playback screen will only display images created on the D750: if you insert a memory card containing images captured on a different model of camera (even another Nikon DSLR) they will not be visible. This can be changed using this menu.

	Playback folder options
ND810 (default)	Displays images in all folders created by the D750.
All	Displays images in all folders on the memory card.
Current	Displays images in the current folder only. (The current or active folder is chosen through the Photo Shooting menu, see page 102.)

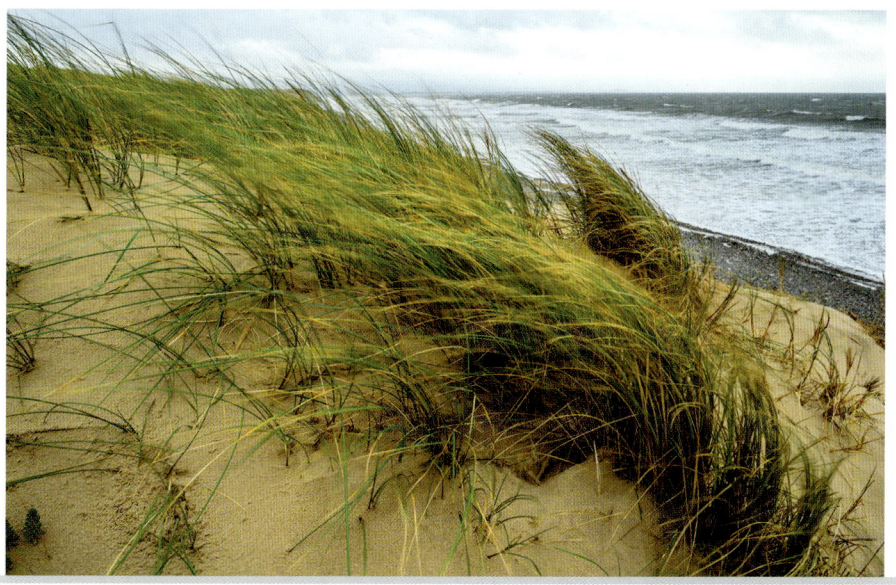

› Hide image

Hidden images are protected from deletion and cannot be seen in normal playback; the only way to access them is through this menu. The procedure for selecting images is just as described under **Delete** step 3 on page 98. Selected images will be tagged with 🔲.

Again, images from the two card slots are displayed separately and you will need to repeat the procedure to hide image(s) on both cards.

› Playback display options

This lets you choose what (if any) information about each image will be displayed on playback. See page 84 for more, including a table showing all the options. To enable or disable any option, press ▶ to check or uncheck it. To make these choices effective, press **OK**.

› Copy image(s)

This allows image(s) recorded on one memory card to be copied to the other card, provided there is space on the destination card.

Select source determines which card images will be copied from; the other card then automatically becomes the destination. **Select image(s)** allows you to select individual images or entire folders for copying. Having selected a folder, **Deselect all/Select all** allows you to check or uncheck individual images. **Select destination folder** determines which folder on the destination card will be used (you can also create a new folder).

While backing up precious images is good, this is a slow way to do it. If you use this item repeatedly, consider enabling automatic backup as images are taken (see **Role played by card in Slot 2** in the Photo Shooting menu, page 103).

› Image review

If Image review is **On** (the default setting), images are automatically displayed on the monitor after shooting. If **Off**, images are only displayed by pressing ▶. This can economize battery power.

› After delete

Determines "what happens next" after an image is deleted in normal playback. **Show next** means that the next image in the order of shooting will be displayed. **Show previous** means that the previous image in the order of shooting will be displayed. **Continue as before** means that the next image to be displayed is determined by the order in which you were viewing images before deleting; if you were scrolling back through the sequence, the previous image will be displayed, and vice versa.

› Rotate tall

This determines whether portrait format ("tall") images will be displayed the "right way up" during playback. If set to **OFF**, which is the default, these images will not be rotated, so you'll need to turn the camera through 90° to view them correctly, but they will use the full screen area. If set to **ON**, portrait images will be displayed in correct orientation but will appear smaller.

› Slide show

Lets you display images as a slide show on the camera's own screen or through a TV (see page 233). All images in the folder or folders selected for playback (see **Playback Folder**, above) will be played in chronological order. Before starting,

ensure the playback screen is set to **Image only** (see page 84) for an uncluttered slide show.

You can choose a Frame interval of 2, 3, 5, or 10 seconds. Select **Start** and press (OK).

When the show ends, a dialog is displayed. Select **Restart** and press (OK) to play again. You can also return to the Frame interval dialog or exit.

If you press (OK) during the slide show, the show is paused and the same dialog screen appears, but if you select **Restart** and press (OK), the show resumes where it left off.

› DPOF print order

This allows you to select image(s) to be printed when the camera is connected to, or the memory card is inserted into, a suitable printer, i.e. one that complies with the DPOF (Digital Print Order Format) standard. See Chapter 9, page 232.

» PHOTO SHOOTING MENU

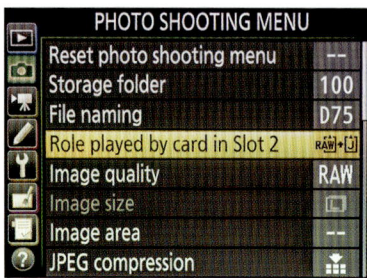

The Photo Shooting menu contains numerous options, but many are also accessible through other means and have already been discussed.

› Reset Photo Shooting menu

This is simply a quick way to restore Photo Shooting menu settings to the camera's original default settings. Use with caution as it can wipe out settings that you have carefully created.

1) In the Shooting menu, select **Reset shooting menu** and press (OK).

2) Select **Yes** and press (OK). Or select **No** to make no changes.

› Storage folder

If you alternate different memory cards, they will all end up holding folders of the same name. This isn't usually a problem but you might wish to avoid it. You might also want to create specific folders for specific shoots. On extended trips when you may be storing thousands of images on your memory cards, creating an ordered series of folders may be helpful.

You can't name folders freely—only the first three digits are editable and only numbers can be used.

To create a new folder number
1) In the Photo Shooting menu, select **Storage folder** and press (OK) or ▶.

2) Choose **Select folder by number** and press (OK) or ▶.

3) Edit the three-digit number: press ▶ or ◀ to highlight a digit, ▲/▼ to change it. (If the indicated number is already in use, a "blocked folder" icon appears.)

4) Press (OK) to create a new folder. It automatically becomes the active folder.

To change the Storage folder
1) In the Photo Shooting menu, choose **Select folder from list** and press (OK) or ▶.

2) Select the desired folder and press (OK) or ▶.

› File naming

By default image files are named as follows: if **Color space** is sRGB, the name begins DSC_; if **Color space** is AdobeRGB, the name begins _DSC. This is followed by a four-digit number and a three-letter extension (e.g. .JPG for JPEG files). You can edit the initial three-letter string, perhaps replacing it with your initials, so that instead of DSC_4567.JPG a file could be CJS_4567.JPG. The text editing procedure is the same as described above.

› Role played by card in Slot 2

When memory cards are present in both slots, Slot 2 can be used in three ways. By default (Overflow), images are only recorded to Slot 2 when the card in Slot 1 is full. **Backup** means that each image is written to both cards simultaneously. **RAW Slot 1 - JPEG Slot 2** is slightly more complicated. If Image quality is **NEF (RAW)+JPEG**, then the NEF version of each shot is recorded to Slot 1 and the JPEG version to Slot 2. At other Image quality settings, this option behaves like **Backup**.

› Image quality

Use this to choose between NEF (RAW) and JPEG options, as described on page 74.

› Image size

Choose between Small, Medium, and Large image sizes, as described in more detail on page 77. This choice applies to JPEG images only.

› Image area

Use this to choose between FX, 1.2x, and DX image areas, as described on page 76. You can also **Enable** or **Disable Auto DX Crop**. I always disable it.

› JPEG compression

Choose how JPEG images are compressed. **Size priority** means all images are compressed down to a set size (dependent on settings for Image area, Image quality, and Image size). Optimal quality means that image sizes are allowed to vary, allowing for better file quality.

› NEF (RAW) recording

Governs how NEF (RAW) files are recorded. There are two submenus, as follows.

Type

There are two options for NEF (RAW) file compression. The default is **Lossless** compressed, where RAW files are compressed by about 20–40% with no detectable effect on image quality. To save card space you can select **Compressed**, which compresses files by around 40–55%, with a very small effect on image quality.

NEF (RAW) bit depth

This allows you to select between 12-bit or 14-bit depth. See page 75.

› White balance

This menu allows you to set the white balance, as already discussed on page 62.

› Set Picture Control and Manage Picture Control

These menus govern the use of Nikon Picture Controls, as already discussed on page 90.

› Color space

Choose between sRGB and Adobe RGB color spaces (see page 61 for an explanation).

› Active D-Lighting

Choose level of Active D-Lighting, as already discussed on page 88.

› HDR (high dynamic range)

Enable and control HDR shooting, as described on page 92.

› Vignette control

Vignetting is a darkening, or fall-off in illumination, towards the corners of the image, most obvious in even-toned areas like clear skies. Almost all lenses show slight vignetting at maximum aperture, but it usually disappears when the lens is stopped down. The D750 can compensate for vignetting during the in-camera

> ***Note:***
> Vignette control only operates when Type D, G, or E lenses are attached. It does not work with DX lenses, or when shooting DX-format images or movies.

processing of JPEG images. Use this menu to choose between **Normal** (the default setting), **High**, **Low**, and **Off**.

› Auto distortion control

If **ON**, this automatically corrects for distortion (see page 196), which may arise with certain lenses. It's available only with Type D, G or E lenses (see page 204), excluding fisheye and perspective-control (PC) lenses, and does not apply when shooting movies.

> **Tip**
>
> When using DX lenses, ensure that **Auto DX crop** is **On**, or **Image area** is set to **DX**; otherwise Auto distortion control may produce undesirable results.

› Long exposure NR

Photos taken at long shutter speeds can suffer from increased noise (see page 58) so extra image processing is available to counteract this. If Long exposure noise reduction is **On**, it operates when exposure times are 1 sec. or longer. During processing, **Job nr** blinks in the displays.

The time this takes is roughly equal to the shutter speed in use, and you can't take another picture until processing is complete. This can obviously cause significant delays, so many users prefer to use post-processing to reduce image noise instead. Long exp. NR is **Off** by default.

› High ISO NR

Photos taken at high ISO settings can also show significant noise. The default setting is **Normal**, which can be changed to **Low** or **High**. High ISO NR can also be set to **OFF**, but even then a modest amount of NR will be applied to images taken at the highest ISO settings.

NIGHT NOISE ⩔
High ISO was inescapable for this night-time shot, but I had High ISO NR turned off, shot RAW, and tackled noise in post-processing (actually, very little was needed).
100mm, 1/125 sec., f/5.6, ISO 3200.

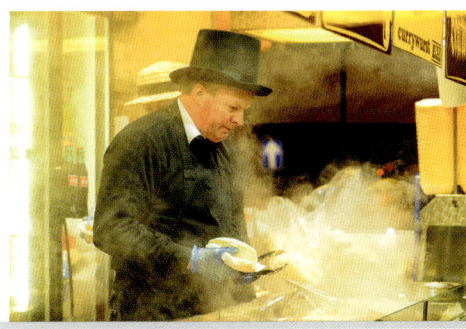

› ISO sensitivity settings

Governs ISO settings, as already discussed in depth on page 58.

› Remote control mode (ML-L3)

Unlike other models, such as the D610, there is no dedicated remote control position on the Release mode dial, so you must visit this menu item in order to use the optional ML-L3 remote control with the D750.

If you don't use the ML-L3 for a while, the camera will revert to the release mode selected with the Release mode dial and you'll need to return to this menu to use the ML-L3 again. To determine the interval before this happens, use Custom Setting c5 (page 117).

› Multiple exposure

When you can merge images on the computer, precisely and flexibly, it might seem that cameras like the D750 hardly need a multiple exposure facility. However, the Nikon manual states "multiple exposures produce colors noticeably superior to those in software-generated photographic overlays." This is debatable, especially if you shoot individual RAW images for careful post-processing before merging on the computer, but clearly this feature does offer an effective way to combine images for immediate use, e.g. as JPEG files for printing.

To create a multiple exposure

1) Select **Multiple exposure** and press ▶.

2) Select **Multiple exposure** mode and press ▶. Select **On (series)** to keep

Setting	Description
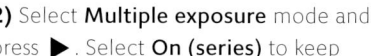 **Delayed remote**	Shutter fires approximately 2 sec. after remote is tripped.
Quick response remote	Shutter fires immediately when remote is tripped.
Remote mirror-up	Press remote once to raise the mirror; press it again to take the picture.
Off	Camera does not respond to the remote.

shooting multiple exposures or **On (single photo)** to shoot just one. Press (OK).

3) Select **Number of shots** and use the multi-selector to choose a number (between 2 and 10) then press (OK).

4) Select **Auto gain** and choose **ON** or **OFF** (see below for explanation) then press (OK).

5) Select **Done** and press (OK).

6) Frame the photo and shoot normally. In continuous release modes, the designated number of images will be exposed in a single burst. In single frame release mode, one image in the sequence will be exposed each time the shutter-release button is pressed. Normally the maximum interval between such shots is 30 sec. This can be extended by setting a longer monitor-off delay in Custom setting c4.

Auto gain

Auto gain (**On** by default) adjusts the exposure, so that if you are shooting a sequence of three shots, each is exposed at ⅓ the exposure value required for a normal exposure. You might turn it off where a moving subject is well lit but the background is dark, so that the subject is well exposed and the background isn't overlightened.

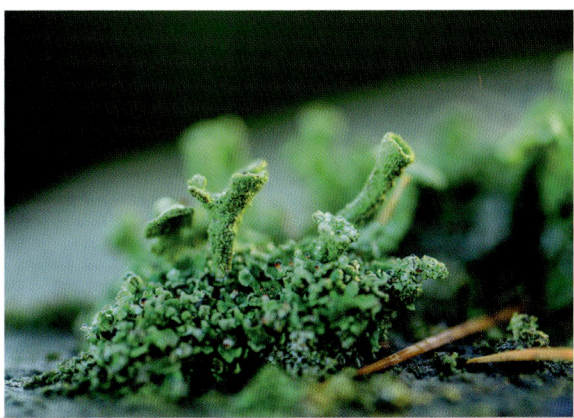

REMOTE CONTROL   «
The ML-L3 remote control (see the opposite page) is one option when you want to minimize camera shake. *100mm macro, 1/40 sec., f/8, ISO 100, tripod.*

3

› Interval timer shooting

The D750 can take a number of shots at predetermined intervals. If **Multiple exposure** is activated first, they will be combined into a single image; otherwise they will be recorded as separate images.

Set up the camera; a tripod is recommended. An appropriate fixed white balance setting (i.e. not Auto) should ensure you don't see unexpected color shifts in the end result. If you expect the light to remain fairly constant, use Manual mode for consistent exposure. If the light is likely to vary—for instance, you're shooting a time-lapse through sunrise and the advance of day—you might use one of the other modes. Aperture-priority mode is often recommended. If using an auto mode, use the supplied eyepiece cap once you've framed the image.

1) Select **Interval timer shooting** and press ▶ or (OK).

2) Select **On** and press ▶.

3) Select **Start options** and press ▶. Use the multi-selector to set the date and time of the start (up to a week ahead), or select **Now**. Press (OK).

4) Select **Interval** and press ▶. Use the multi-selector to set the interval between shots (the default is 1 min.). Press (OK).

5) Select **No of intervalsxshots/interval** and press ▶. Use the multi-selector to set the number of intervals, and the number of shots to be taken at each interval. The screen shows the resulting total number of shots. Press (OK).

6) Select **Exposure smoothing** and choose **Off** or **On**. Exposure smoothing aims to minimize brightness differences between successive shots. Press (OK) to complete setup and reach the primary Interval timer shooting screen.

7) Highlight **Start>On** and press (OK). If you selected **Now** under **Start options**, shooting begins in about 3 sec.

Tip

If planning a large number of shots and/or long intervals, ensure that the battery is fully charged or the camera is connected to a mains adapter, and that there is sufficient space on the memory card.

» MOVIE SHOOTING MENU

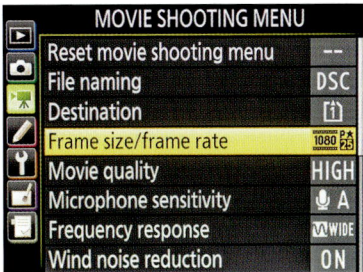

The Photo Shooting menu contains numerous options, but many are also accessible through other means and have already been discussed.

› Reset Movie Shooting menu

Resets all options in this menu to original default values.

› File naming

Set naming options for movie files, just as with stills (page 103). The default for the initial three-letter string is DSC, which you can change; the extension is .MOV, which you can't change.

› Destination

Determines which card slot is used for recording movies. Unlike stills, you cannot record movies to both slots simultaneously. It may make sense to use one card for stills

and one for movies. The settings screen shows available recording time for each card at current settings.

› Frame size/frame rate

Select the frame size for movies: either 1920 x 1080 pixels (Full HD), denoted **1080p**, or 1280 x 720 pixels, denoted **720p**. The frame rate options vary according to the size chosen.

› Movie quality

Sets the compression level (see page 178); options are **High** or **Normal**.

› Microphone sensitivity

Determines the sensitivity of the built-in microphones (or an external microphone if attached). The options are: **Auto sensitivity**, **Manual sensitivity** (in steps from 1-20), and **Off**. The menu includes an audio-level display, facilitating a "soundcheck".

› Frequency response

Again, this applies both to the built-in microphones or an external one. **Wide range** (the default) picks up a broad frequency range, which may capture all kinds of ambient sound. **Vocal range** is tailored more narrowly to the normal frequencies of human speech and can give cleaner sound when recording dialog.

› Wind noise reduction

This applies only to the built-in microphones. Enabling it can indeed reduce the level of wind noise but may also impair the quality of other sound.

› Image area

Determines whether movies use the full width of the sensor, denoted **FX**, or a smaller **DX** area (see page 76).

› White balance

Sets white balance for movie shooting. The procedure, and the options, are just the same as for stills (page 62), except for one extra item, **Same as Photo settings**. This will match movie white balance to the current still photography setting.

› Set Picture Control and Manage Picture Control

Again, these are exactly equivalent to corresponding items in the Photo

Shooting menu (page 104), except for the addition of **Same as Photo settings**.

› High ISO NR

Again, does the same job as the corresponding item in the Photo Shooting menu (page 105).

› Movie ISO sensitivity settings

In almost all shooting modes, ISO control is automatic. However, if you shoot in mode M you can set the ISO yourself using **ISO sensitivity (mode M)**. You can also opt for **Auto ISO control (mode M)**. This is the same as Auto ISO sensitivity control in stills shooting (page 59).

Finally, **Maximum sensitivity** allows you to set an upper ISO limit to the ISO which auto control can set—from 200 to Hi2.

Time-lapse photography

Time-lapse photography shoots a series of still frames and combines them into a silent movie. Camera setup is similar to Interval timer photography (see page 108) and it's advisable to start with a fully charged battery or mains adapter.

1) Select **Time-lapse photography** and press ▶.

2) Select **Interval** and press ▶. The default interval between shots is 5 sec.; change this using the multi-selector. Press (OK).

3) Choose the **Shooting time**. The default is 25 min.; use the multi-selector to change this. The maximum you can set is 7 h. 59 min. Press (OK).

4) Select **Exposure smoothing** and choose **Off** or **On**. Exposure smoothing aims to minimize brightness differences between successive shots. Press (OK).

5) In the main Time-lapse photography screen, select **Start** and press (OK) to proceed; shooting begins after approximately 3 sec.

MOVIE ISO ⌄

In Mode M, the Movie ISO sensitivity settings item allows full control of ISO settings.

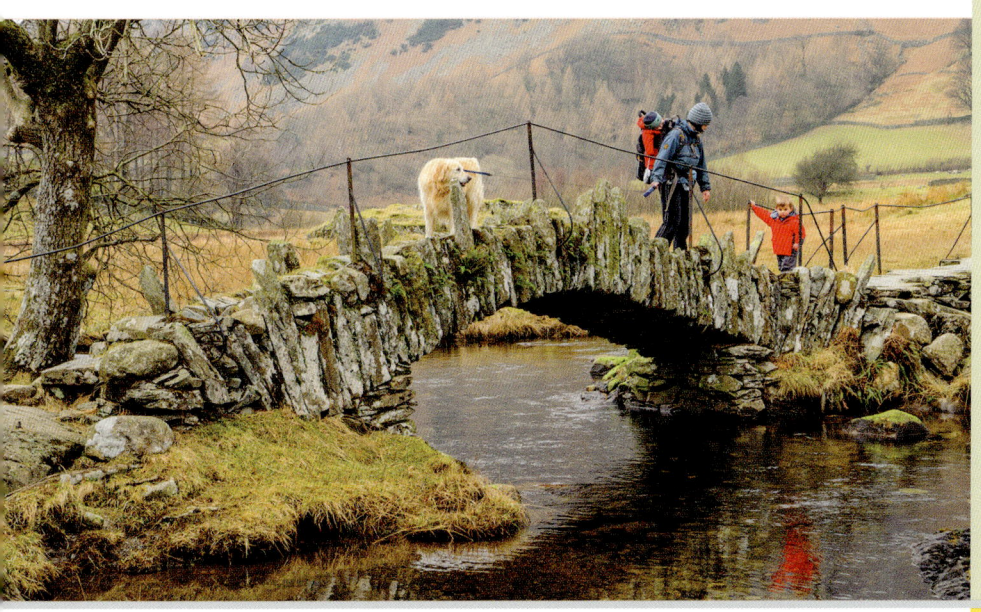

» CUSTOM SETTING MENU

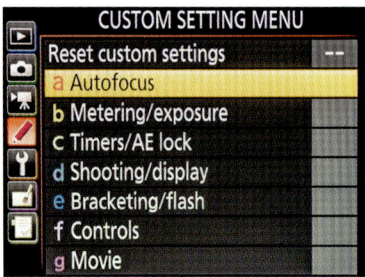

The Custom Setting menu allows you to fine-tune almost every aspect of the camera's operation to suit your personal preferences. The menu is divided into seven submenus, identified by key letters and a color: **a: Autofocus** (red); **b: Metering/Exposure** (yellow); **c: Timers/AE Lock** (green); **d: Shooting/display** (light blue); **e: Bracketing/flash** (dark blue); **f: Controls** (lilac); and **g: Movie** (purple).

Navigating the Custom Setting menu is essentially the same as the other menus. However, from the main menu screen, the first press on ▶ takes you into the list of submenus. Scroll through these to the desired group and press ▶ to see its constituent items.

Although the menu is organized into seven groups, individual items do appear as a continuous list, so you can scroll straight down from a10 to b1, and so on. By scrolling up you can jump directly from a1 to g4.

The Custom Setting identifier code (e.g. a4) is shown in the appropriate color for that group. If you change the setting from default value, an asterisk appears over the initial letter of the code.

› Reset Custom Setting

Select **Yes** and press (OK) to restore all Custom Settings to standard default values.

› a: Autofocus

a1 AF-C priority selection and
a2 AF-S priority selection

Normally, in AF-C (Continuous-servo) release mode, the camera can take a picture even if it has not acquired perfect focus (**release priority**). Custom setting a1 allows you to choose focus priority instead, meaning that pictures can only be taken once focus is acquired.

Similarly, Custom setting a2 allows you to change the priority setting for AF-S (Single-servo AF), but the default is **focus priority**.

a3 Focus tracking with lock-on

This governs how rapidly the camera reacts to sudden large changes in the distance to the subject (for example, when other objects pass in front of the intended subject). If this is **Off**, the camera reacts instantly to such changes, but this means it can be fooled. Longer delays reduce its sensitivity to such intrusions. Options run from **5 (Long)** via **3 (Normal)**, which is the default setting, to **1 (Short)** as well as **Off**.

a4 Focus point illumination

It's a shame Nikon didn't call this "Focus point display", to make a clearer distinction between it and item a5. This item determines when and how the focus point(s) are visible. There are separate options for different focus modes.

Manual focus mode

Choose **On** or **Off** to determine whether the active focus point is displayed when you are focusing manually. Focus points are irrelevant, and may be a distraction, when you're purely using the focusing screen. However, if you are using focus confirmation (see page 68), you do need to know where the focus point is.

Dynamic-area AF display

If you select **On**, when Dynamic-area AF (see page 70) is in use the camera will show the focus points surrounding the one you have selected, as these may also be used to aid focus. If you select **Off**, only the selected focus point is shown.

When 3D tracking is in use, if this item is **On**, the camera displays a dot at the center of the active focus point.

Group-area AF illumination

Determines how the focus points are indicated when Group-area AF (page 70) is in use—they can be displayed as large rectangles, as they are in other focusing modes, or as much smaller ones, which can give a clearer view of the subject.

a5 AF Point illumination

This determines whether the active focus point is illuminated in red in the viewfinder. If not, it's outlined in black. The default is **Auto**, which means the focus point is illuminated only when this will give better contrast with the background. Alternatively, it can be **On** or **Off**.

a6 Focus point wrap-around

This governs whether the active focus point wraps to the opposite edge of the available area (see page 72). The options are **Wrap** or **No wrap** (default).

a7 Number of focus points

This governs the number of focus points available when selecting the focus point manually (see page 72). By default it uses the full **51 points**, but you can opt to use just **11 points** to speed up the selection process.

> *Note:*
> Even with **11 points** selected here, the camera still uses all 51 points for automatic selection, focus tracking, and so on.

a8 Store by orientation

This enables the camera to remember different selections for the initial placement of the focus point according to the orientation of the camera. You might use this in fast-moving shooting where you want to switch quickly between two views. For example, when shooting running or cycling, you'll often want to use the uppermost focus point to focus on a competitor's face, as this is usually high in the frame. But what counts as "high in the frame" changes according to whether the camera is in portrait or landscape orientation. To enable this function, select **Focus point** in this menu.

You can also select **Focus point and AF-area mode**. This allows you to choose quite different AF operation for "landscape shots" and "portrait shots", e.g. using Group-area AF when the camera is in portrait orientation and 3D tracking when it is in landscape orientation.

a9 Built-in AF-assist illuminator

This determines whether the AF-assist illuminator (see page 69) operates. Options are **On** (default) or **Off**. It's unnecessary most of the time, and can add to battery drain.

b1 ISO sensitivity step value

This governs the increments you use when setting ISO sensitivity value (see page 58). Options are ⅓ step (default), 1 step, or ½ step. Larger intervals make it a bit quicker to scroll from, say, 100 to 1600.

b2 EV steps for exposure cntrl

This governs the increments which the camera uses for setting shutter speed and aperture, as well as for bracketing, and so on. Again, the options are ⅓ step (default), 1 step, or ½ step. Setting a larger step can speed up operation, but taking out the intermediate steps seems more drastic in this case.

b3 Easy exposure compensation

This determines how you can apply exposure compensation (see page 54) in P, S, and A modes. When it's Off (the default setting), you must press ⊡ and rotate the main command dial. When it's On, you can apply exposure compensation simply by rotating the sub-command dial (in P and S modes) or main command dial (in A mode).

Auto reset means that compensation setting(s) made in this way return(s) to Off when the camera or meter turns off.

(Settings made using ⊡ still don't reset automatically.)

b4 Matrix metering

Use this to turn Face detection On or Off. Face detection can be handy when shooting individual or group portraits as it means that the metering prioritizes correct exposure for the face(s).

This selection has no impact when using center-weighted or spot metering, nor in Live View or movie shooting.

b5 Center-weighted area

This governs the diameter of the primary area when Center-weighted metering is in use (see page 52). The options are 8mm, 12mm (default), 15mm, 20mm, and Average. Average means metering is based equally on the entire frame. With non-CPU lenses only 12mm and Average are available.

b6 Fine tune optimal exposure

This allows for a sort of permanent exposure compensation; you can apply separate settings for each of the four metering methods (Matrix, Center-weighted, Spot, and Highlight-weighted—see page 52) in steps of 1/6 Ev, up to +/-1 Ev.

Usually the regular exposure compensation procedure is preferable, but this option could be useful for specific needs. You might, for example, prefer portraits to have a consistently lighter feel, and could fine-tune the center-weighted setting for this purpose.

You will need to remember that this is in effect as the normal exposure compensation indicator will not be displayed; you can only confirm the setting by revisiting this menu item.

c1 Shutter-release button AE-L

This determines whether you can lock exposure by half-pressure on the shutter-release button. By default, this item is **Off**, half-pressure locks focus only (see Focus lock, page 72), and you can only lock exposure with *AE-L/AF-L* (see page 55).

c2 Standby timer

This governs the interval before the exposure meter turns off when the camera is idle (i.e. you don't take any pictures, or operate any of the other controls). A shorter delay benefits battery life.

The default is **6 sec.**; other options range from **4 sec.** up to **30 minutes** plus **No limit**, which means the meter remains active until you turn the camera off.

c3 Self-timer

This has three submenus governing the operation of the self-timer.

Self-timer delay determines the interval between pressing the button and

LONELY ROAD »
I've found self-timer sequences very handy when walking or cycling alone. Although they don't allow for critical timing of action shots, shooting nine frames at 0.5-sec. intervals gives a reasonable chance that one or two will be keepers. I wasn't carrying a tripod on this outing, so kept an eye out for places to set the camera, like the dry-stone wall used here.
28mm, 1/320 sec., f/9, ISO 200.

the shot being taken. The default is **10 sec.**; alternatives are **2**, **5**, and **20 sec**.

You can take a single shot, or shoot several with one press of the release button. **Number of shots** can be set from **1–9**, and **Interval between shots** can be set to **0.5**, **1**, **2**, or **3 sec**.

c4 Monitor off delay

Governs how long the LCD monitor screen remains illuminated when the camera is idle. Shorter delays improve battery economy. You can set the delay separately for **Playback**, **Menus**, **Information display**, **Image review**, and **Live view**. For most, the options range from **4 sec** to **10 min**. For Image review there's also a **2 sec** option. For Live View the range is **5 min** to **30 min**, plus **No limit**.

c5 Remote on duration (ML-L3)

When using the optional ML-L3 remote control (see page 213), this governs how long the camera will remain on standby for a signal from the remote before remote control mode turns off. Options range from **1 min** (default) to **15 min**. Shorter delays improve battery economy.

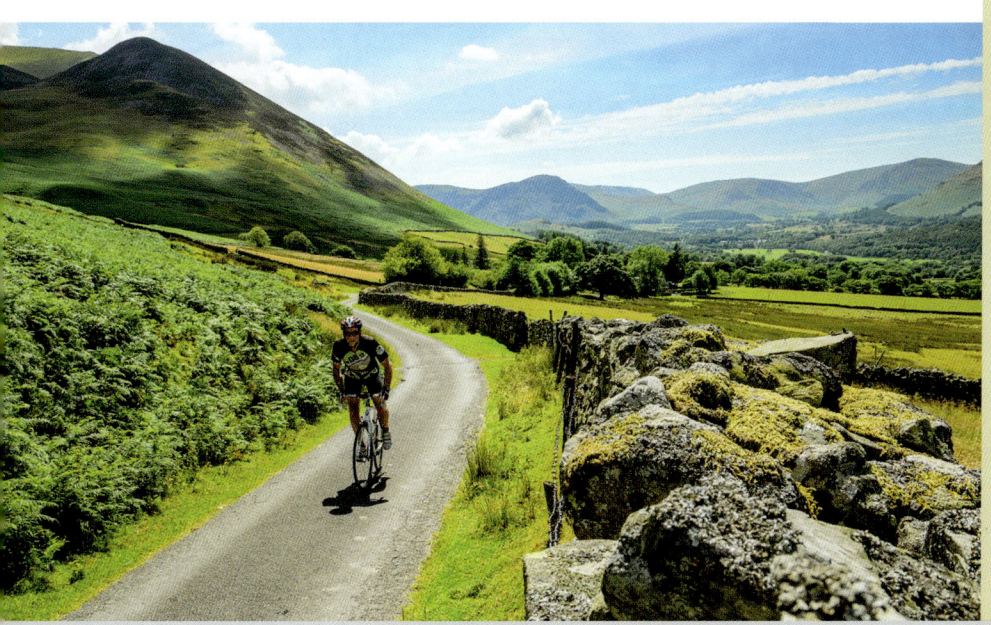

d1 Beep

If you wish, the camera can emit a beep when the self-timer operates, and to signify focus acquisition when shooting in AF-S mode. This is (rightly!) **Off** by default. There are two submenus. **Volume** includes the **Off** setting; enable the beep by selecting **1**, **2**, or **3**. **Pitch** can be **High** or **Low**.

d2 Continuous low speed

Governs the frame rate when using CL (Continuous Low speed) release mode (see page 31). The default is **3fps** (frames per second), and options run from **1** to **6fps**.

d3 Max continuous release

This determines the maximum number of shots that you can take in a single burst when using CL, CH, or QC release mode. The upper limit is **100**. You can take it right down to **1** if you wish, but that would defeat the object of continuous release mode.

> **Note:**
> The 100-shot limit mostly applies when shooting JPEG. Buffer capacity (see page 32) usually sets a lower limit to bursts when shooting RAW.

d4 Exposure delay mode

You can create a delay of **1s**, **2s**, or **3s** when you press the shutter-release button. This is a possible alternative to the self-timer or mirror lock-up to reduce vibration when shooting on a tripod. It's **Off** by default.

d5 Flash warning

In P, S, A, or M modes, determines whether the flash-ready symbol will blink in the viewfinder to indicate that flash may be required. It's **On** by default. (In other modes flash either activates automatically or remains off.)

d6 File number sequence

This controls how image numbers are set. If it's **Off**, file numbering is reset to 0001 whenever you insert a new memory card, format an existing card, or create a new storage folder (see page 102). If it's **On**— which is the default—numbering continues from the previous highest number used. **Reset** creates a new folder, and also begins numbering from 0001.

d7 Viewfinder grid display

This allows the camera to display grid lines in the viewfinder; these can help you keep the camera level and assist with precise framing. They can also alert you if a lens is delivering noticeable distortion (see page 196). The options are **Off** (default) and **On**.

d8 Easy ISO

This allows you to change the ISO setting simply by rotating one of the command dials. In A mode, you use the main command dial; in S or P mode you use the sub-command dial. This has its attractions, but you can't use it in Manual, when both command dials are required for their primary purpose, so it can also be confusing. It's **Off** by default.

d9 Information display

Determines the appearance of the information display. By default (**Auto**) the camera switches automatically from **Dark on light** to **Light on dark** to suit lighting conditions, but you can manually select to apply one or the other at all times.

d10 LCD illumination

This governs illumination of the top-plate control panel. By default (**Off**), it is only illuminated when you move the power switch to ☀. **On** means the control panel will be illuminated whenever the exposure meter is active. Clearly, **Off** is more economical for battery life.

d11 MB-D16 battery type

If you're using an optional MB-D16 battery pack with AA batteries, set this to match the type of cells. Options are: **LR6 (AA alkaline)**; **HR6 (AA Ni-MH)**; **FR6 (AA lithium)**.

d12 Battery order

Again, this applies if you're using an optional MB-D16 battery pack. It determines whether the camera will draw on its own battery first, or on those in the MB-D16. The latter is the default setting.

e1 Flash sync speed

This determines the fastest flash synchronization speed (see page 158 for an explanation). Settings run from **1/200s** (the default) down to **1/60s**.

There are also settings of **1/250s (Auto FP)** and **1/200s (Auto FP)**. These enable flash sync at any shutter speed when a Nikon Speedlight is attached (see High speed flash sync, page 165).

e2 Flash shutter speed

The previous item controls the fastest shutter speed which can be used with flash. This one determines the slowest shutter speed which the camera can set when using flash in P or A exposure modes

(see page 158). The options run from **1/60s** (default) to **30s** in 1 Ev steps. In M or S modes, any speed down to 30 sec. can be set anyway.

e3 Flash control for built-in flash

This governs how the built-in flash is regulated.

e4 Exposure comp. for flash

This determines how exposure compensation (see page 160) operates when flash is active. If you select **Background only**, the compensation setting only affects the ambient exposure; flash output is unchanged. If **Entire frame** is selected (which is the default), flash

Main setting	Explanation	Sub-menu options
TTL (default)	Flash output is regulated automatically by the camera's metering system.	
Manual	You determine the strength of the flash.	From **Full** down to **1/128** power.
Repeating flash	Fires the flash multiple times during a single exposure, giving a stroboscopic effect.	**Output** (flash power) **Times** (number of flashes) **Frequency** (number of flashes per second).
Commander mode	Uses the built-in flash as a trigger for remote flash unit(s) (see page 164).	Set **Mode** and **Compensation** for Built-in flash and external units/groups; select **Group** and **Channel** for external units.

output is also increased or reduced by the same amount.

e5 Modeling flash

This applies when the built-in flash is active or you attach a compatible optional flash unit. If it's **On** (which is the default), the flash emits a pulse of light when you press the Pv button, giving an indication of the flash effect. It's limited, but you can see where shadows fall.

e6 Auto bracketing set

Bracketing is discussed in detail on pages 56 and 161. The options are: **AE & flash** (default), **AE only**, **Flash only**, **WB bracketing**, and **ADL bracketing**.

e7 Bracketing order

This determines the order in which auto-bracketed exposures are taken: by default, the first shot is taken at the metered exposure (**MTR> under> over**). The alternative (**Under> MTR> over**) places the metered exposure in the middle of the sequence, which seems more logical.

LIGHT ROCK ⌄
Fill-in flash was very useful here, but had to be toned down using flash compensation.
36mm, 1/100 sec., f/11, ISO 250.

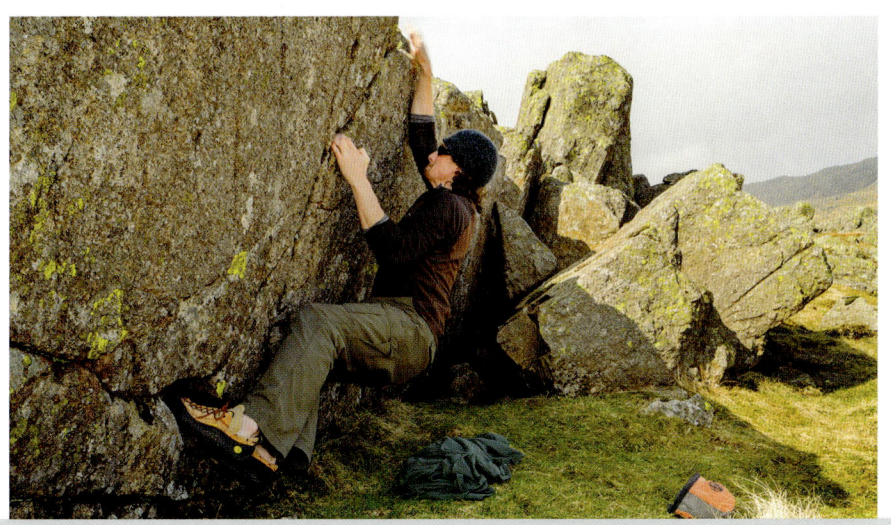

f1 OK button

This governs which functions are activated, in different modes, when you press (OK).

f2 Assign Fn button

Various functions can be assigned to the Fn button, both on its own and in conjunction with the command dials. These include functions which are normally assigned to other buttons (e.g. depth of field preview, normally assigned to the Pv button).

There are separate lists of options for a simple press and for using the button in conjunction with a command dial; however, some options in the two lists are incompatible. For example, if you pick a **Press** option that is incompatible with the one you picked under **Press + command dials**, your earlier choice is deactivated, and an error message will be displayed.

f3 Assign preview button

The same wide range of functions can be assigned to the Pv button as to the Fn button (above). The only difference is in the default settings.

For **Press**, the default setting (not surprisingly!) is **Preview**.

For Assign Preview button: **Press + Command dials**, the default setting) is **None**. As with f2, some Press options are incompatible with some **Press + command dials** options.

f4 Assign AE-L/AF-L button

Again, you can assign a wide range of different functions to *AE-L/AF-L*. The list of options is shorter than for Fn and Pv.

Under Press + Command dials, the following are available: **AE/AF lock** (default), **AE lock only**, **AE lock (Hold)**, **AF lock only**, **AF-ON**, **FV lock**, **None**.

f1: OK button	
Shooting mode	Select center focus point (default)
	Highlight active focus point
	None
Playback mode	Thumbnail on/off (default)
	View histograms (see page 86)
	Zoom on/off (see page 86)
	Choose slot and folder
Live View	Select center focus point (default)
	Zoom on/off (see page 86)
	None

f2: Assign Fn button: Press

Preview	Fn activates depth of field preview.
FV lock	Fn locks flash value (compatible flashguns only)— see page 160. Press again to cancel.
AE/AF lock	Exposure and focus both lock when you press Fn.
AE lock only	Exposure locks while you hold Fn.
AE lock only	Exposure locks when you press Fn and remains locked. until you press it again, or release the shutter, or standby timers expire.
AE lock (Hold)	Exposure locks when you press Fn and remains locked until you press it again, or standby timers expire.
AF lock only	Focus locks when you press Fn.
AF-ON	Pressing Fn activates focus; focus can't be activated with half-press on shutter release.
🚫	Flash will not fire while Fn is pressed.
Bracketing burst	Fn activates a bracketing burst at last used settings.
+NEF (RAW)	When Image quality is set to JPEG, pressing Fn ensures a NEF copy of the next shot will also be recorded.
Matrix metering	Hold Fn to activate matrix metering (see page 52).
Center-weighted metering	Hold Fn to activate center-weighted metering (see page 52).
Spot metering	Hold Fn to activate spot metering (see page 53).
Highlight-weighted metering	Hold Fn to activate highlight-weighted metering (see page 53).
Viewfinder grid display	Press Fn to show/hide framing grid in viewfinder.
Viewfinder virtual horizon	Press Fn to show a virtual horizon in viewfinder (see pages 79 and 136).
MY MENU	Press Fn to display My Menu.
Access top item in My Menu	Press Fn to go straight to Item 1 in My Menu.
Playback	Fn duplicates function of ▶.
NONE (default)	Pressing Fn has no effect.

f2: Assign Fn button: Press + Command dials	
Choose Image area (default)	Press Fn and rotate either command dial to select FX, 1.2x, or DX image areas (see page 76). You can also use this menu item to uncheck any of the available areas in this list: e.g. uncheck 1.2x so that using Fn and dial simply toggles between FX and DX.
1 step spd/aperture	If Fn is pressed while command dials are rotated, changes to aperture/shutter speed are made in 1 Ev steps.
Choose non-CPU lens number	Use Fn and either command dial to select among lenses specified using Non-CPU lens data (see page 136).
Active D-Lighting	Press Fn and rotate either command dial to select between Active D-Lighting options (see page 88).
HDR (high dynamic range)	Press Fn and rotate main command dial to choose HDR mode (single photo or series). Press Fn and rotate sub-command dial to choose HDR strength (see page 92).
Exposure delay mode	Press Fn and rotate either command dial to select an exposure delay (see page 30).
NONE (default)	Rotating a command dial while pressing Fn has no effect.

For Press + Command dials, the options are: **Choose image area**, **Choose non-CPU lens number**, and **None**.

f5 Customize command dials

You can change the operation of the command dials in various ways. There are five submenus.

Reverse rotation

This reverses the effect of rotating the dials in a given direction. You can customize this separately for Exposure compensation and for Shutter speed/aperture settings.

Change main/sub

Normally, when shooting in modes A, S, and M, the main command dial sets shutter speed and the sub-command dial sets aperture—this item modifies these roles.

Under **Exposure setting**, **On** reverses the usual roles completely. Alternatively, you can select **On (Mode A)** to use the main command dial for aperture selection in mode A, while retaining normal operation in other modes.

Similarly, under **Autofocus setting**, you can reverse the normal effect of rotating the command dials while holding ⊕. If this is **On**, holding ⊕ and rotating main command dial selects AF-area mode, and ⊕ and sub-command dial selects AF mode.

Aperture setting

This determines whether the aperture ring (where present, i.e. on older lenses) can be used to set apertures, or the sub-command dial. See page 28. On non-CPU lenses, only the aperture ring can be used anyway.

Menus and playback

This allows you to use the main command dial to navigate playback images and menus. **On** allows you to use it to scroll through individual images in image review and playback. **On (image review excluded)** allows the dial to be used only in playback initiated with ▶, not with images displayed immediately after shooting. With either option enabled, the sub-command dial can be used to skip from page to page when images are displayed as thumbnails.

In menu navigation, with either option enabled, the main command dial can be used to scroll through menu items, while the sub-command dial can be used to enter submenus (rotate right) or go up a level (rotate left).

Sub-dial frame advance

This gives the sub-command dial a function during playback. If you're using the main command dial to scroll through images on playback, you can set the sub-command dial to jump forward or back by **10** or **50** images, or to jump to the next **Folder** (assuming there is more than one folder on the memory card).

f6 Release button to use dial

Normally, buttons such as ⊕☰/**WB** must be kept pressed while you rotate the appropriate command dial to make changes. If you activate this option by selecting **Yes**, you can continue to make changes with the dial alone after releasing the button, though only until you press the shutter-release button, press the relevant control button again, or until the camera goes onto standby.

Other buttons to which this applies are **ISO**, ☒, ☰, ⚡, **BKT**, and ⊕.

The same also applies to the Fn, Pv, **AE-L/AF-L**, and ⊙ buttons if you've given them a function using **Press + Command dials** (see page 124).

f7 Slot empty release lock

By default (**Enable release** selected in this menu), the shutter can be released even if no memory card is present. Images are held in the buffer and can be displayed on the monitor (demo mode), but are not recorded.

Alternatively you can select **Release locked** instead. This means that the shutter can't be released unless there's a memory card in the camera. The obvious lack of response protects you against shooting away happily for hours, only to discover later that none of your images have been recorded.

The default setting is useful when cameras are on display at a shop or trade show, but not in normal use. I always change it when I receive a new camera.

f8 Reverse indicators

This governs the display of exposure indicators in the viewfinder, control panel, and information display. By default (**−0+**) overexposure is indicated by bars on the right side and underexposure on the left.

+0− reverses the indicators.

f9 Assign movie record button

This gives ⊙ a function during normal photography and still-image Live View. The default is **None**, i.e. this button remains inactive. There are three other options, all under **Press + command dials**: **White balance**, **ISO sensitivity**, and **Choose image area**.

f10 Assign MB-D16 AE-L/AF-L button

If you're using an optional MB-D16 battery pack, this allows you to allocate a range of a functions to its **AE-L/AF-L** button. The range of options is more limited than those available for the camera's own **AE-L/AF-L** button (see Custom setting f6), and there are no Press + command dials options.

f11 Assign remote (WR) Fn button

Similarly, this lets you assign various functions to the Fn button on some Nikon wireless remote controls.

f10: Assign MB-D16 AE-L/AF-L button

AE/AF lock (default)	Exposure and focus both lock when you press Fn.
AE lock only	Exposure locks while you hold Fn.
AE lock (Hold)	Exposure locks when you press Fn and remains locked until you press it again, or standby timers expire.
AF lock only	Focus locks when you press Fn.
AF-ON	Pressing Fn activates focus; focus can't be activated with half-press on shutter release.
FV lock	Locks flash value (compatible flashguns only)—see page 72. Press again to cancel.
Same as Fn button	Duplicates the function selected for Fn on the camera (see Custom setting f2).

f11: Assign remote (WR) Fn button

Preview	Activates depth of field preview.
FV lock	Locks flash value (compatible flashguns only)—see page 72. Press again to cancel.
AE/AF lock	Exposure and focus both lock when you press Fn.
AE lock only	Exposure locks while you hold Fn.
Flash off	Flash will not fire while Fn is pressed.
+NEF (RAW)	When Image quality is set to JPEG, pressing Fn ensures a NEF copy of the next shot will also be recorded.
Lv	Pressing Fn activates Live View.
=Fn	Duplicate function selected for Fn on the camera (see Custom setting f2).
=Pv	Duplicate function selected for Pv on the camera (see Custom setting f3).
= AE-L/AF-L	Duplicate function selected for Fn on the camera (see Custom setting f4).
NONE (default)	Pressing Fn has no effect.

› g: Movie

This menu allows you to assign functions to certain key buttons. These only apply when the camera is in Movie mode and can be completely different from the functions performed by the same button when shooting stills.

g1 Assign Fn Button

This governs the function performed by Fn when camera is in Movie mode. The following are available: **AE/AF lock, AE lock only, AE lock (Hold), AF lock only, AF-ON, FV lock, None** (default). In addition there are three options relevant only to movie shooting. See the table below.

g2 Assign preview button

You can assign exactly the same range of functions to the Pv button, but the default is **Index marking**.

g3 Assign AE-L/AF-L button

You can also assign the same range of functions to *AE-L/AF-L* , except that **Power aperture** is not included. The default is **AE/AF lock**.

g4 Assign shutter button

This determines the behavior of the shutter-release button when the Live View selector is set to ⬛.

By default (**Take photos**), fully pressing the shutter-release button ends movie recording (if in progress) and takes a still photo (see page 188). Alternatively, you can select **Record movies**. When you do this, half-pressure on the button begins movie Live View (effectively duplicating the function of ⬛Lv). Fully pressing the button begins recording a movie clip, and a second press ends it; this effectively duplicates the function of ⦿. If you're shooting movies

g1: Assign Fn Button	
Power aperture (open)	Opens the aperture when you press Fn (see page 183).
Index marking	Press Fn during movie shooting to add an index mark, which can be used to jump to specific points when playing and editing movies.
View photo shooting info.	Press Fn to show current still photo settings (shutter speed, aperture, ISO); press again to show current movie settings.

seriously, this can streamline the operation, but leaves you no quick way to capture a still photo. This setting also allows you to use a remote cord or wireless remote controller (but not the ML-L3) to start and end movie shooting.

Note:
If you select Power aperture (open) in g1, setting g2 is automatically set to Power aperture (close), and vice versa.

REFLECTIVE MOMENTS ⌄
Index marking, which can be assigned to the Fn button, can make it easier to find specific moments in a clip during editing.

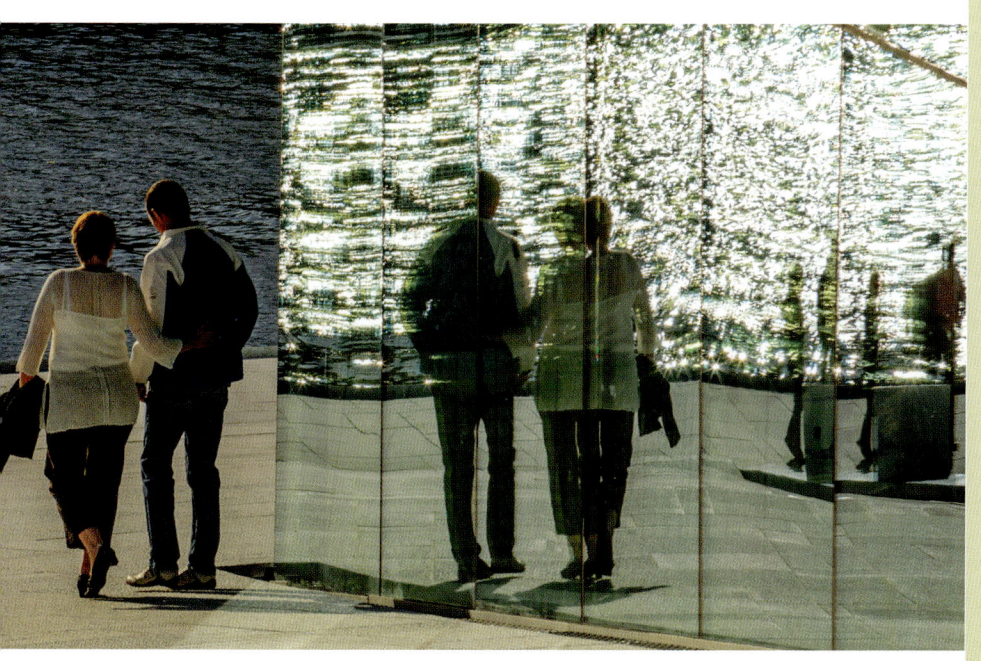

» SETUP MENU

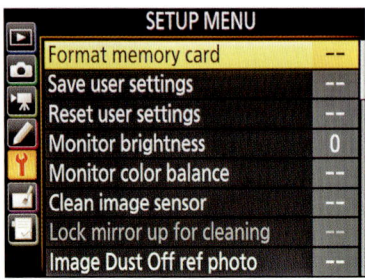

```
              SETUP MENU
  Format memory card              --
  Save user settings              --
  Reset user settings             --
  Monitor brightness               0
  Monitor color balance           --
  Clean image sensor              --
  Lock mirror up for cleaning     --
  Image Dust Off ref photo        --
```

The Setup menu controls a number of important camera functions, although many are ones you will need to access only occasionally.

› Format memory card

This is one Setup menu item that you may use regularly. Some may prefer the alternative "two-button" method (page 24), but I find this way quicker and more convenient.

To format a memory card
1) Select **Format memory card** and press ⒪ⓚ or ▶.

2) Select **Slot 1** or **Slot 2** and press ⒪ⓚ or ▶.

3) Select **Yes** and press ▶.

› Save user settings/ Reset user settings

See page 94 for a detailed explanation of saving and resetting user settings.

› Monitor brightness

Change the brightness of the rear LCD display with ▲/▼. This has no effect on the images themselves (e.g. as viewed on your computer). The point is to adapt the display to changing ambient light levels. The screen shows a "step-wedge" with 10 bands ranging from very dark to very light gray. It should be possible to distinguish clearly between all of them.

Monitor brightness for Live View/movie shooting is adjusted separately (see the table on page 80).

> **Tip**
>
> *Nikon warns that the monitor may display colors less accurately with the highest brightness settings (+4 or +5).*

› Monitor color balance

Adjust the color balance of the monitor using the multi-selector.

When you enter this menu, the screen shows the most recent image taken. There are obvious pitfalls in using a photo for reference—if colors in the image look wrong, it could be that it was shot using an inappropriate white balance setting. In this case, adjusting screen settings to make it look right only masks the fact that colors in the image itself are wrong.

If there are no images on the memory card, the screen shows a gray rectangle instead. For the reasons just given, I use prefer to use this to judge the color balance of the screen, so would use this menu when there are no images on the card(s) in the camera. If necessary, simply remove the card(s) for the few seconds it takes to use this menu.

› Clean image sensor/ Lock mirror up for cleaning

For more details see page 217.

› Image Dust Off Ref photo

Nikon Capture NX-D (see page 227) can automatically remove dust spots on images, by comparing them to a reference photo which maps dust on the sensor. This can save a lot of "grunt-work" compared to manually removing spots from individual images. This menu item allows you to take a suitable reference photo.

To take a dust-off reference photo
1) Fit a lens (preferably full-frame and at least 50mm focal length). With a zoom lens, use the longest setting. Locate a featureless white object such as a sheet of paper, large enough to fill the frame.

2) Select **Image Dust Off Ref photo** and press ▶.

3) Select **Start** or **Clean sensor and then start** and press (**OK**). (Select **Start** if you have already taken the picture(s) from which you want to remove spots.)

4) Frame the white object at a distance of about 10cm. Press the shutter-release button halfway; focus is automatically set to infinity, creating a soft white background against which dust spots stand out clearly.

5) Press the shutter-release button fully to capture the reference image.

3

› Flicker reduction

Some light sources can produce visible flicker in the Live View screen image and in movie recording. To minimize this, use this menu to match the frequency of the local mains power supply; **60Hz** is common in North America; **50Hz** is normal in the European Union, including the UK. The **Auto** setting will normally adjust automatically.

› Time zone and date

Sets date, time, and time zone, and specifies the date display format (Y/M/D, M/D/Y, or D/M/Y). First set your usual time zone, then set the time correctly. If you travel to a different time zone, change the time zone setting and the time will be corrected automatically.

> **Note:**
> If a GPS receiver is attached (see page 230), it can set the clock using the very accurate data from the satellite system. Enable this in the **Location data** menu item (page 136).

› Language

Set the language which the camera uses in its menus and dialogs.

› Auto image rotation

If set to **ON** (default), information about the orientation of the camera is recorded with every photo taken, ensuring that they appear the right way up when viewed with Nikon View NX2, Nikon Capture NX-D, or most third-party imaging applications.

› Battery info

Displays information about battery status, including charge level, number of shots taken since last charge, and overall age of battery (assessed against nominal lifespan). The information displayed may change if an optional battery pack is fitted.

› Image comment

You can append brief comments (up to 36 characters) to images. Comments appear in the info page on playback (see page 84) and can be viewed in Nikon View NX2 and Nikon Capture NX-D. To attach a comment, select **Input comment** and press ▶. Use the multi-selector to input text.

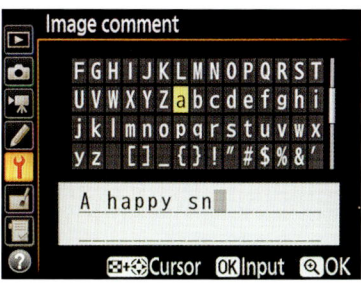

When finished press ⊕ ⬛⬛. Select **Attach comment**, then select **Done** and press (OK). The comment will be attached to all new shots until turned off again.

› Copyright information

Copyright is a fundamental right, and exists automatically in every photo you take. There should be no need to "copyright" images. However, making a clear statement that your images are copyright is still worthwhile. It doesn't confer any additional rights, but may make it easier to enforce the rights you already have.

This menu allows copyright information to be embedded into metadata, using the usual text input method, described above.

There are separate fields for **Artist** (i.e. photographer) and **Copyright**; however, in most jurisdictions, they are usually one and the same person, as copyright automatically belongs to the person

creating the image. There is often an exception for photographers shooting in the course of permanent employment (not freelancers under contract), when copyright belongs to the employer. Copyright law does vary internationally, and it is wise to familiarize yourself with local law where you work.

To attach copyright information to all subsequent photos, select **Attach copyright information**, then press (OK).

Tip

Copyright normally exists in any photo you take, without registration. However, in the US and a few other countries, registration—although a cumbersome bureaucratic process—can add extra protection.

› Save/load settings

This allows you to save many camera settings (see the table below) to a memory card. If the same card (or another to which the settings file has been copied) is inserted later, the saved settings can be quickly restored. This could be useful, for instance, if you lend the camera to a friend, or send it away for servicing. It can also be used to transfer settings to another D750, but not to any other model. The settings file is named "NCSETUPG" and the procedure will fail if the file name is changed.

Menu	Settings
Playback	Playback display options
	Image review
	After delete
	Rotate tall
Photo Shooting	File naming
	Role played by card in Slot 2
	Image quality
	Image size
	Image area
	JPEG compression
	NEF (RAW) recording
	White balance (including fine-tuning)
	Set Picture Control
	Color space
	Active D-Lighting
	Vignette control
	Auto distortion control
	Long exposure NR
	High ISO NR
	ISO sensitivity settings
	Remote control mode (ML-L3)
Movie Shooting	Destination
	Frame size/frame rate
	Movie quality
	Microphone sensitivity

Menu	Settings
Movie Shooting	Frequency response
	Wind noise reduction
	Image area
	White balance
	Set Picture Control
	High ISO NR
	Movie ISO sensitivity settings
Custom Setting	All Custom Settings
Setup	Clean image sensor (auto settings)
	Flicker reduction
	Time zone and date display format
	(does not reset the time and date themselves)
	Language
	Auto image rotation
	Image comment
	Copyright information
	Non-CPU lens data
	HDMI
	Location data
	WiFi
	Eye-Fi upload
My Menu/Recent Settings	All My Menu items
	All recent settings
	Choose tab

› Virtual horizon

Displays a horizon indicator on the monitor to assist in leveling the camera. Green bars indicate when the camera is level.

The virtual horizon display shows both left–right tilt (roll) and front–back tilt (pitch). The tilt indicator can be really useful in ensuring that horizons will be level when shooting landscapes and seascapes, for example. The pitch indicator helps keep the camera-back vertical, to avoid converging verticals when shooting architecture and similar subjects (see page 203).

Alternatively, the viewfinder's analog display can be used as a tilt-meter, in conjunction with the Fn button: enable this in Custom setting f2 or f3.

› Non CPU lens data

Many older Nikon lenses, often rugged and optically excellent, can be used on the D750. When lenses lack a built-in CPU, little information is available to the camera and shooting options are drastically reduced. Important functions can be restored by specifying the focal length and maximum aperture of a given lens in this menu. Data can be stored for up to nine such lenses.

› AF fine-tune

AF fine-tune allows the camera to compensate for slight variations in autofocus performance (back-focus or front-focus) between different lenses (CPU lenses only). The camera can store details for up to 20 lenses and will subsequently recognize them automatically.

AF fine-tune should be used only when you are certain that back-focus or front-focus exists. It is OFF by default.

Detecting back- or front-focus requires careful testing. One method is to compare results using standard AF with those from Live View. Use a solid tripod to avoid camera movement and ensure the same focus point is being targeted by both AF systems.

› HDMI

You can connect the camera to HDMI (High Definition Multimedia Interface) TVs and monitors (see page 233). This menu allows you to set the camera's output to match the HDMI device; see the specifications for the device.

› Location data

Set up a connection with a compatible GPS device (see page 230).

› WiFi

This item will only be visible if an Eye-Fi card is inserted (see page 224). It allows you to Enable (default) or Disable wireless upload of photos

› Network

This menu item is normally grayed out and inaccessible. It is relevant only when the D750 is connected to a Communication Unit UT-1 and either an Ethernet cable or a wireless transmitter (see page 225).

› Conformity marking

Displays some technical networking standards with which the camera complies. It's for information only; there are no options to choose from.

› Firmware version

Firmware is the onboard software which controls the camera's operation. Nikon issues updates periodically. This item shows the version presently installed, so you can verify whether it is current.

When Nikon releases new firmware, download it and copy it to a memory card. Insert this card in the camera then use this menu to update the camera's firmware.

Note:
Firmware updates may include new functions and new menu items, which can make this *Expanded Guide* (and the Nikon manual) appear out of date.

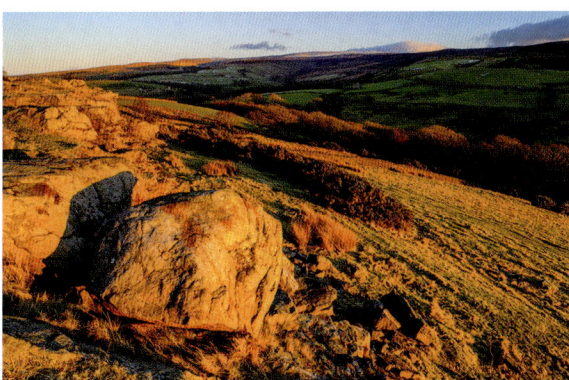

ON THE LEVEL «
The virtual horizon (for an illustration of the Live View version see page 79) is really useful in leveling the camera when there is no obvious horizon line in the scene to refer to.
24mm, 1/8 sec., f/14, ISO 200, tripod.

» RETOUCH MENU

The Retouch menu lets you make corrections and enhancements to images, including cropping, color balance, and much more. The original image remains untouched; instead, a copy is created to which the changes are applied. Further retouching can be applied to the new copy, but you can't apply the same effect twice to the same image.

Copies are always created in JPEG format but the size and quality depends on the format of the original (a few exceptions, such as **Trim** and **Resize**, produce copies smaller than the original).

› To create a retouched image

Retouching can begin either from the Retouch menu, or from normal playback.

1) If starting from the Retouch menu, select the desired retouch option and press ▶. A screen of image thumbnails appears. Select the required image using the multi-selector, as in normal image playback. Press (OK). If subsidiary options appear, make a further selection and press ▶ again. A preview of the retouched image appears.

2) If starting from normal playback, select the required image and press ◄**🔘**▶ , then select **Retouch** and press ▶. Now select the desired retouch option and press ▶ again. If subsidiary options appear, make a further selection and press ▶ once more. A preview of the retouched image appears.

3) Depending on the type of retouching to be done (see details below), there may be further options to choose from.

4) Press (OK) to create a retouched copy.

› Side-by-side comparison

This option is not part of the regular Retouch menu; it only appears if you display the menu by pressing ◄**🔘**▶ when a retouched copy, or its source image, is selected in full-frame playback. It displays the copy alongside the original source image. Highlight either image with ◄ or ▶ and press ⊕**🔲** to view it full frame. Press ▶ to return to normal playback; to return to the playback screen with the highlighted image selected, press (OK).

Format of original photo	Quality and size of copy
NEF (RAW)	Fine, Large
JPEG	Quality and size match original

› D-Lighting

D-Lighting should not be confused with Active D-Lighting (page 88), though there are similarities in the final effect. Active D-Lighting is applied before shooting, and has an effect on the original exposure; D-Lighting is applied later and simply lightens the shadow areas of the image. The D-Lighting screen shows a side-by-side comparison of the original image and the retouched version; a press on ⊕▦ zooms in on the retouched version. Use ▲/▼ to select the strength of the effect—**High**, **Medium**, or **Low**.

› Red-eye correction

This is aimed at dealing with the notorious problem of "red-eye", caused by on-camera flash (see page 158). This option can only be selected for photos taken using flash. The camera then analyzes the photo looking for evidence of red-eye; if none is found the process ends. If red-eye is detected a preview image appears and you can use the multi-selector and the zoom controls in the usual way to view it more closely.

› Trim

This allows you to crop an image to eliminate unwanted areas or to better fit it to a print size. When this option is selected, a preview screen appears, with the crop area marked by a yellow rectangle. Change the aspect ratio of the crop by rotating the main command dial. Adjust the size of the cropped area by pressing ⊖▦ to reduce the size, ⊕▦ to increase it. Adjust its position using the multi-selector. Figures at the top left give the pixel dimensions of the copy. Press ▦ to preview the cropped image. Press (OK) to create a cropped copy.

› Monochrome

Create monochrome copies—straight Black-and-white, Sepia (a brownish-toned effect), or Cyanotype (a bluish-toned effect). For Sepia or Cyanotype, you can make the toning effect stronger or weaker with ▲/▼.

3

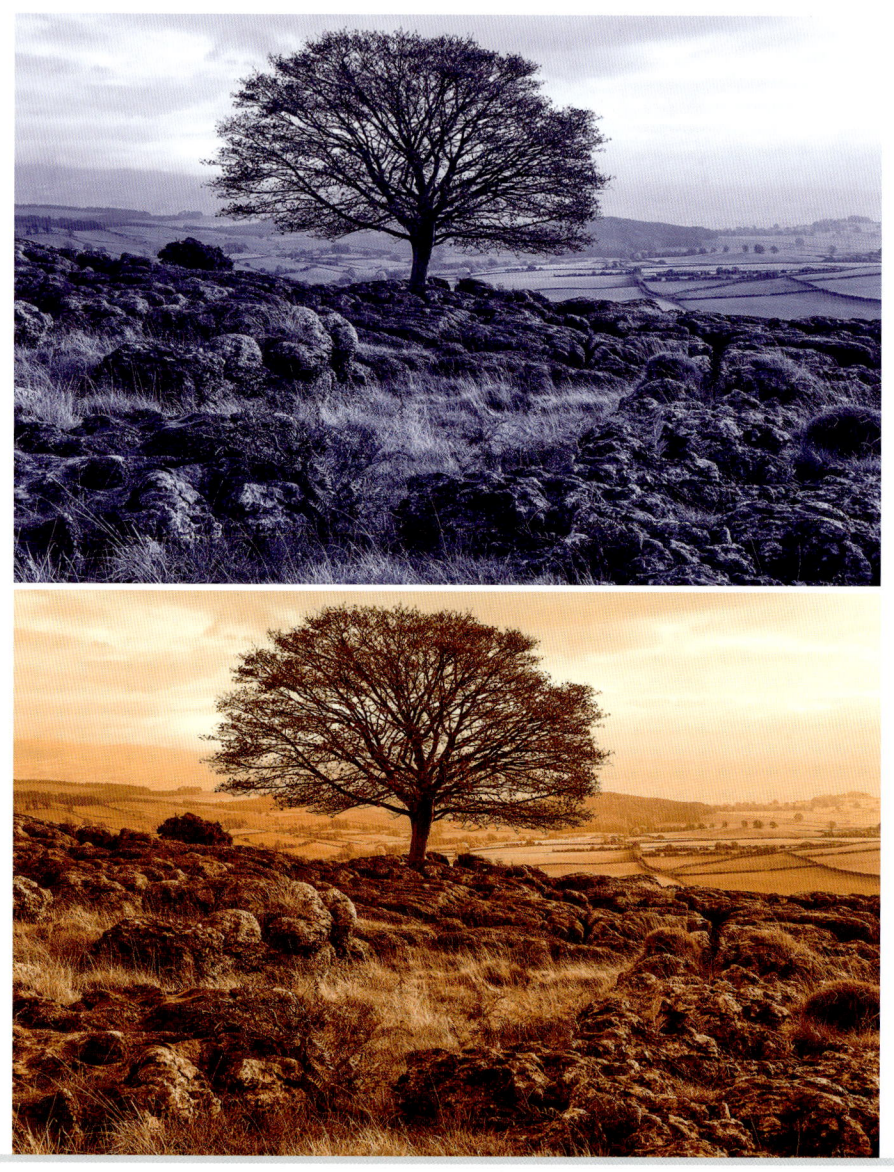

› Filter effects

This mimics several common photographic filters (perhaps we should say "once common", i.e. in the days of film). **Skylight** reduces the blue cast which can affect photos taken on clear days with a lot of blue sky. Applied to other images, its effect is very subtle, even undetectable. **Warm filter** has a much stronger warming effect. **Red**, **Green**, and **Blue intensifier** are all fairly self-explanatory, as is **Soft**.

Cross screen, however, is an enigmatic name—surely "Star" would have been better. It creates a "starburst" effect around light sources and other very bright points, like sparkling highlights on water. There are multiple options within this item, including the number, angle, and length of the star points.

› Color balance

Creates a copy with adjusted color balance. Use the multi-selector to move around a color grid; the effect is shown in a (zoomable) preview and histograms.

MONOCHROME   **«**
Cyanotype (top) and Sepia (bottom).

› Image overlay

This allows you to create a new combined image from two existing photos. Image overlay can only be applied to originals in NEF (RAW) format, but Nikon claim (debatably) that the results are better than combining the images in an application like Photoshop because Image overlay makes direct use of the raw data from the camera's sensor. You can also create a new RAW image by this method—it's the only Retouch menu option which allows you to do this.

> ### Tip
>
> *Although Image overlay works from RAW images, the size and quality of the copy are not automatically set to Fine, Large. Make sure the **Image Quality** and **Image Size** options are as required.*

To create an overlaid image
1) In the Retouch menu, select **Image overlay** and press ▶. The next screen has panels labeled **Image 1**, **Image 2**, and **Preview**. Initially, **Image 1** is highlighted. Press **OK**.

3

2) The camera displays thumbnails of RAW images on the memory card. Select the first image required for the overlay and press (OK). Press ▶ to move to Image 2 and select the second image.

3) Use the **Gain** control below each image to determine its "weight" in the final overlay. You can press (OK) to change the selected image in either position.

4) Press ▶ to highlight the Overlay panel. With **Overlay** highlighted, press ⊕▦ to preview the overlay. Return to the main screen by pressing ⊕▦. To save the combined image, highlight **Save** and press (OK).

› **NEF (RAW) processing**

This menu creates JPEG copies from images originally shot as RAW files. It doesn't replace full RAW processing on computer (see page 226), but it does allow you to create quick copies for immediate sharing or printing. Options available for the processing of RAW images are displayed in a column to the right of the preview image (see the table below).

To finish, select **EXE** and press (OK) to create the JPEG copy. Pressing ▶ exits without creating a copy.

Option heading	Description
Image quality	Choose Fine, Normal, or Basic (see page 74).
Image size	Choose Large, Medium, or Small (see page 76).
White balance	Choose a white balance setting; options are similar to those described on page 62.
Exposure compensation	Adjust exposure (brightness) levels from +2 to −2.
Set Picture Control	Choose any of the range of Nikon Picture Controls (see page 90) to be applied to the image. Fine-tuning options can also be applied.
High ISO NR	Choose level of noise reduction where appropriate (see page 105).
Color space	Choose color space (see page 61).
Vignette control	Apply Vignette control (see page 104).
D-Lighting	Choose D-Lighting level (High, Normal, Low, or Off)—see page 139.

Option	Size	Description
2.5M	1920 x 1280	Display on HD TV, larger computer monitor, recent iPad
1.1M	1280 x 856	Display on typical computer monitor, older iPad
0.6M	960 x 640	Display on standard TV, iPhone 4/5
0.3M	640 x 424	Display on majority of mobile devices

› Resize

Resize can be accessed from the Retouch menu or from Image playback, but there are slight differences in the procedure. From the Retouch menu, you first select a picture size and destination slot and then select the picture(s) to be copied at that size. From Image Playback, you select a picture first and then choose the copy size; this way you can only copy one picture at a time.

Tip

*Resize creates copies using the full image area of the original image, and therefore with the same aspect ratio. To create cropped copies, or copies with a different aspect ratio, use **Trim**.*

› Quick retouch

Provides basic one-step retouching for a quick fix, boosting saturation and contrast. D-Lighting is applied automatically to retain shadow detail. Use ▲/▼ to increase or reduce the strength of the effect, then press (OK) to create the retouched copy.

› Straighten

It's best to get horizons level at the time of shooting, and the virtual horizon (page 79) can help. However, errors can still happen. This option offers a fallback, with correction up to 5° in 0.25° steps. Use ▶ to rotate clockwise, ◀ to rotate anticlockwise. Inevitably, this crops the image.

› Distortion control

Some lenses create noticeable curvature of straight lines (see page 196)—this menu allows in-camera correction, but inevitably crops the image slightly.

3

Auto allows automatic compensation for the known characteristics of Type G and D Nikkor lenses; it can't be used on images taken with other lenses. **Manual** can be applied whatever lens was used; use ▶ to reduce barrel distortion, ◀ to reduce pincushion distortion. The multi-selector can also be used for fine-tuning after **Auto** control is applied.

› Fisheye

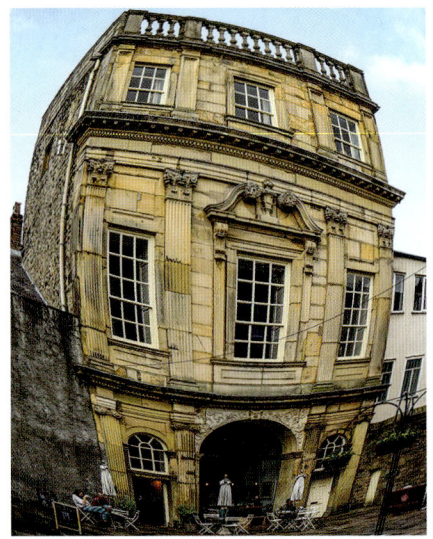

FISHEYE ⌃

Instead of correcting distortion, this menu exaggerates it to give a fisheye lens effect. Use ▶ to strengthen the effect, ◀ to reduce it.

› Color outline

This detects edges in the photograph and uses them to create a "line-drawing" effect. There are no options to alter the effect.

› Color sketch

This creates a copy resembling a colored pencil drawing. Controls for **Vividness** and **Outlines** adjust the strength of the effect.

› Perspective control

Corrects the convergence of vertical lines in photos taken looking up, for example, at tall buildings. Grid lines aid in assessing the effect, and the strength of the effect is controlled with the multi-selector. The process inevitably crops the original image, so if you're shooting an image where you plan to use perspective control later, make sure to leave room around the subject. For alternative approaches to perspective control, and an illustration, see page 203.

› Miniature effect

This option mimics the fad—already done to death—for shooting images with extremely small and localized depth of field (see page 49), making real landscapes or city views look like miniature models. It usually works best with photos taken from a high viewpoint, which generally have clearer separation of foreground and background. A yellow rectangle shows the area which will remain in sharp focus; you can reposition this using ▲/▼. Use ▶/◀ to make the "in-focus" zone wider or narrower and ◉▦ to flip it through 90°.

Press ◉▦ to preview the results and press (OK) to save a retouched copy.

› Selective color

You can select up to three specific color(s) to be preserved in the retouched copy; other hues are changed to monochrome.

1) Choose **Selective color** in the Retouch menu. Press ▶.

2) Select an image from the thumbnail screen and press (OK).

3) Use the multi-selector to place the rectangular cursor over an area of the desired color. Press **AE-L/AF-L** to choose that color.

4) Turn the main command dial and then use ▲/▼ to adjust the color range (i.e. to be more or less selective with the color). A preview shows the effect.

5) To select another color, turn the main command dial again to highlight another "swatch" and repeat steps 3 and 4.

6) To save the image, press (OK).

› Edit movie

This item has a rather inflated title; it merely allows you to trim the start or end of a movie clip. It's nothing like proper editing (see page 188), but has its uses.

To trim a movie clip

1) Select a movie clip in full frame playback (do not play the movie).

2) Press ▣ ; select **Edit Movie** and press ▶.

3) Select **Choose start/end point** and press ▶.

4) Press (OK) to start playing the movie. Press ▼ to pause. Rotate the main command dial to jump forward or back in 10-second steps.

5) Press **WB** to toggle between start and end. You can see in the progress bar below the image that the start or end point is highlighted in yellow.

6) Press ▲ to trim the clip at the selected start or end point. Select **Save as new file** and press (OK) to save the trimmed clip as a copy; the original is retained. Or select **Overwrite existing file** and press (OK) to save the trimmed clip in place of the original—use care as this is irrevocable.

7) If you need to trim both ends of a clip, repeat the process on the clip you've already trimmed once.

3 ›› MY MENU AND RECENT SETTINGS

My Menu is a convenient way to speed up access to menu items and settings that you use frequently. Items from other menus can be added to My Menu to create a handy shortlist, up to a maximum of 20 items.

Alternatively, you can activate the Recent Settings menu, which stores the 20 most recent settings made using the other menus. This requires less effort than adding items to My Menu, but the most recent items aren't always the ones you use most frequently over the longer term. For example, if you've been busy in the Retouch menu, Recent Settings may fill up with things like Selective Color and Trim, which will be of little use to you if you want quick access to shooting settings when out in the field.

› To add items to My Menu

1) In My Menu, highlight **Add items** and press ▶.

2) A list of the other menus now appears. Select the appropriate menu and press ▶.

3) Select the desired menu item and press (OK).

4) The My Menu screen reappears with the newly added item at the top. Use ▼ to move it lower down the list if desired. Press (OK) to confirm the new order.

› To remove items from My Menu

1) Highlight **Remove items** and press ▶.

2) Highlight any item and press ▶ to select it for deletion. A checkmark appears beside the item.

3) Select additional items in the same way.

4) Highlight **Done** and press (OK). A confirmation dialog appears. To confirm the deletion(s) press (OK) again. To exit without deleting anything, press **MENU**.

> ### *Tip*
>
> *To delete a single item, highlight it and press 🗑. To confirm deletion press 🗑 again.*

› To rearrange items in My Menu

1) Highlight **Rank items** and press ▶.

2) Highlight any item and press (OK).

3) Use ▲/▼ to move the item up or down; a yellow line shows where its new position will be. Press (OK) to confirm the new position.

4) Repeat steps 2 and 3 to move further items. When finished, press **MENU** to exit.

› Recent settings

The Recent Settings menu stores up to 20 items. You must activate Recent Settings before any items can be recorded. It only stores items from the menus. It does not record changes made using the buttons and dials.

To activate Recent Settings

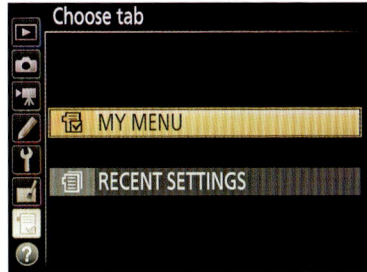

CHOOSE TAB
Choose tab switches between My Menu and Recent Settings.

1) In My Menu, select **Choose tab** and press (OK).

2) Select **Recent Settings** and press (OK). The name of the menu changes to Recent Settings.

To revert to My Menu, repeat the **Choose tab** procedure.

To remove items from the Recent settings menu

It is possible to delete items from the list, perhaps to bring your "favorite" shooting settings back to the top of the list.

Highlight any item in the list and press 🗑 to delete. To confirm, press 🗑 again.

Deleting items simply makes the list shorter; older items do not reappear. If you regularly find yourself editing the Recent Settings list in this way, consider reverting to My Menu.

4 FLASH

Unlike top pro models like the D4s, the D750 has a built-in flash. It has limited value as a main light; its range is short and the light is ugly. However, it can play a serious role by providing fill light and by acting as a "commander" in multi-flash wireless setups. Whether using the built-in flash or a compatible flashgun, the D750 is very capable at managing flash exposure automatically. Still, to get the best from flash, and make informed decisions about when to use it and when to do without, we need to understand some basic principles.

» PRINCIPLES

All flashguns are small; all flashguns are weak. This is especially true for built-in units like the D750's; compact camera flashes are typically even smaller and weaker. Being small, the flash produces very hard light and equally hard shadows, although we can often modify it using diffusers or reflectors.

As flash is fundamentally weak, its range is limited. Accessory flashguns are generally more powerful than built-in units, but still only extend the range by a few meters.

Built-in flash units are also fixed in position close to the lens, making their light one-dimensional—and the same for every shot. Fortunately, accessory flashguns offer various additional options.

There's a key distinction between using flash as the main/only light source and using it for supplementary light, e.g. for fill light (see page 152).

RACE FACE »
This shot was taken using two Speedlight SB-700s. One was used "naked" from the left of the picture, giving a fairly hard-edged light, and the other with a HONL diffuser (see page 167) at lower power on the right to illuminate that side of the face.
200mm, 1/200 sec., f/5.6, ISO 100.

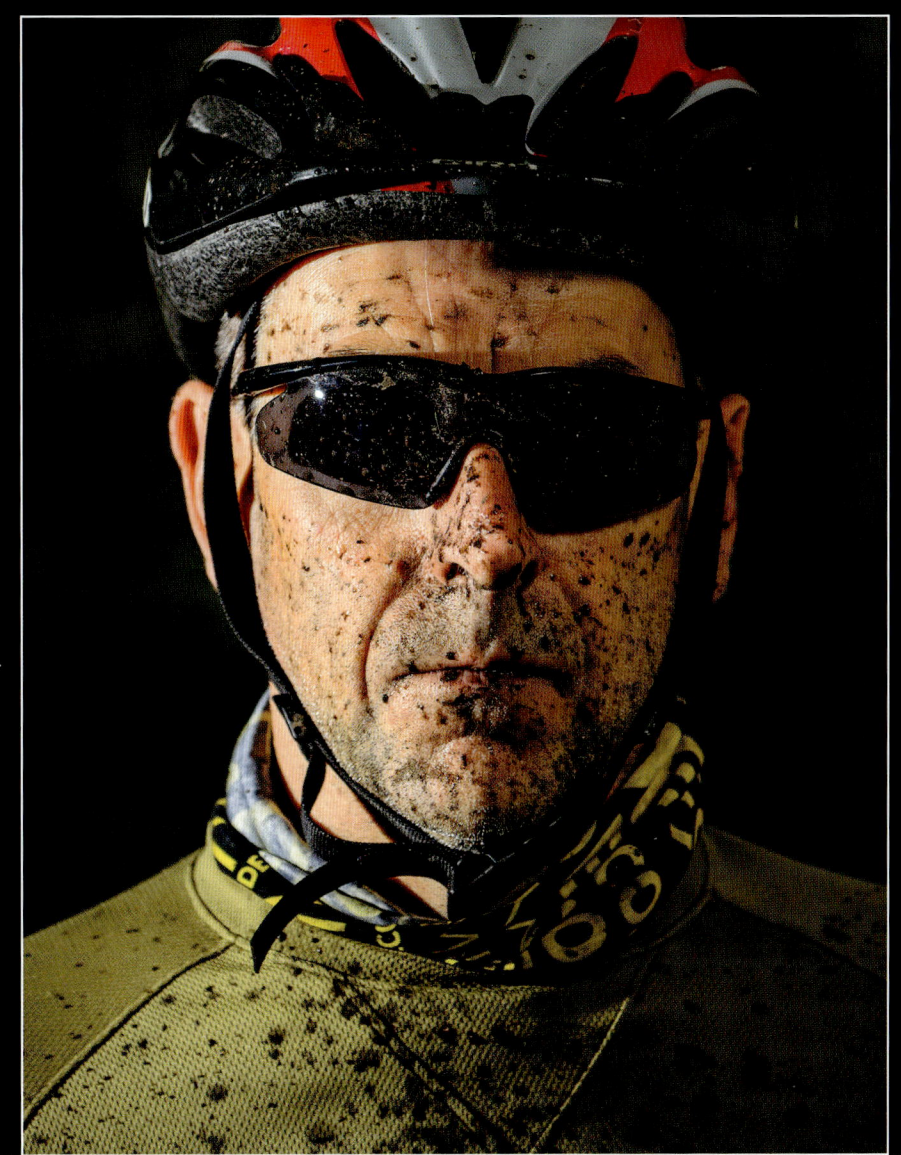

» BUILT-IN FLASH

As just observed, the built-in flash has a limited range, and its flat, harsh light is rarely pleasing. It's certainly better than nothing at times, but its real value is for fill-in light. Its other great asset is that it can be used to trigger remote flashguns.

The built-in flash covers the field of lenses up to 24mm (16mm if using DX-crop). With wider lenses, the corners of the frame will not be covered by the flash. Some lenses may block part of the flash output, especially at close range; removing the lens hood often helps.

FLASH POP-UP BUTTON ⚡   ⌄

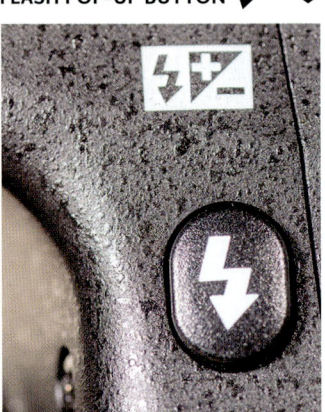

D750 BUILT-IN FLASH IN USE   ⌄

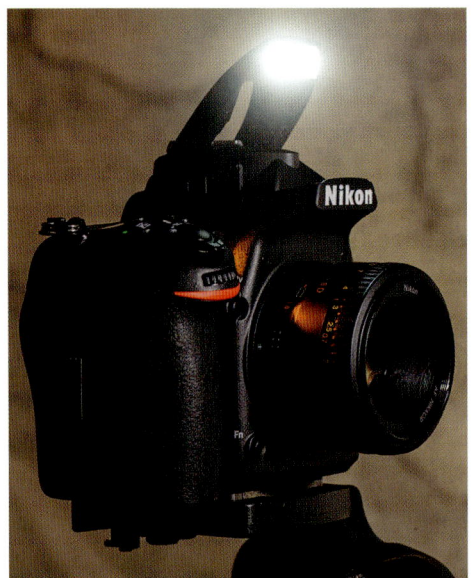

Activating the built-in flash

1) Press ⚡ and the flash will pop up and begin charging. When it is charged, the ready indicator ⚡ is displayed in the viewfinder.

2) Choose a flash mode by pressing ⚡ and rotating the main command dial until the appropriate icon appears in the Information display. See page 158 for an explanation of flash modes.

3) Half-press the shutter-release button to meter and focus; fully depress it to take the photo.

4) When finished, lower the flash. Press down gently until it clicks into place.

» NIKON CREATIVE LIGHTING SYSTEM

Nikon's Creative Lighting System (CLS) was launched in 2003, embodying several innovations to make using flash both easier and more flexible. These include i-TTL flash metering, FV (flash value) lock, advanced wireless control, and auto FP high-speed sync, all of which we'll cover in this chapter.

CLS requires both a compatible camera (like the D750) and one or more compatible flashguns. These include all current Nikon Speedlights plus several earlier models which are now discontinued. The current models are described in more detail on page 166.

Many older Nikon flashguns can also be used with the D750 but advanced CLS functions such as wireless flash control will not be available. The first table on page 166 lists such units.

FLASH PAST »
Using flash while panning gives a sharp image of the rider combined with a blurred background for a strong impression of speed.
75mm, 1/60 sec., f/8, ISO 200.

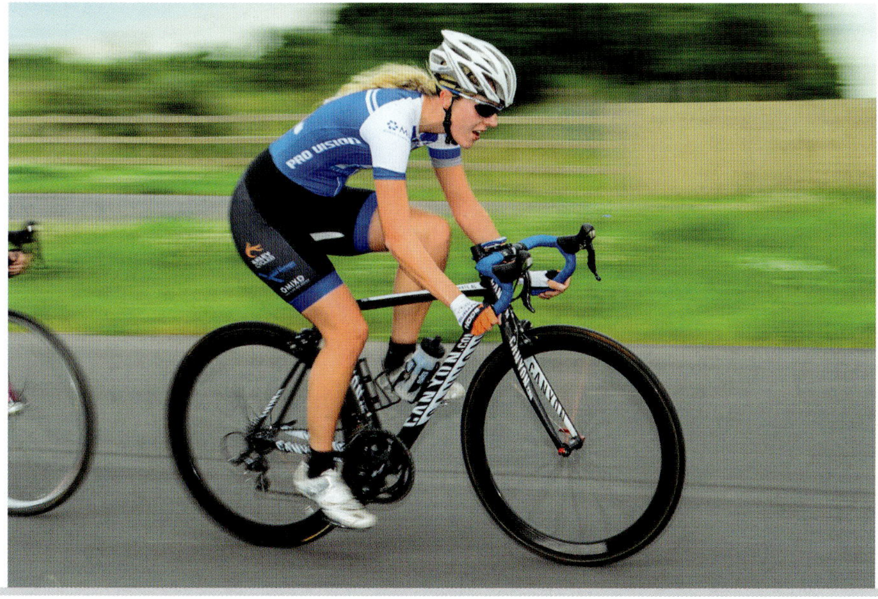

› Fill-in flash

A key application for flash is for "fill-in" light, giving a lift to dark shadows like those cast by direct sunlight. This is why pros regularly use flash in bright conditions (to the mystification of the uninitiated).

Fill-in flash doesn't need to illuminate the shadows fully, only to lighten them a little. This means the flash can be used at a smaller aperture, or greater distance, than when it's the main light (averaging around 2 Ev smaller, or four times the distance).

i-TTL balanced fill-flash for DSLR

i-TTL balanced fill-flash helps achieve natural-looking results when using fill-in flash. It applies automatically provided (a) matrix or center-weighted metering is selected, and (b) a CPU-equipped lens is attached.

FILL-IN FLASH ⌄
The background exposure is the same for both shots. The flash lightens the foreground (left) but has no visible effect in other areas. *24mm, 1/40 sec., f/11, ISO 200.*

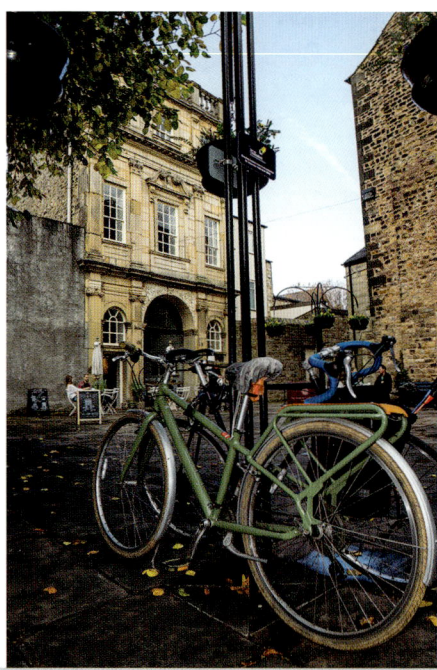
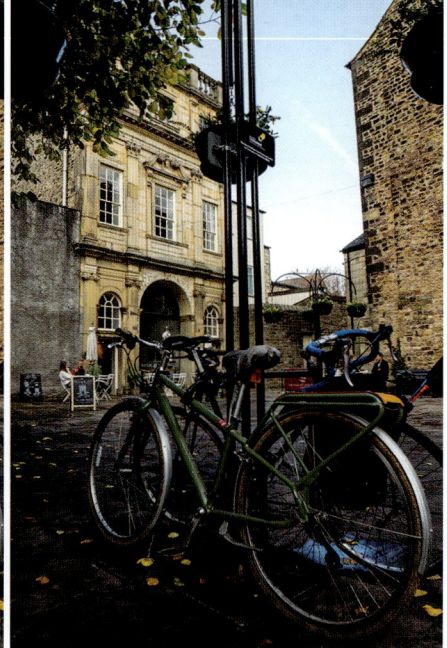

The flash (built-in or compatible flashgun) emits a series of virtually invisible pre-flashes immediately before exposure. Light reflected from these is detected by the metering sensor and analyzed together with the ambient light. If Type D or G lenses are used, distance information is also incorporated.

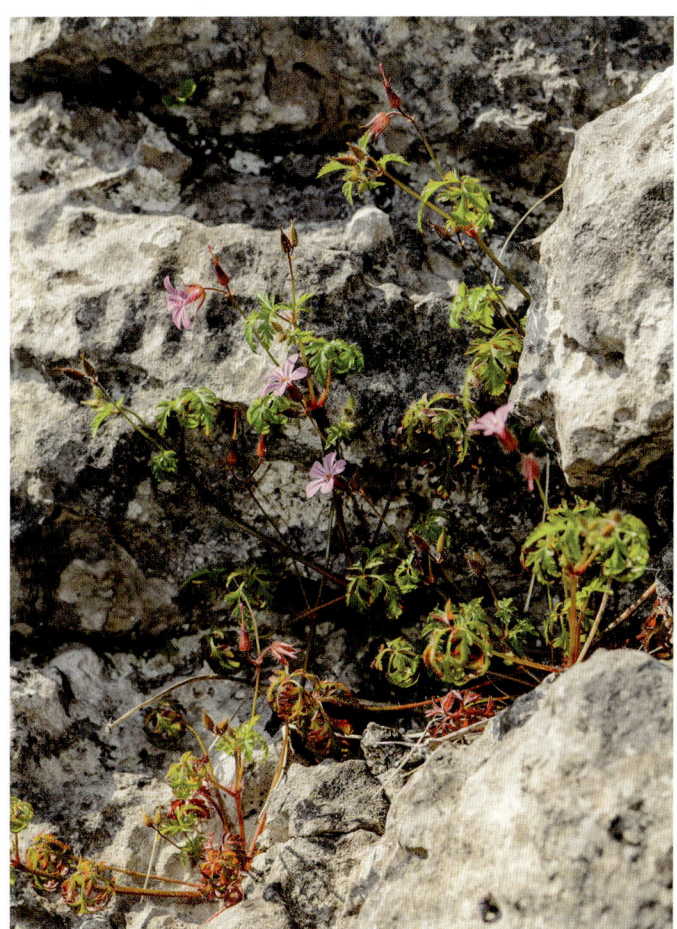

FILL-FLASH »
i-TTL balanced fill-flash for DSLR gives a very natural result; it's not overly obvious that flash has been used at all, but without it the shadows would be much darker.
100mm macro, 1/160 sec., f/11, ISO 100, tripod.

4 » FLASH EXPOSURE

Whether the shutter speed is 1/200 sec. or 20 sec., the flash normally fires just once and therefore delivers the same amount of light to the subject. If there's no other light, the subject will look the same whatever the shutter speed. However, in most cases, there is some other light around, which we call ambient light. Whenever there's ambient light, shutter speed becomes relevant, as slower shutter speeds give ambient light more chance to register.

Aperture, however, affects both flash and ambient exposure. If you use a smaller aperture, but don't change the flash output or ISO, the image will look darker. The camera's flash metering takes this into

FLASH COMPARISON ⌄
Both shots use the same aperture setting, giving identical results on the facing flower, lit only by the flash. However, varying the shutter speed makes a difference in the daylit background.
120mm, 1/100 (left) and 1/13 sec., f/11, ISO 100, tripod.

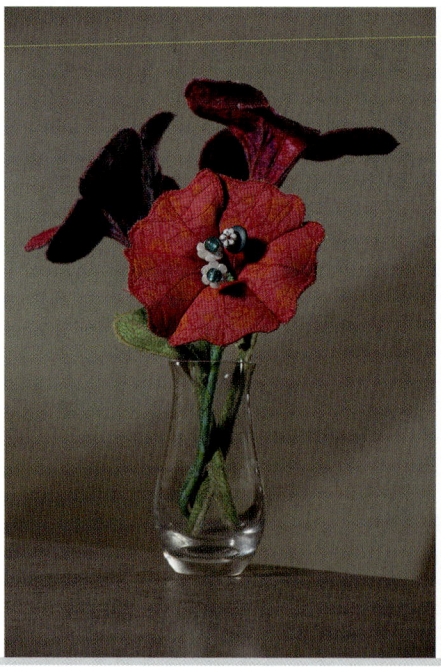
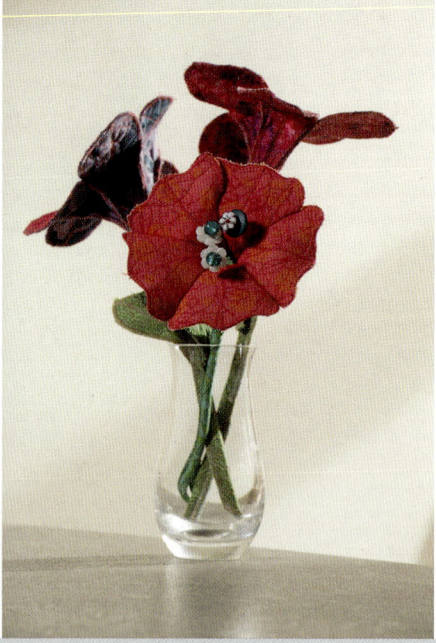

account but it is useful to understand this distinction for a clearer sense of what's going on, especially with slow-sync shots.

The possible combinations of shutter speed and aperture when using flash depend on the current Exposure mode.

Note:
Under some circumstances flash can be used with shutter speeds faster than 1/200 sec.—see High-speed flash sync (page 158).

Exposure mode	Shutter speed	Aperture
P	Set by camera. The normal range is between 1/200 and 1/60 sec., but in certain flash modes all settings up to 30 sec. are available.	Set by camera.
A	Selected by user. All settings between 1/200 sec. and 30 sec. are available. If user sets a faster shutter speed, the D750 will fire at 1/250 sec. while the flash is active.	Set by camera.
S	Set by camera. The normal range is between 1/200 and 1/60 sec., but in certain flash modes all settings up to 30 sec. are available.	Selected by user.
M	Selected by user. All settings between 1/200 sec. and 30 sec. are available. If user sets a faster shutter speed, the D750 will fire at 1/250 sec. while the flash is active.	Selected by user.
AUTO 🏞,🌷,🍃,🌃,🐕,🍴,🍶	Set by camera, between 1/200 and 1/60 sec.	Set by camera.
👤	Set by camera, between 1/200 and 1/60 sec. (1/30 sec. when Vibration Reduction is in use).	Set by camera.
🌠	Set by camera, between 1/200 and 1 sec.	Set by camera.

4 » FLASH RANGE

The usable range of any flash depends on its power, the ISO sensitivity setting, and the aperture selected. If the flash does not reach far enough, you can increase its effective range by setting a higher ISO and/or a wider aperture—but only up to a point.

The table below shows the approximate maximum range of a Nikon SB-700 for selected distances, apertures, and ISO settings, assuming a 50mm lens. This is based on Nikon's published figures, verified by practical tests. Without needing to memorize all these figures, it is helpful to have a general sense of the range limitations that apply when using flash. In specific situations, a few test shots will quickly establish a workable shooting range.

› Guide Numbers

The Guide Number (GN) is a measure of the power of a flash. GNs may be specified in feet or meters and also vary with the ISO rating. They can be used to calculate flash exposures and working range, but with the Nikon CLS this is rarely necessary.

GNs are useful for comparing different flashguns. For instance, the GN for the built-in flash is 12 (meters, ISO 100); for the Nikon SB-910 it is 34, indicating almost three times the power. This allows shooting at three times the distance, at a lower ISO, or with a smaller aperture.

ISO setting						Maximum range	
100	200	400	800	1600	3200	(meters)	(feet)
1.4	2	2.8	4	5.6	8	19.8	65'
2	2.8	4	5.6	8	11	14.2	47'
2.8	4	5.6	8	11	16	9.8	32'
4	5.6	8	11	16	22	7	23'
5.6	8	11	16	22	32	4.9	16'
8	11	16	22	32		3.5	11' 6"
11	16	22	32			2.6	8'
16	22	32				1.6	5'

FLASH RANGE ⌄

The limited range of the flash is apparent, illuminating the wall and the dead tree, but having no discernible effect further away.
32mm, 1/40 sec., f/11, ISO 200, tripod.

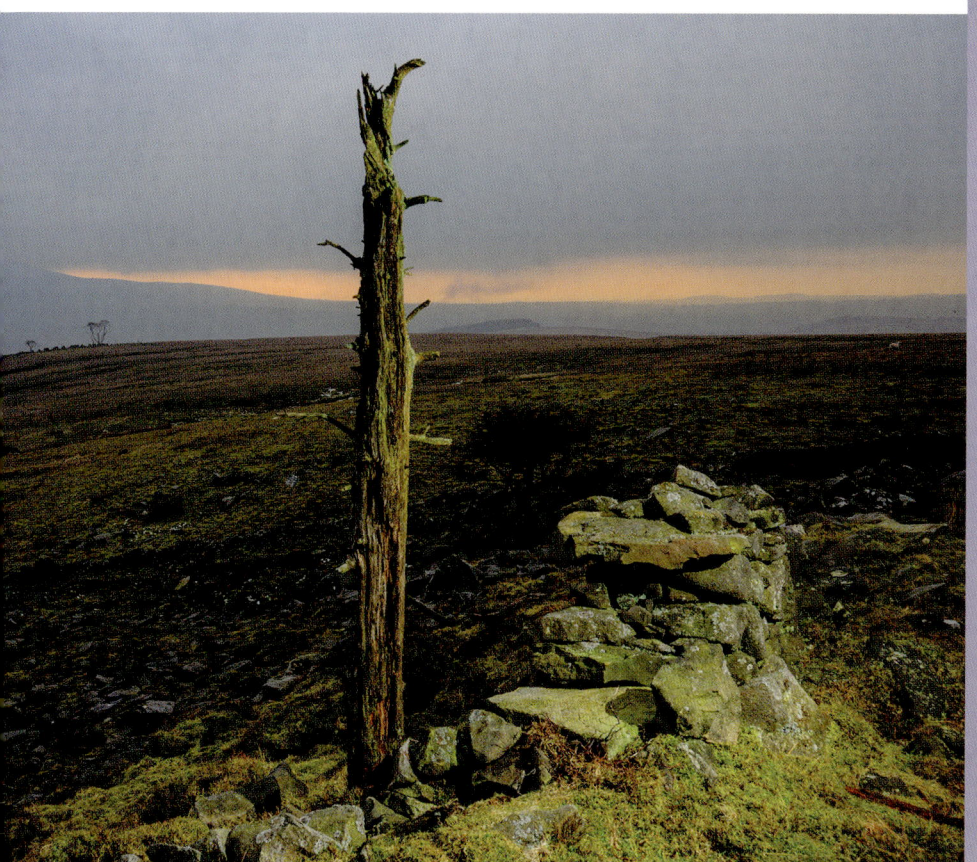

» FLASH SYNCHRONIZATION AND FLASH MODES

To cover the whole image frame, the flash must fire when the shutter is completely open. However, at faster shutter speeds DSLRs do not expose the whole frame at once; for the D750, the fastest shutter speed where this normally applies is 1/200 sec. This is known as the sync speed.

Flash modes are distinguished by how they regulate synchronization and shutter speed. To choose flash mode, press 🔲🔀 and rotate the main command dial.

Standard flash mode (front-curtain sync)

Nikon labels this basic flash mode "fill flash". This is accurate when using matrix or center-weighted metering, but not with spot metering (see page 53). It's called "front-curtain sync" because the flash fires as soon as the shutter is fully open, i.e. as soon as possible after the shutter-release button is pressed. In most exposure modes, the camera will automatically set a shutter speed between 1/60–1/200 sec.

The "opposite" of front-curtain sync is, naturally enough, rear-curtain sync (see next page).

Red-eye reduction

On-camera flash, especially from built-in units, often creates "red-eye", where light reflects off the subject's retina (in animals you may see different colors).

Red-eye reduction works by shining a light (the AF-assist illuminator) at the subject just before the exposure, causing the subject's pupils to contract. This causes a delay, making it unsuitable for moving subjects and killing spontaneity. It's usually better to remove red-eye using **Red-eye correction** in the Retouch menu (see page 139) or on the computer. Better still, use a separate flash, away from the lens axis, or set a high ISO and don't use flash at all.

Slow sync

This mode allows longer shutter speeds (up to 30 sec.) to be used in P and A exposure modes, so that backgrounds can be captured even in low ambient light. Movement of the subject or camera can result in a partly blurred image combined with a sharp image where the subject is lit by the flash. This may be unwanted, but is often used for specific creative effect. This mode is unavailable in S and M exposure modes, because longer shutter speeds can then be set directly.

A limited version (longest exposure 1 sec.), labeled **Auto slow sync**, is available in 🌃 Night portrait mode.

Red-eye reduction with slow sync

This combines the two modes named, allowing backgrounds to register. This may help shots look more natural than red-eye reduction mode alone, but is still subject to delay.

Rear-curtain sync

Rear-curtain sync triggers the flash not at the first possible instant (as in front-curtain sync) but at the last. With moving subjects, this makes any image created by ambient light appear to trail behind the subject, which usually looks more natural than when it extends ahead. In P and A modes it also allows you to select slow shutter speeds (below 1/60 sec.), becoming **slow rear-curtain sync**.

At slow shutter speeds, rear-curtain sync is tricky, as you need to predict where your subject will be at the end of the exposure, rather than at the moment you press the shutter-release button.

LIGHT TRAILS ⌄
Front-curtain sync (left) makes the blurred elements appear to run ahead of the sharp flash image, rear-curtain sync (right) lets them trail behind it.
Left: 14mm, 1/160 sec., f/11, ISO 400.
Right: 24mm, 1/60 sec., f/11, ISO 1250.

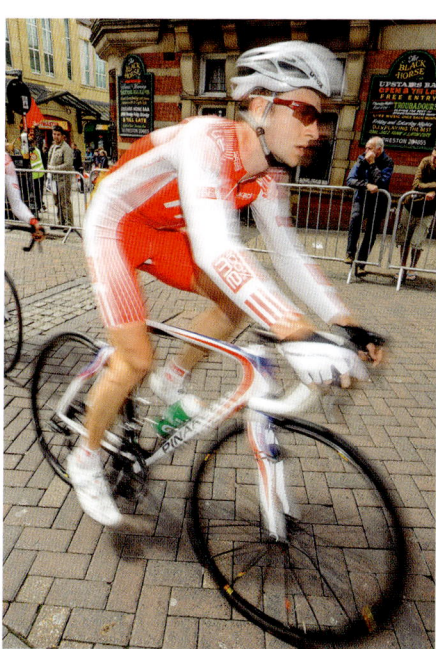 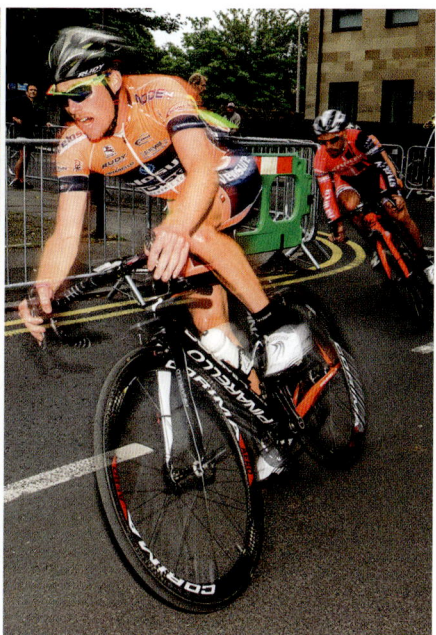

4 » FLASH COMPENSATION

Although the D750 has excellent flash metering, it's not completely infallible. You may also want to adjust flash output for creative effect. Flash compensation (and FV lock) work with compatible Speedlights or the built-in flash.

To use flash compensation, rotate the sub-command dial while pressing **+/−**; settings can be seen in the control panel, information display, and viewfinder. Flash compensation can be set from −3 to +1 Ev in ⅓ Ev steps. Negative compensation reduces the brightness of flash-lit areas, without affecting ambient-lit areas.

Positive compensation brightens areas lit by the flash, again leaving other areas unaffected. However, if the subject is already at the limit of flash range, positive compensation can't help; instead use a wider aperture, set a higher ISO, or move closer to the subject.

Manual flash

Using Custom setting e3 **Flash control for built-in flash>Manual** (page 160), you can precisely control flash output from Full power down to 1/128. With external Speedlights, manual power settings use the unit's own controls.

FV lock

FV lock is analogous to exposure lock (page 55), allowing you to lock flash output and then reframe the image. It's most useful when you want to use flash with an off-center subject.

However, using FV lock is somewhat involved. You must first assign the FV lock function to one of the control buttons: Fn, Preview, or **AE-L/AF-L**, via Custom setting f2, f3, or f4 respectively. This means flash compensation is usually more convenient.

If you do assign a button to FV lock, the procedure is very like that for exposure lock.

Make sure the built-in flash (or CLS-compatible flashgun) is charged, with the flash-ready indicator **⚡** showing in the viewfinder. Position the subject centrally in the frame and half-press the shutter-release button to activate metering, then press the assigned control button. A pre-flash is fired to set the flash level, and FV lock icons appear in the displays.

Reframe the image and shoot. The flash level remains locked for succeeding shots. To release FV lock, press the assigned button again.

Flash bracketing

Flash bracketing is another way to ensure you have exactly the right level of flash illumination. It works just like exposure bracketing (see page 56), and indeed you can bracket both flash and main exposure simultaneously; set Custom setting e6 **Auto** bracketing set to **Flash only** (to vary flash level only) or **AE & flash** (to vary the main exposure as well).

You then proceed exactly as for exposure bracketing, using **BKT** and the main command dial to select the number of shots in the bracketing burst. **BKT** and the sub-command dial set the difference in flash output between shots.

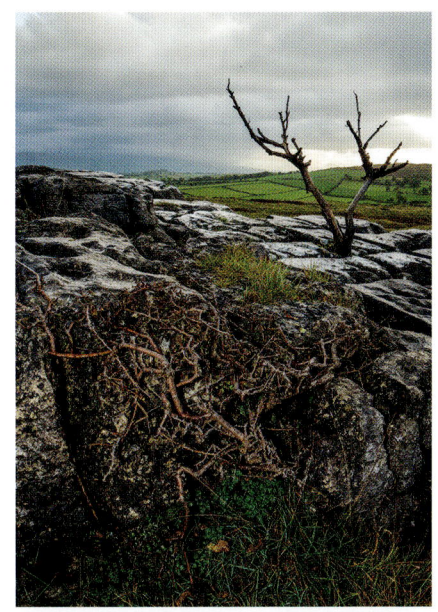

TURNING IT DOWN »
With flash, "less is more", and negative compensation has been here used to tone it down below the camera's default setting. *24mm, 1/20 sec., f/11, ISO 100, tripod.*

COMPENSATION ≫
The background exposure is the same for these three shots, with flash compensation set to (from left to right): −1, 0, and +1. *78mm, 1/200 sec., f/11, ISO 100.*

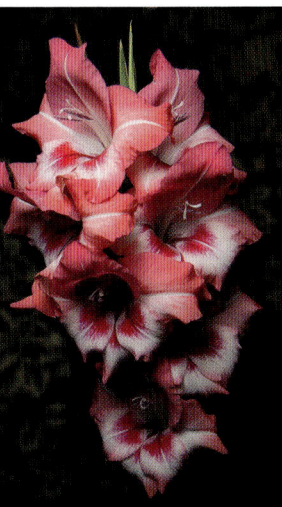
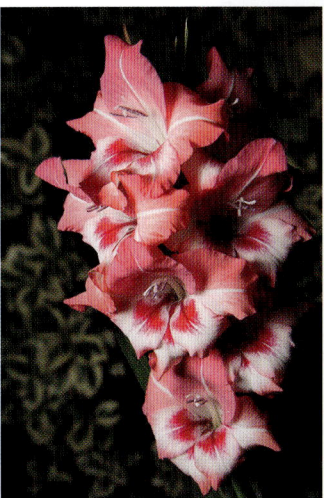
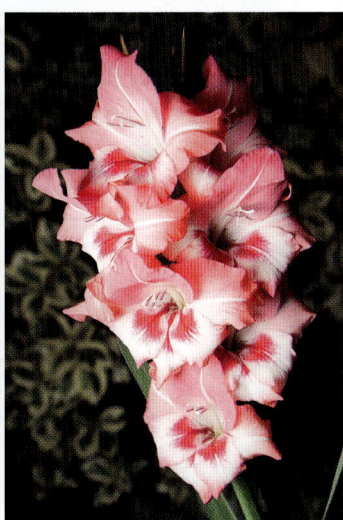

4

» ACCESSORY FLASHGUNS

Compared to the built-in flash, accessory flashguns, which Nikon calls Speedlights, bring much greater power and flexibility. Nikon Speedlights integrate with Nikon's Creative Lighting System for outstanding results. Independent makers such as Sigma offer alternatives, many of them also compatible with i-TTL flash control. However, such dedicated units tend to be expensive.

Using non-Nikon units

Nikon issues dire warnings about using other brands of flash with its cameras, and it's true that some flashguns may use too high a trigger voltage or even the wrong polarity, which could damage the camera's circuitry. It's best to avoid mounting or connecting any non-Nikon flashgun unless it's from a reputable maker like Sigma or Metz, and their information clearly states that it is compatible.

The risk of encountering excessive voltages is even more pronounced with studio flash units. When using Nikon DSLRs with studio flash—for instance, shooting images of the camera for this book—I never connect them directly but use the built-in flash to trigger the studio flash in "slave" mode.

There are many possibilities with cheap, basic flashguns, which you may find lurking at the back of a cupboard, or in the local

camera shop's bargain bin. Even without i-TTL metering, great results are possible with a little trial and error. If you use certain setups regularly, as you may for portraits and close-ups, you can easily record and replicate the flash settings. However, take note of the warning above; be wary of flashguns that are not certified compatible. You can still make good use of

D750 WITH SB-700 ˅

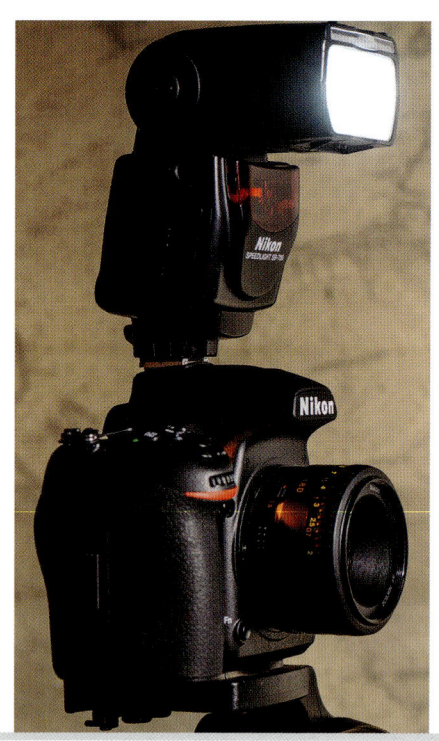

such units (triggering with slaves, for example), but they should not be mounted in the hotshoe.

› Mounting an external flashgun

Check the flashgun is switched off, then slide its foot into the camera's hotshoe. If you feel resistance, check that the mounting lock on the flashgun is released. Lock it once the unit is mounted, then switch on the flashgun. Once it is charged and ready, a ⚡ icon appears in the viewfinder.

› Bounce flash and off-camera flash

Mounting a flashgun in the hotshoe is a start, but its light is still harsh and still quite close to the lens axis, and red-eye remains a common issue.

You can dramatically alter the quality of flash light by bouncing it off a ceiling, wall or reflector, or by taking the flashgun off the camera entirely.

Bounce flash
Bouncing the flash light off a suitable surface spreads the light, softening the shadows, and changes its direction, giving more varied and interesting results.

Many flashguns have heads that can be tilted and swiveled, allowing light to be bounced off walls, ceilings, and other surfaces. Most surfaces will absorb some light, and the light also has to travel further to reach the subject; i-TTL metering will automatically compensate, but the working range is reduced.

> ### Tip
>
> *Colored surfaces affect the color of the bounced light. This can be exploited for creative effect, but for neutral results choose a white or silvered surface. Portrait photographers often use gold reflectors for warmer results.*

SPEEDLIGHT SB-910

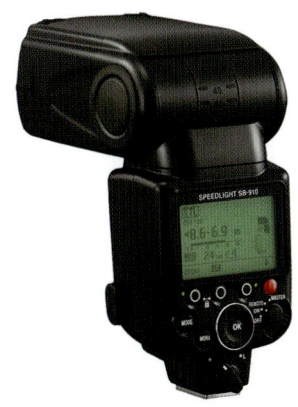

Off-camera flash

Taking the flashgun off the camera gives complete control over the direction of its light. The flash can be fired wirelessly (see below) or using a flash cord; Nikon's dedicated cords (see page 213) preserve i-TTL metering.

› Wireless flash

Many external flash units can be fired wirelessly using a "slave" attachment, but there's no other communication between camera and flash, and no direct control over flash output. However, CLS-compatible flashguns can communicate fully with the camera and its powerful metering system. The D750's built-in flash can act as the "commander" unit,

controlling multiple Speedlights in one or two separate groups.

To enable Commander mode, and tune the output of the remote Speedlight(s), use Custom setting e3 **Flash cntrl for built-in flash**. To allow the camera to regulate flash output set **Mode** to **TTL** for each unit or group. **Comp** settings are exactly like Flash compensation (page 160).

Many professionals prefer radio-control systems, which offer greater range and

LIGHT EXPERIMENT ⌄

The first shot (left) was taken using the built-in flash; there's an ugly shadow yet the subject itself looks a bit flat. The second (center) uses off-camera flash high on the left, giving a more 3D result. The third (right) uses bounce flash, giving a softer, more even light.
100mm, 1/200 sec., f/11, ISO 200, tripod.

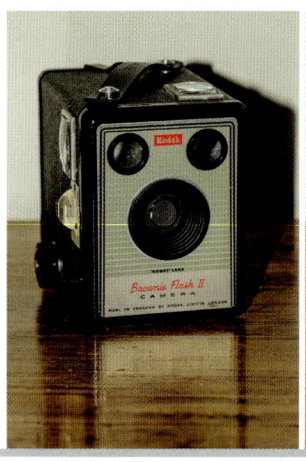
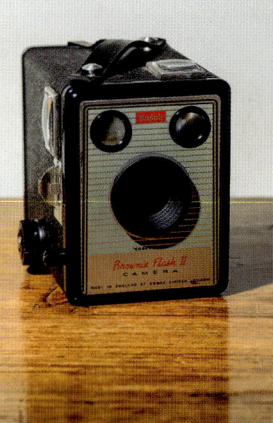
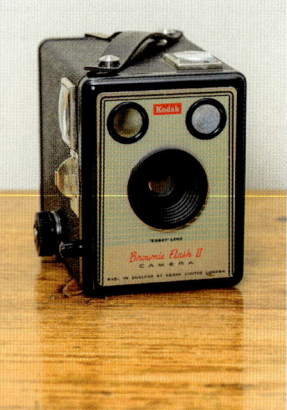

allow you to use third-party flashguns. Pocket Wizard systems have a good reputation, while I've had excellent results using the less expensive Phottix Odin setup.

Using multiple flashes in a wireless system gives terrific power and flexibility, but it's not easy to visualize all the possible permutations. It's wise to have a few dry-runs before using such a setup on an important shoot.

› High-speed flash sync

Most Nikon Speedlights offer Auto FP High Speed sync. This enables the flash output to be phased or pulsed, allowing flash to be used at all shutter speeds. Combining flash with fast shutter speeds is useful, for instance, when ambient light levels are high or you wish to use a wide aperture, or when using fill-in flash with fast-moving subjects.

Enable Auto FP High Speed sync using Custom setting e1: set either **1/250s (Auto FP)** or **1/200s (Auto FP)**. If a suitable Speedlight is attached, flash can then be used at any shutter speed from 30 sec. to 1/8000 sec. However, the effective power (and therefore working range) of the

Speedlight will reduce as the shutter speed gets faster. See the manual for the individual Speedlight for more details, and take test shots and review them on the monitor if at all possible.

SPIDER   ⌄
Wireless flash was used to backlight this spider. I used the built-in flash in commander mode. Similar results are possible using a sync lead or a radio system.
150mm, 1/200 sec., f/32, ISO 100.

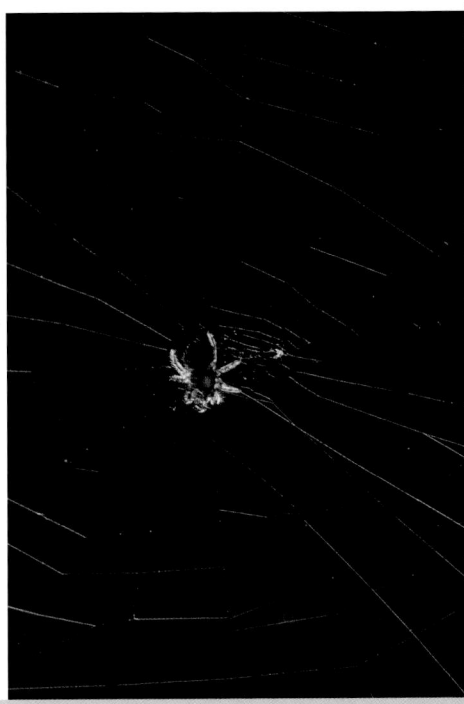

» NIKON SPEEDLIGHTS

The table below shows CLS-compatible
Speedlights made by Nikon, both current
and discontinued. The second table
summarizes key features of current models.

CLS-compatible Speedlights

	Guide Number for ISO 100 (meters)	Use as commander unit?	Current or discontinued
SB-910	34	Yes	Current
SB-700	28	Yes	Current
SB-500	24	Yes	Current
SB-300	18	No	Current
SB-R200	10	No	Current
SB-900	34	Yes	Discontinued
SB-800	38	Yes	Discontinued
SB-600	30	No	Discontinued
SB-400	21	No	Discontinued

Current Nikon Speedlights

	SB-910	SB-700	SB-500	SB-300	SB-R200
Flash coverage (lens focal length range) with D750	17– 200mm	24– 120mm	24mm	18mm	
Guide Number (meters, ISO 100)	34	28	24	18	
Tilt/swivel	Yes	Yes	Yes	Tilt only	No
Dimensions (width x height x depth, mm)	78.5 x 145 x 113	71 x 126 x 104.5	67 x 114.55 x 70.8	57.4 x 65.4 x 62.3	80 x 75 x 55
Weight (without batteries)	510g	360g	273g	120g	120g
Use as Commander?	Yes	Yes	Yes	No	No*

Cannot be used in camera hotshoe, only as a slave within Creative Lighting System

» FLASH ACCESSORIES

Flash accessories such as diffusers, reflectors, and remote leads allow yet more flexibility and control over lighting effects, while power packs increase flash capacity.

› Speedlight stand AS-19

Allows Speedlights to stand on flat surfaces or to be mounted on a tripod.

› Flash diffusers

Flash diffusers are a simple, economical way to spread and soften the hard light from a flash head. Many flashguns are supplied with a small dome-type diffuser; larger third-party units like those from Honl give almost a "soft-box" effect.

   Diffusers inevitably reduce the light reaching the subject; flash metering will compensate, but the effective range is reduced.

› Flash brackets

Nikon's Speedlights can be mounted on a tripod or stand on any flat surface using the AS-19 stand, but for more portable support many photographers prefer a flexible arm or bracket attached to the camera; Novoflex produces a wide range.

SHOOTING WITH A DIFFUSER ❯❯
The bottom image resulted from the setup in the top picture. The light is clearly directional but much softer than if taken with a "naked" Speedlight.
100mm macro, 1/8 sec., f/22, ISO 200, tripod.

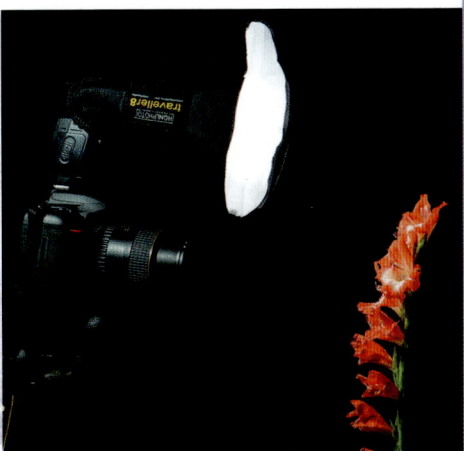

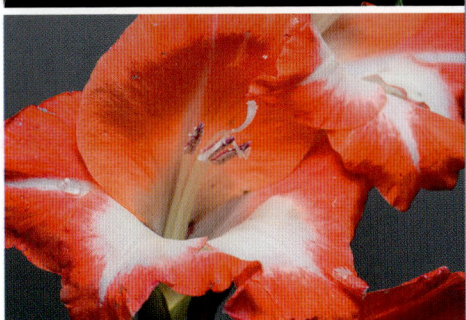

5 CLOSE-UP

Close-up photography is a fascinating branch of the craft, but it certainly has its challenges. A key issue is depth of field (see page 49), which becomes narrower as you move closer to the subject. This often necessitates using small apertures, which can make long exposures essential. Narrow depth of field also means that the slightest movement of either subject or camera can completely ruin focus. A tripod or other solid camera support is often required, and sometimes you'll want to immobilize the subject (within ethical limits).

» MACRO PHOTOGRAPHY

"Close-up" is a vague term, but "macro" has a precise meaning; it strictly means photographing objects at life-size or larger, i.e. with a reproduction ratio (see page 170) of 1:1 or better. Some lenses are badged "macro" when their reproduction ratio is only 1:4, or 1:2 at best. There's still plenty of close-up potential, but it isn't classically macro.

You can explore true macro photography without the expense of a dedicated macro lens (see page 174).

› Focusing

With minimal depth of field, focusing becomes critical. Rather than merely focusing on "the subject", you must decide which part of the subject to focus on. The D750's 51 AF points cover a good spread, but Live View has much to offer. In Live View (see page 81) you can set the focus point anywhere in the frame, and zoom in for greater precision. This makes manual focus easy and ultra-precise; I almost never use AF for macro work.

BOUNDED IN A NUTSHELL »
Close-up photography opens up a whole new world, or at least a new way of seeing the world. *125mm, 1/60 sec., f/6.3, ISO 400.*

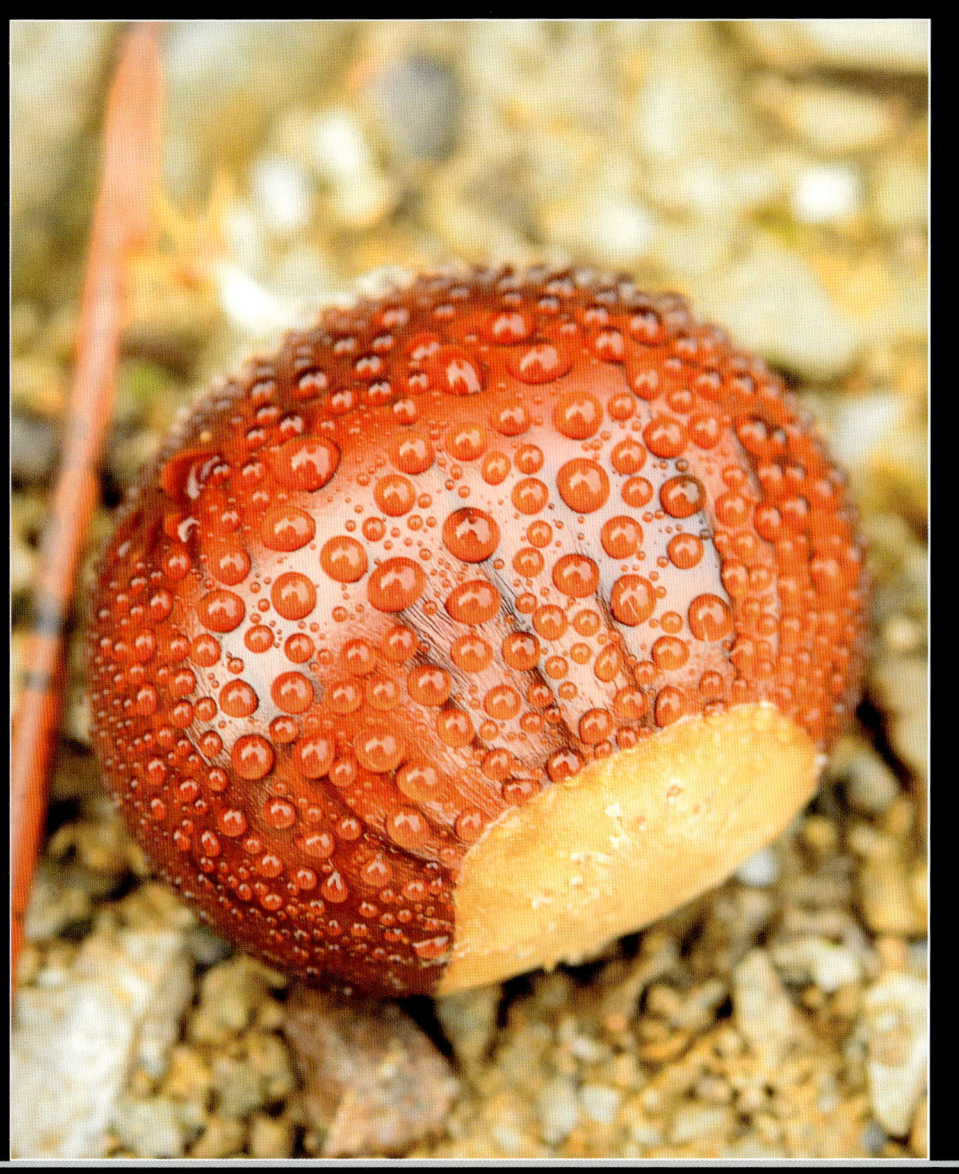

› Reproduction ratio

The reproduction ratio is the ratio between the actual size of the subject and the size of its image on the D750's sensor. This measures 35.9 x 24mm. At 1:1 an object of this size will fill the image frame exactly. To take a handy example, an SD memory card (32 x 24mm) will almost span the long axis of the frame and fill the short axis.

› Working distance

The working distance is the distance required for a desired reproduction ratio with any given lens. It is directly related to the focal length of the lens: a 200mm macro lens doubles the working distance for 1:1 reproduction compared to a 100mm. Extra distance can be helpful when photographing living subjects, especially mobile ones, as well as ones which might be damaged by accidental contact.

Working distance, and the minimum focus distance of a lens, are measured from the subject to the focal plane, i.e. the position of the sensor (marked with ⊖ on the top of the camera). The front of the lens may be much closer to the subject.

For any given lens, working distance will be shorter with an FX-format camera like the D750 than a DX-format model. Consider switching **Image area** to **DX** (see page 76); the resulting images are still more than adequate for most purposes.

BOX BROWNIE ⌄
Comparison of close-up at 1:1 (left) and 1:4.

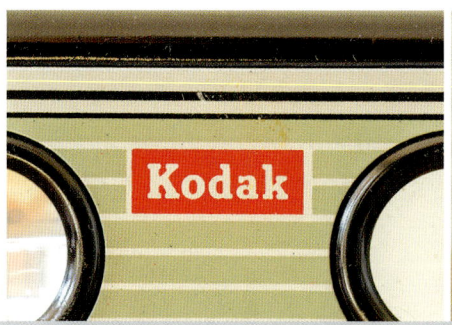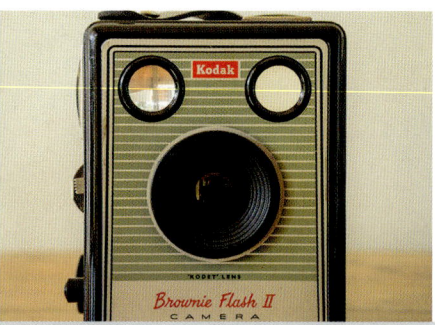

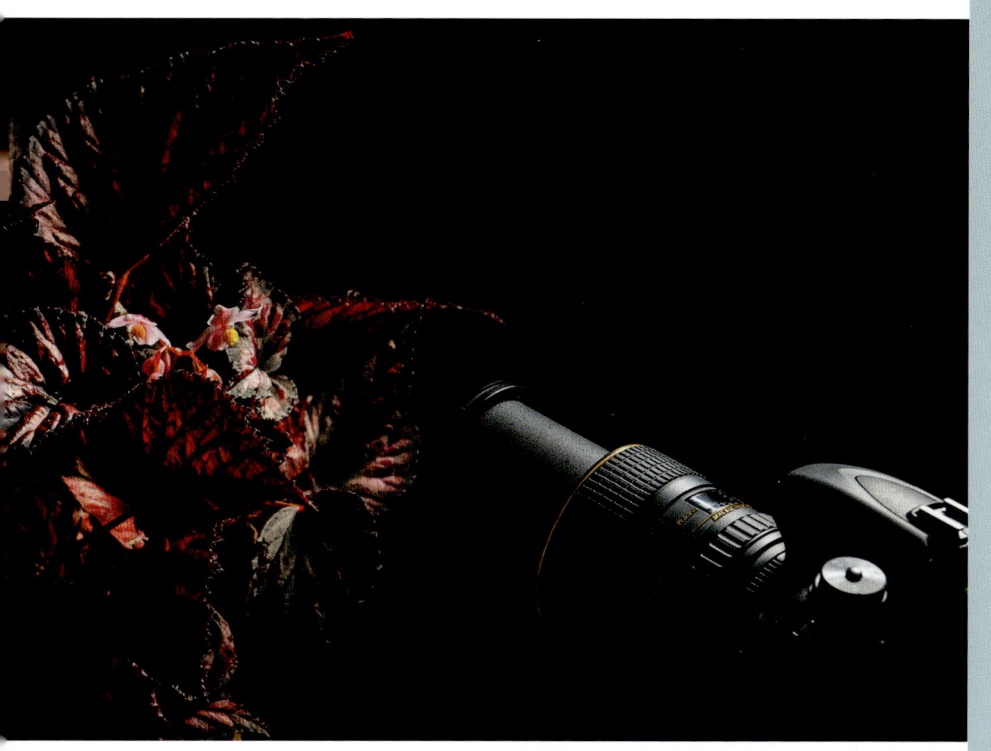

FOLIAGE

Even with a 100mm macro lens, the working distance for 1:1 reproduction is such that the lens is in among the foliage.

5 » MACRO LIGHTING

Much fine close-up photography is done using available light, but your own shadow, or the camera's, often intrudes. For this and other reasons, more precisely directed light is often needed. Regular Speedlights mounted in the hotshoe may not light the subject at all, and the built-in flash is equally useless at short working distances.

Ring-flash units encircle the lens, giving even illumination on ultra-close subjects (they're also favored by some portrait photographers). They are available from Sigma, Nissin, and others.

Nikon prefers a twin-flash approach with its Speedlight Commander Kit R1C1 and Speedlight Remote Kit R1. Both use Speedlight SB-R200 flashguns, mounting either side of the lens. The R1C1 includes a Wireless Speedlight Commander SU-800, which fits into the camera's hotshoe, while the R1 needs a separate commander (possibly the built-in flash).

› LED light

LED lights, like the Sunpak DSLR67 LED Macro Ring Light, are a much cheaper alternative. It's only suitable for close subjects, but that's all you need in a macro light. You may need fairly high ISO ratings to achieve fast shutter speeds for mobile subjects.

CLOSE-UP LIGHTING ⌄
The image resulting from the setup in the previous picture. It gives even illumination on the subject, but doesn't reach very far, so the background (actually a light wall) appears dark.
100mm macro, 1/8 sec., f/22, ISO 200, tripod.

RING LIGHT ⌄
D750 and Sunpak LED Macro Ring Light (this is an older version, not the DSLR67).
100mm macro, f/13, ISO 64.

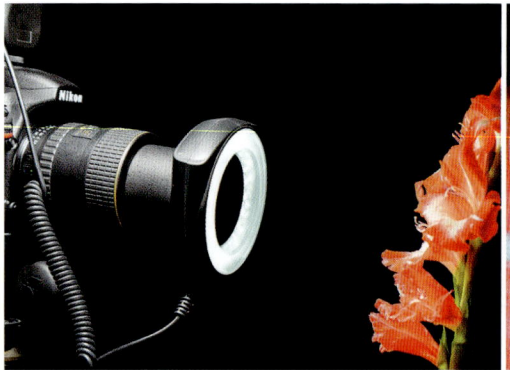

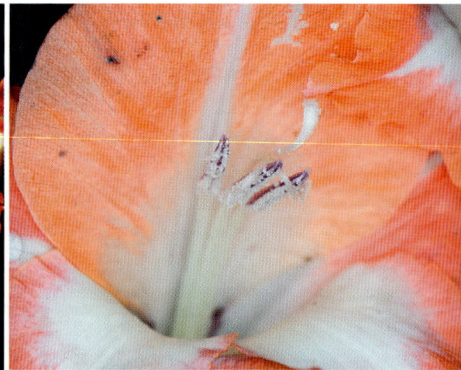

» EQUIPMENT FOR MACRO PHOTOGRAPHY

› Close-up attachment lenses

Close-up attachment lenses are simple magnifying lenses that screw into the filter thread of the lens. They are light, inexpensive, and fully compatible with the camera's exposure and focusing systems. Results are generally best in conjunction with prime lenses (see page 204).

Nikon produces six close-up attachment lenses (see the table below).

› Extension tubes

Extension tubes, or extension rings, are another simple, economical, way of extending a lens's close-focusing capabilities. In essence they are simple tubes fitting between the lens and the camera. They decrease the minimum focusing distance, thereby increasing the magnification factor. They are light, compact, and easy to carry and attach. Nikon produces four Extension rings— PK-11A, PK-12, PK-13, and PN-11—which extend the lens by 8mm, 14mm, 27.5mm, and 52.5mm respectively. The PN-11 incorporates a tripod mount. They are an

elderly design and also quite expensive. A set of three compatible extension tubes (12mm, 20mm, and 36mm) from Kenko costs little more than one of the Nikon items. They support metering and auto-exposure but not autofocus with all lenses, but that's a minor issue in most macro work.

› Bellows

Like extension tubes, bellows extend the spacing between the lens and the camera body, but in a greater range. Again, there's no extra glass to impair optical quality. However, bellows are expensive, heavy, and slow to set up. They are usually employed in a studio or other controlled setting.

› Reversing rings

Also known as reverse adapters or inversion rings, these allow lenses to be mounted in reverse, allowing much closer focusing than normal. They are ideally used with a prime lens, such as the classic 50mm f/1.8, Nikon's BR-2A fits its 52mm filter thread. You'll lose all automatic functions, so you need a lens with an aperture ring.

Product number	Attaches to filter thread	Recommended for use with
0, 1	52mm	Standard lenses
3T, 4T	52mm	Short telephoto lenses
5T, 6T	62mm	Telephoto lenses

» MACRO LENSES

True macro lenses give reproduction ratios of 1:1 or better and are optically optimized for close-up work, though very capable for general photography too. This is certainly true of Nikon's Micro Nikkor lenses. Of course, other makers produce alternative macro lenses; the lens used for all the close-up illustrations in this book is a 100mm Tokina.

The **60mm f/2.8G ED AF-S Micro Nikkor** is an upgrade to the previous 60mm f/2.8D. Advances include ED glass for superior optical quality and Silent Wave Motor for ultra-quiet autofocus.

The **105mm f/2.8G AF-S VR Micro Nikkor** also features internal focusing, ED glass, and Silent Wave Motor, but arguably its most notable attribute is VR (Vibration Reduction). As the slightest camera shake is magnified at high reproduction ratios, VR is invaluable, and—at least in theory—it allows you to employ shutter speeds up to

four stops slower than otherwise possible. However, at close range the slightest change in subject-to-camera distance can completely ruin the focus, so a tripod is still invaluable.

The **200mm f/4D ED-IF AF Micro Nikkor** is an older design, but its longer working distance makes it particularly suited to photographing wildlife.

There are also two DX-format Micro Nikkor lenses.

The **40mm f/2.8G AF-S DX Micro Nikkor** has the attraction of being Nikon's lightest, and least expensive, macro lens. However, its working distance at 1:1 reproduction ratio is just 6.2in. (16cm), leaving very little room between the subject and the front of the lens.

The **85mm f/3.5G ED VR AF-S DX Micro Nikkor** has a more versatile focal length and internal focusing, ED glass, and Silent Wave Motor.

60MM F/2.8G ED AF-S MICRO NIKKOR ⌄

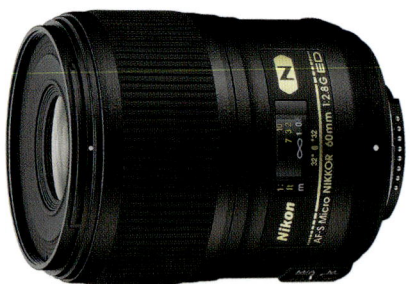

105MM F/2.8G AF-S VR MICRO NIKKOR ⌄

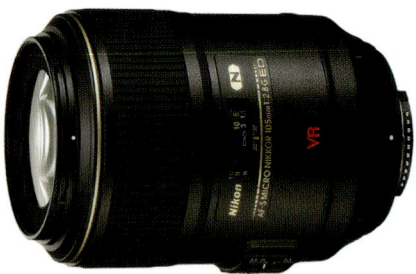

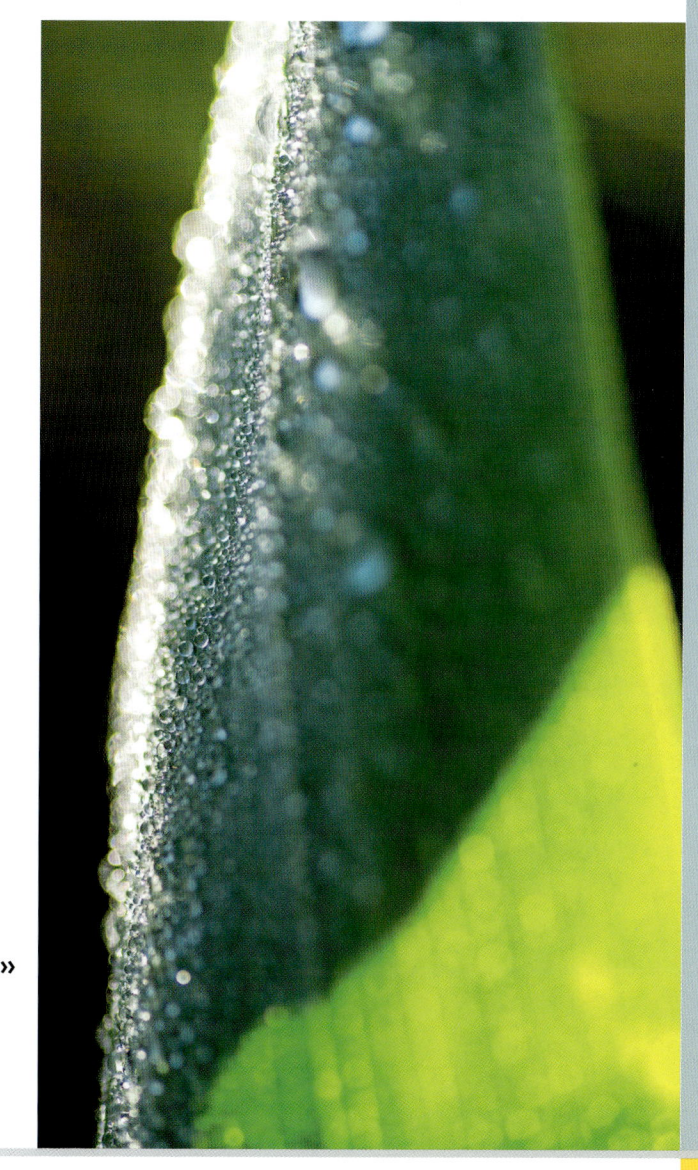

SHALLOW SHOOTING »
This image exemplifies
the minimal depth of
field obtained in extreme
close-up shooting.
100mm macro, 1/80 sec.,
f/6.3, ISO 100, tripod.

6 MOVIES

Nikon pioneered DSLR movies with the D90 (2008). For many, the true purpose of the DSLR is to shoot stills and its ergonomics are still best for this, but the addition of video is no mere sideshow. Professional movie makers have embraced DSLRs because their large sensors deliver image quality that's superior—and just plain different—to standard camcorders, while photojournalists welcome the ability to shoot high-quality stills and video on the same camera. However, still photography and movies are very different media, and require distinctly different approaches for best results.

› Advantages

DSLRs in general, not least the D750, have some real advantages over standard camcorders. One is the large sensor's ability to give very shallow depth of field (see page 49); movie-makers have eagerly embraced this "DSLR look". The large sensor also brings greater dynamic range (page 92) and better quality at high ISO ratings, extending the possibilities for shooting in low light.

Another plus is the D750's ability to use the entire array of Nikon-fit lenses (see chapter 7, page 190): in particular, it can use wide-angle lenses which go well beyond the range of most camcorders.

Digital camcorders often claim enormous zoom ranges but these are only achieved by "digital zoom", a software function that enlarges the central portion of the image—inevitably losing quality. "Optical zoom" range is what matters, and interchangeable lenses cover all normal angles of view. The widest range currently available in a single Nikon lens is 18–300mm. Tamron produces a 16–300mm.

LEGIONARY »
It's much easier to get really shallow depth of field than with most video cameras.
300mm, f/5.6, ISO 400.

HIGH AND WIDE »
On a full-frame camera like the D750, a 15mm focal length gives a wide and dramatic view.
25mm, f/14, ISO 400.

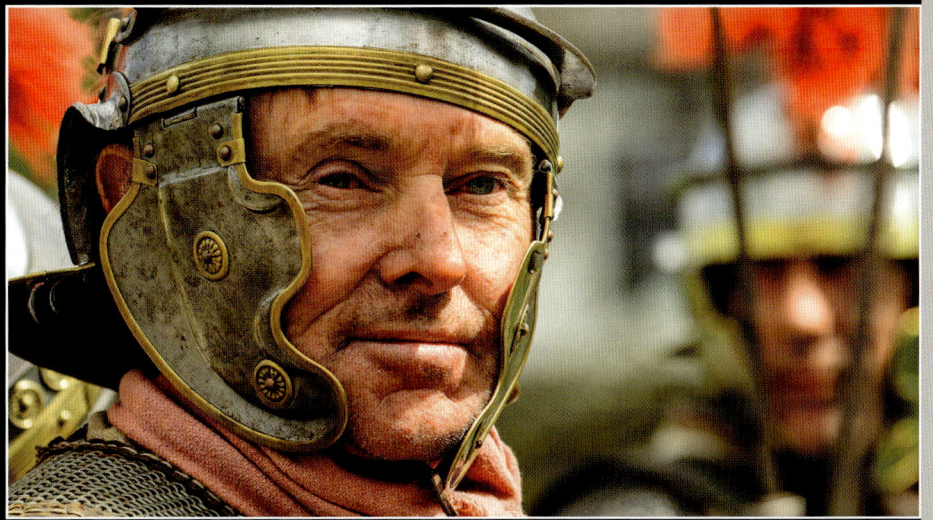

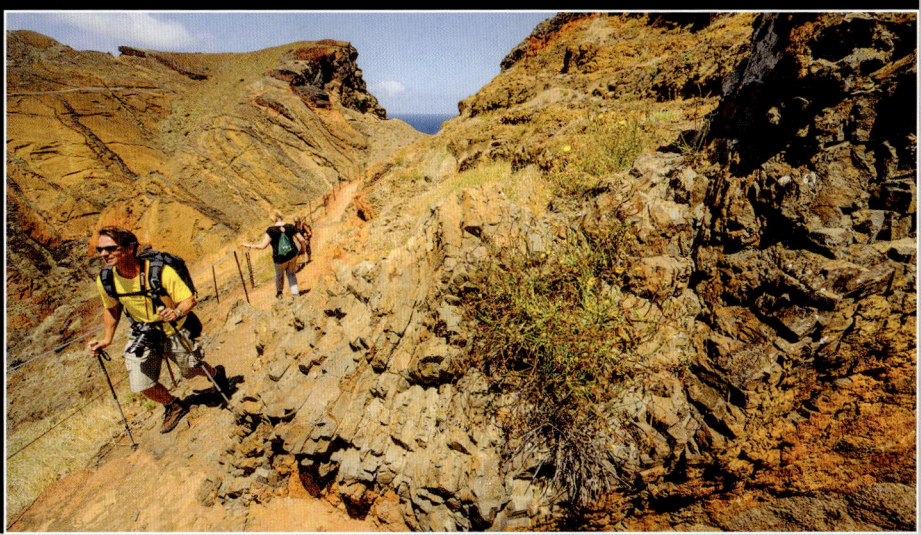

» MAKING MOVIES

› Quality

Before shooting, select settings in the Movie Shooting menu (see pages 109–111).

Frame size/frame rate is a key choice. The D750 can shoot movies in Full HD (High Definition) quality with a frame size of 1920 x 1080 pixels. Full HD is a general benchmark of video resolution, although the 720p standard (1280 x 720 pixels) looks excellent on most computer screens and mobile devices and gives much smaller file sizes. It is the norm on Vimeo.com, a prime online outlet for quality video.

However, Retina iPads have a 2048 x 1536 display—over 50% more pixels than Full HD. With displays like this becoming common, and with "4K" video (equivalent to around 8 megapixels) becoming available on affordable cameras, 720p may look inadequate as time goes on. Available frame rate options vary according to the size chosen. (See also **Image area**, below.)

Movie quality sets the compression level; **High** quality equals low compression. Footage recorded to a memory card is always compressed, though High quality is fine for most purposes. For professional applications, the D750 can also export uncompressed footage when a compatible recorder is connected to the camera's HDMI port.

You cannot record a clip longer than 20 minutes in High quality or 30 minutes in Normal quality. This is hardly ever a problem—for viewers, 20 minutes is an enormously long time for a single clip!

The D750 records movies with a "widescreen" aspect ratio of 16:9. Normally these use the full width of the sensor. However, if **Image area** (page 76) is set to **DX**, or **Auto DX Crop** is **On** and a DX lens attached, the camera employs a smaller area (see the diagram below). This does not affect the output size; you can still record Full HD as well as smaller frame sizes. This allows the use of DX lenses—which can be light, inexpensive, and have very wide zoom ranges—but also gives a "teleconverter" effect (see page 201).

IMAGE AREAS ⌄
Movie image areas superimposed on the full screen.

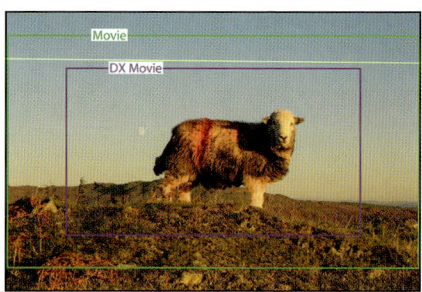

› Picture Controls

The Picture Control should also be set in advance; you can do this quickly in Movie Live View—see **Movie Live View options**, below. If you're planning to adjust the look of the movie in post-processing ("grading"), then the Flat Picture Control (page 92) gives most latitude for this, but if you're likely to use the footage more or less as is, then pick the Picture Control which gives the look you want.

PICTURE CONTROL
Picture Control selection in Movie Live View.

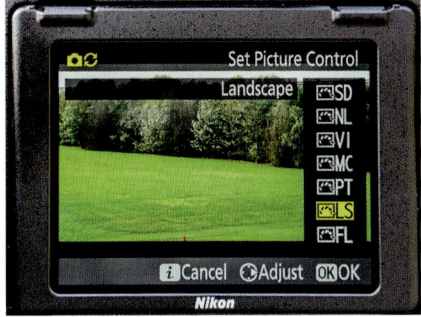

› Movie Live View options

Most of the Movie Shooting menu options, except **Movie ISO sensitivity settings**, can also be accessed from Movie Live View (but not while actually shooting a clip) by pressing ◄**i**►. In addition, you can access options for **Monitor brightness**, **Highlight display**, and **Headphone volume**.

1) In Movie Live View, make sure that the screen is showing information indicators—if not, press info to cycle through the screens, as in normal Live View (page 78).

2) Press ◄**i**► to reveal a list of items on the right of the screen. Use ▲/▼ to scroll through the list.

3) Press ► to see options for the selected item; select from among them with ▲/▼.

4) Press OK to confirm and return to the screen of step 2.

5) Press ◄**i**► again to exit.

› Focus options

The focus modes and AF-area options for movie shooting are the same as for Live View (page 81). In Full-time servo AF (AF-F), the D750 will automatically maintain focus during movie recording, though Live View AF is nowhere near agile enough for fast-moving subjects. It's important to be aware of this limitation—sometimes you just have to work round it and plan alternative shots that don't stress the AF system so far.

In Single-servo AF (AF-S) the camera will only refocus when you half-press the shutter-release button.

Manual focusing is also possible, but can be yet another recipe for wobbly pictures. A tripod helps, especially with longer lenses, where focusing is more critical and wobbles are magnified. Some lenses have a smoother manual focus action than others. The physical design of older lenses often makes them more suitable, with large and well-placed focus rings. There are attachments (often

BLUES BROTHERS ⌄
With the performers staying roughly the same distance from the camera, a fixed focus was perfectly adequate.
180mm, f/5.6, ISO 1600.

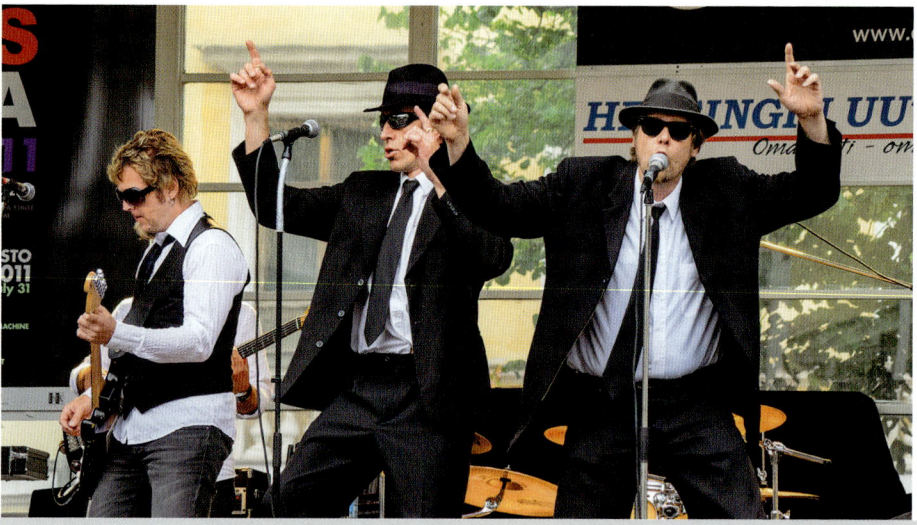

expensive!) which allow you to control focus more smoothly and precisely.

Unexpected or inaccurate shifts in focus can be very disconcerting when viewing the footage. Fortunately, it is often not necessary anyway. Using a fixed focus is perfectly viable for many shots, especially when depth of field is good. To employ fixed focus, use AF-S (Single-servo AF), set focus in Live View before shooting the clip, and avoid pressing the shutter-release button while shooting. Or just use manual focus.

› Exposure

In Program or Shutter-priority mode, exposure levels can be adjusted by ±3 Ev using ![icon] and the main command dial. Shutter speed, aperture, and ISO are set automatically. The only other exposure-related option you can change is the metering pattern (page 52). In fact, for movies there is no functional difference

---

Tip

To avoid sudden changes in brightness in your footage, you can lock exposure by holding **AE-L/AF-L** *, just as in stills photography.*

---

between P and S modes. Scene modes have similar options (or lack of them), except that you can't change the metering pattern. In Full Auto and Effects modes exposure is entirely automatic.

More extensive exposure control is only available in A and M modes. In Aperture-priority mode, aperture can be manually adjusted during shooting. Shutter speed and ISO are set automatically. Aperture control is vital if you're seeking to create "DSLR-look" footage with slender depth of field.

Manual mode gives you direct control over aperture, shutter speed, and ISO sensitivity. The shutter speed does affect how moving subjects are recorded, so this can be very important. However, the available shutter speed range is limited (see below).

Although these options are welcome, actually making adjustments while shooting is fiddly. It can cause shake unless the camera's on a solid tripod, and the built-in microphones may also capture the sounds of these operations, though power aperture (see page 183) is pretty quiet. Just as with focusing, it is often best to get these things right beforehand and use a fixed exposure, but with some shots changes in brightness levels (e.g. panning from a shadowy area towards a brighter one) leave you no option.

› Shutter speed

You can (in good light) set shutter speeds right up to 1/4000 sec., but there are inescapable limits to the slowest speed you can select. For instance, if frame rate is 24 or 25, the slowest possible speed is 1/25 sec.; you obviously can't shoot 25 x ½ sec. exposures in one second! Similarly, the slowest possible shutter speed at 50p is 1/50 sec., and 1/60 sec. for 60p.

Still photography experience suggests that faster shutter speeds give sharper pictures. In movies it works differently. If you shoot at 1/500 sec., you will find that each frame may appear sharp when examined individually, but the clip appears jerky when played. This is because you have recorded 25 discrete slices of continuous action (assuming 25p frame rate). 25 times 1/500 sec. is just 5% of the action. The nearer the shutter speed is to 1/25 sec., the nearer you get to capturing 100% and the smoother the motion appears on playback.

SLOW TRAIN ⌄
A slow shutter speed helps to render movement more smoothly.
135mm, 1/50 sec., f/11, ISO 160.

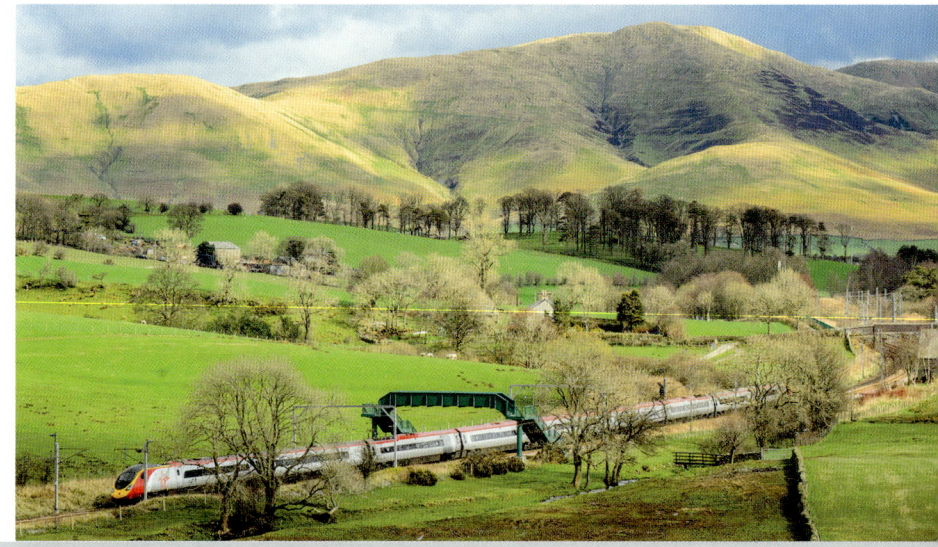

However, in bright conditions, you can't shoot at 1/30 sec. and at the same time use a really wide aperture for shallow depth of field, even at ISO 100—unless there's a neutral density filter (page 212) handy.

› Highlight display

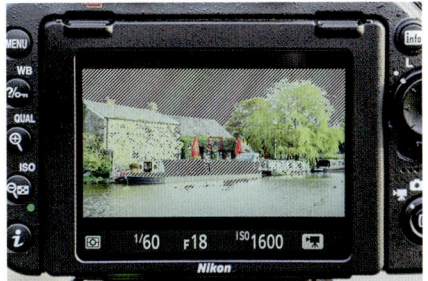

THE MOVIE HIGHLIGHTS DISPLAY   ⌃

Most of the usual methods of judging exposure are available in Movie Live View—and the D750 has an extra trick up its sleeve, specifically for movies. If you press ◀🔲▶ in Movie Live View and select **Highlight display>On**, the camera will display diagonal "zebra stripes" in areas which may be blown out or "clipped" (see page 87).

› Power aperture

You can use the Fn and Pv buttons to govern aperture. Use Custom setting g1 and select **Power aperture (open)**. This automatically sets g2 to **Power aperture (close)**. Now, each press on Fn widens the aperture, while each press on Pv makes it smaller. This is smoother and much quieter than using the sub-command dial. Power aperture is only available in A and M modes.

› Index marking

Adding index marks at key points during a take can facilitate editing. Use Custom setting g1, g2, or g3 and select **Index marking**. Now, pressing the chosen button during recording adds an index mark—up to 20 for each clip. If using Power aperture (see above), you'll have to use *AE-L*/*AF-L* for index marking, set via Custom setting g3.

› Sound

Often, you can identify skilled or professional video footage not with your eyes but with your ears. Good sound quality and the absence of extraneous noise are vital for enjoyable movies.

The D750's built-in microphones give reasonable quality stereo output but readily pick up any sounds you make operating the camera (focusing, zooming, even breathing). If you want to include dialog or "talking heads", keep subjects close to the camera and ensure that background noise is minimized.

Fortunately the D750 also allows you to attach an external microphone. External microphones connect to a standard 3.5mm socket under the cover on the camera's left side. This automatically overrides the internal microphones.

The D750 allows you to monitor sound during shooting by plugging headphones into the appropriate socket. However, you can't manually adjust recording level while shooting, so check and set sound levels beforehand in Live View, or leave on Auto.

› Shooting

1) Set Lv to the 🎥 position. Activate Live View by pressing its center button.

2) Select shooting options, e.g. Picture Control, as above.

3) Choose exposure mode, AF mode, and AF-area mode as for Live View shooting. Set aperture if using A mode, aperture and shutter speed in M mode.

4) Check sound levels. Check framing and exposure. Initialize focus by half-pressing the shutter release (or focus manually).

5) Press ⦿ to start recording the movie. **REC** flashes red at the top of the screen while recording, and an indicator shows the maximum remaining shooting time.

6) To stop recording, press ⦿ again.

7) Exit Live View by pressing Lv.

Tip

*You can also use the shutter-release button to start and end movie recording: see Custom Setting g4 **Assign shutter button**. This removes the option to shoot a still frame directly during movie recording.*

» SHOOTING MOVIES

If a still frame isn't quite right, you can review it, change position or settings, and be ready to reshoot within seconds. To shoot and review even a short movie clip eats up much more time, and you may not get a second chance anyway; so think ahead and aim to get shooting position, framing, and camera settings right beforehand. A short test clip can help verify these. If you're planning to pan or zoom, you can do a dry run in Live View before shooting for real.

If you're new to the complexities of movies, keep it simple. Do one thing at a time; don't try zooming, panning, and focusing simultaneously. Many subjects can be filmed with a fixed camera: waterfalls, birds at a feeder, musicians playing, and loads more. Equally, you can become familiar with camera movements shooting static subjects: try panning across a wide landscape or zooming in from a broad cityscape to a detail of a single building.

› Handling

The tilting screen improves the D750's handling for movie shooting, but the overall balance of a DSLR still makes handheld shooting awkward.

It's impossible to overstress the importance of a tripod for shooting decent movies. VR lens technology can

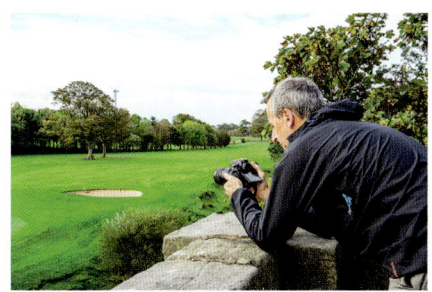

BRACING FOR THE SHOT ⌃

counteract short-frequency shake, but does nothing to eliminate slower (and often larger) wobbles. Of course, even "real" movie directors sometimes use handheld cameras to create a specific feel, but in a controlled way and for deliberate effect. Using a tripod, or other suitable camera support, is the simplest way to give movie clips a polished, professional, look. If one isn't available, look for other alternatives—for instance, by sitting with elbows braced on knees.

A standard tripod with a pan-and-tilt head is fine to start with. For best results, especially when panning, dedicated video tripods (or just tripod heads) are specifically designed to move smoothly.

When a tripod isn't practicable, there are many accessory grips and stabilizers to improve handling and stability, including smaller versions of the legendary Steadicam.

› Panning

The panning shot is a movie-maker's staple. Often essential for following moving subjects, it's also very effective with static subjects—for instance, sweeping across a vast panorama. Handheld panning may be acceptable when following a moving subject, but a wobbly pan across a grand landscape will definitely grate. Sometimes there really is no substitute for a tripod—and it must be properly leveled, or you may start panning with the camera aimed at the horizon but finish seeing nothing but ground or sky.

Panning too rapidly can irritate the viewer and make the shot hard to "read"; keep it slow and steady. Smooth panning is easiest with video tripods, but with care you can do a fair job using a standard model.

With moving subjects, the speed and direction of panning is dictated by the need to keep the subject in frame. Accurate tracking of fast-moving subjects is challenging and takes practice.

PANNING ⌄
A natural subject for a panning shot, but the tripod needs to be properly leveled.

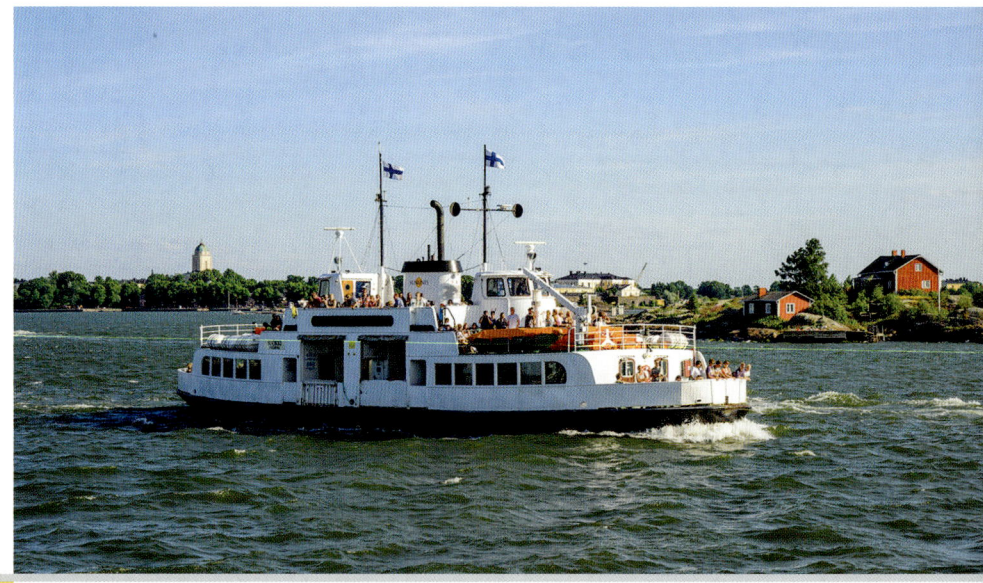

› Zooming

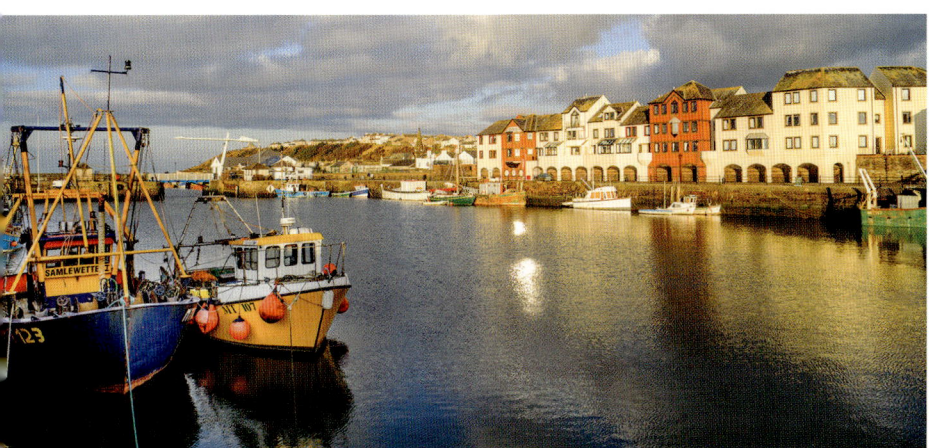

The zoom is another fundamental technique. Moving from a wide view to a tighter one is *zooming in*, the converse *zooming out*. As ever, forward planning makes all the difference—consider how the shot will look at both extremes. When zooming in to a specific subject, check it's central in frame.

No current lenses for the D750 are designed specifically for shooting movies. None have the extreme zoom range of some camcorder lenses but, more seriously, it's hard to achieve a really smooth, even-paced zoom action. Practice helps; mounting the camera on a solid tripod helps even more.

EXPLORING A SCENE ☆
On the face of it, quite a static scene, but the camera can introduce a dynamic element by panning across it or zooming in.

Power aperture has made aperture control much smoother, but there are no current SLR lenses with powered zoom. Nikon already makes power-zoom lenses for its Nikon 1 mirrorless cameras, so watch this space.

When zooming, remember that depth of field decreases toward the telephoto end of the range. Your subject may appear perfectly sharp in a wide-angle view but end up looking soft when you zoom in. Pre-set focus at the telephoto end of the range.

6

» EDITING MOVIES

› Still frame capture

To capture a still frame during movie shooting, simply press the shutter-release button. This ends movie-recording, takes the shot, and returns you to Live View. The resulting image will use the 16:9 aspect ratio. Quality and size are determined by your still-image settings (see the table below).

› Lighting

For obvious reasons, you can't use flash. There are many LED light units specifically designed for DSLR-movie shooting. The D750's ability to shoot at high ISO ratings is also invaluable.

We've referred to the D750 shooting movies, but actually it doesn't. Like all movie cameras, it shoots movie clips. A clip, even a collection of clips, is not a movie, only the raw material. Turning this into a movie requires editing.

Digital editing is non-linear—a grandiose way of saying that clips in the final movie don't have to appear in the order in which they were shot. It is also non-destructive, meaning that it does not affect your original clips (unlike cutting and splicing bits of film in the "old days"). During editing, you work with previews based on the original clips. At the end, the result is exported as a new movie.

› Software

Nikon now provides editing software as part of the View NX2 suite. Nikon Movie Editor is a basic, simple editing package for Mac and Windows.

Other, more sophisticated options are also available at no cost. Mac users have

Image area	Image size setting	Size in pixels
FX movie	Large (or RAW)	6016 x 3376
	Medium	4512 x 2528
	Small	3008 x 1688
DX movie	Large (or RAW)	3936 x 2224
	Medium	2944 x 1664
	Small	1968 x 1112

iMovie, which is included with all new Macs. The Windows equivalent is Windows Movie Maker, a free download from *windows.microsoft.com*. A more advanced (but not free) option, for both platforms, is Adobe Premiere Elements.

All these apps make it easy to trim and reorder your original clips, and to apply transitions such as dissolves, wipes, and fades. You can also adjust the look of any clip or segment of the movie. There are basic controls for brightness, color, and so on, and a range of special effects can be added. Effects and transitions are great fun—and you can experiment to your heart's content—but, for the sake of the audience, it's best to use a limited selection in the final version.

You can add other media, including still photos. You can insert stills individually or create slideshows within the main movie. It's equally easy to add a new soundtrack, like a voiceover or music, to part or all of

NIKON MOVIE EDITOR ⌄

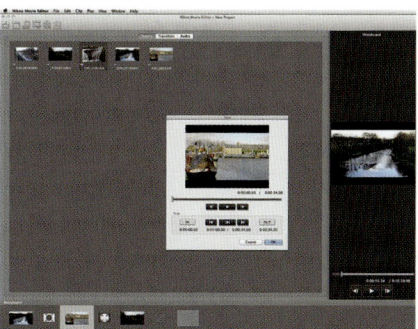

iMOVIE ⌄

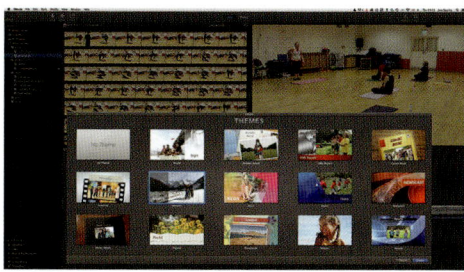

Tip

Unless you created them yourself, still photos, music, and other media are someone else's copyright. Even legitimately purchasing a song online does not give you the right to use it in a public performance (showing your movie). Using unlicenced music can get your video barred by YouTube. Look for open-source material or get the copyright owner's permission to use their work.

the movie. Last but not least, you can also add titles and captions.

› Taking it further

There's far more to movie-making than we can cover in a single chapter. A useful next step would be reading *Understanding HD Video* by Chiz Dakin, from this publisher.

7 LENSES

There are many reasons for preferring a DSLR like the D750 over a compact. One of the most important is the ability to use a vast range of lenses, including Nikon's own legendary system as well as lenses from other makers. Nikon's "F" lens mount is now—in its basic form—50 years old. A philosophy of continuity of design means that most Nikkor lenses will work on the D750, although sometimes with major limitations.

Very early "non-AI" lenses should not be used—unless modified—as they can damage the camera. A few other (rare) lenses should also be avoided. See the maker's manual.

Nikon's classic AI lenses (introduced from 1977) can be used, but they lack a CPU and therefore automatic functions are limited.

There can be optical issues with some older lenses too, as they were designed solely for use with 35mm film, which puts slightly different demands on lenses—not to mention that a 24-megapixel sensor can resolve finer detail than film. Many older lenses will give excellent results, but should be carefully tested for evidence of vignetting and chromatic aberration (color fringing). Wide-angle lenses are usually more susceptible than telephotos. Such shortcomings can to some extent be corrected in post-processing (especially if you shoot RAW files).

DOOR DETAIL
Crisp rendering of detail is important for subjects like this, which can show up any lack of resolution from the lens—or any shortcomings in technique.
80mm, 1/125 sec., f/4, ISO 200.

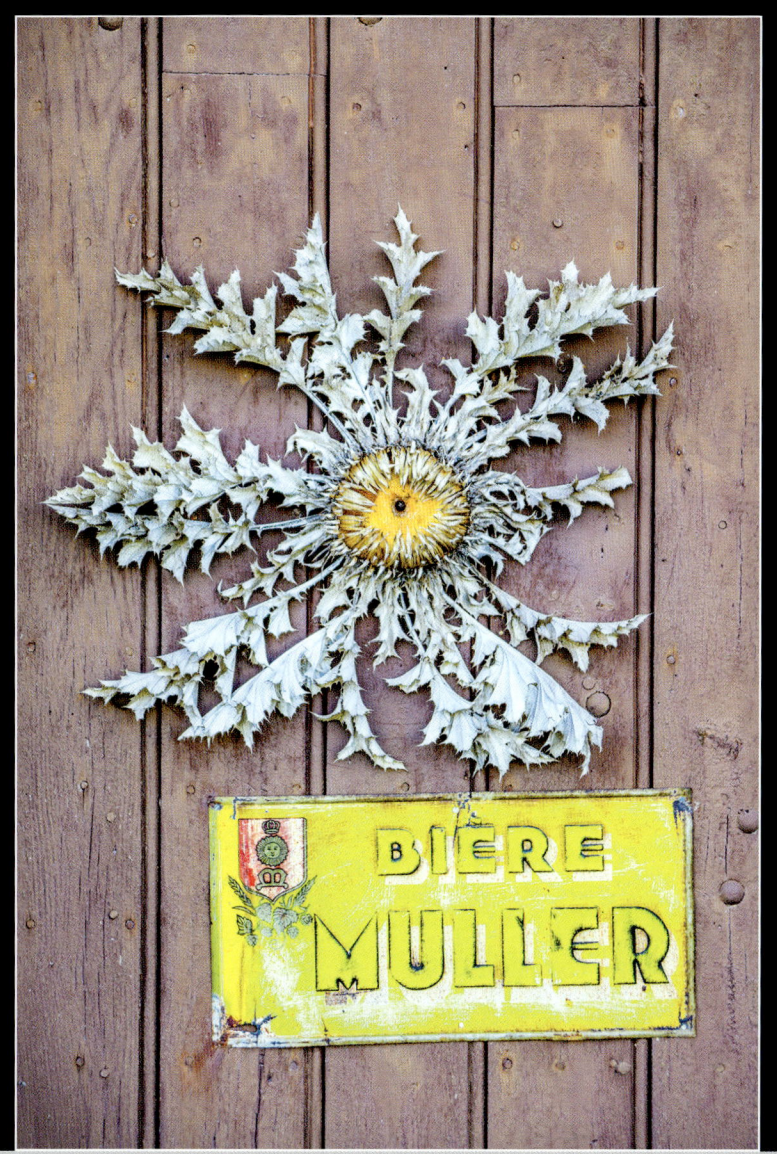

7 » FOCAL LENGTH

Though familiar, the term "focal length" is often misapplied. The focal length of any lens is a fundamental optical property, and is not changed by fitting the lens to a different camera. Unfortunately, as if to promote confusion, the lenses on most digital compact cameras are described not by their actual focal length but by their "35mm equivalent"; i.e. the focal length that would give the same angle of view on a 35mm or full-frame camera.

Of course, zoom lenses have variable focal length—that's what zoom means— but an 18–55mm zoom is always an 18–55 zoom, regardless of whether it's fitted on a DX-format camera like the D7100 or a full-frame (FX) camera like the D750. However, because the D7100 has a smaller sensor than the D750, the recorded image shows a smaller field of view. Exactly the same applies when using the D750's DX-crop function. (See opposite for an illustration of FX and DX image areas.)

› Field of view

The field of view, or angle of view, is the area covered by the image frame. While the focal length of a lens remains the same on any camera, the angle of view seen in the image is different for different sensor formats. The angle of view is usually measured on the diagonal of the frame (as in the table on pages 206–209).

› Crop factor

Shooting on a DX camera, or using the DX-crop function creates a crop factor, also referred to as focal length magnification factor, of 1.5x. **DX-crop** normally applies automatically when a DX lens is fitted but can be turned off; it can also be activated manually (set **Image area** to **DX**). This still yields very usable 13-megapixel images.

Of course, you can crop images later, with greater flexibility, but using DX-crop is handy if you want to use the images immediately. It also reduces file sizes.

The crop factor also allows long-range shooting with relatively light and inexpensive lenses; for example, a 200mm lens gives the same field of view in DX-crop as a 300mm lens on full-frame.

Furthermore, the 51 focus points cover most of the DX image area, improving the chances of keeping a moving subject in focus wherever it may be in the frame.

Some DX lenses have a wider image area than the strict DX crop, giving you the option to obtain larger images with them—set **Auto DX crop** to **Off**, then crop the images later to eliminate the darkened corners. You can do this using **Trim** in the Retouch menu, or in any image-editing app on a computer or tablet.

The next page shows a series of images taken on a Nikon D750, from a fixed position, with a range of lenses from 12mm to 300mm.

CLIMBING FRAME ≈
A shot taken with a Nikkor 35mm DX lens. The DX crop is unnecessarily severe with this lens. I can comfortably use the 1.2x image area or just crop afterwards.

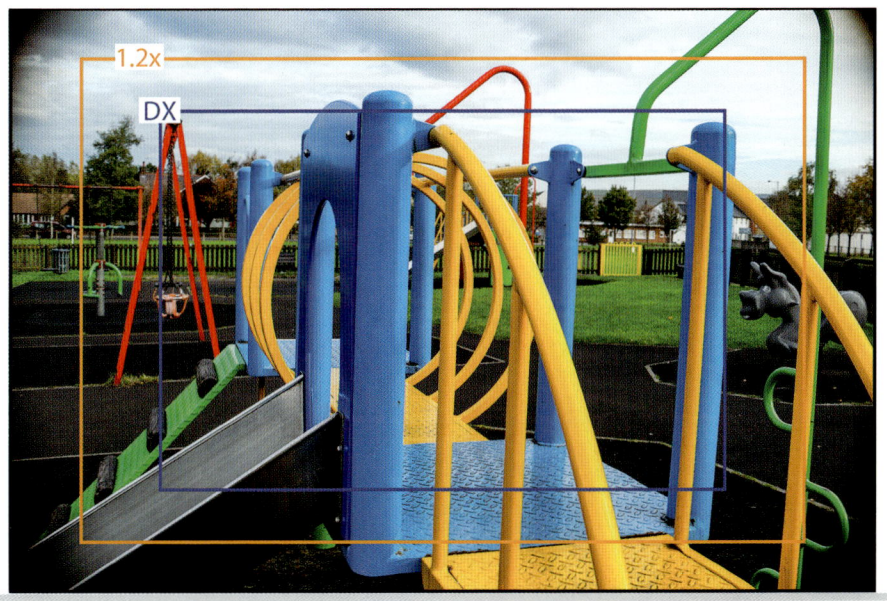

7

CHANGING PERSPECTIVE ⮯

The images were taken with a range of lenses:
12mm; 24mm; 50mm; 100mm; 200mm; 300mm.
1/80 sec., f/11, ISO 100, tripod.

Focal length: 12mm

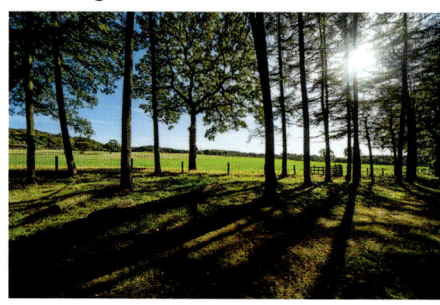

Focal length: 24mm

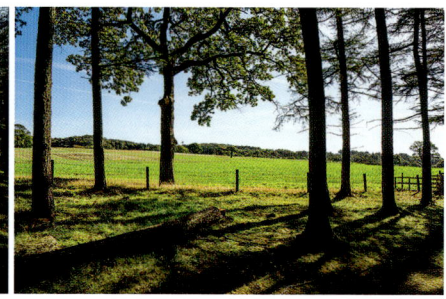

Focal length: 50mm

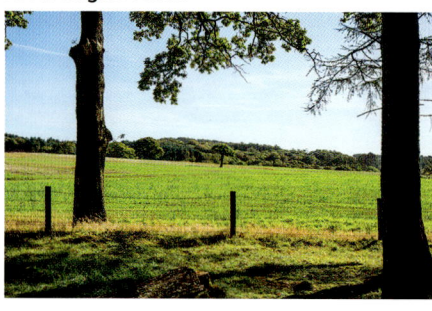

Focal length: 100mm

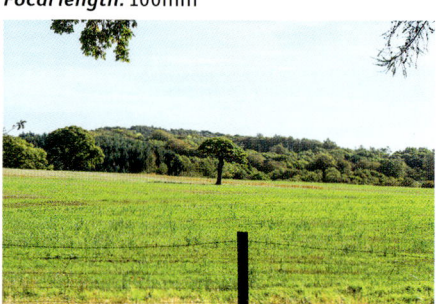

Focal length: 200mm

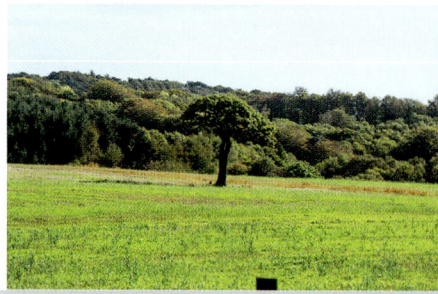

Focal length: 300mm

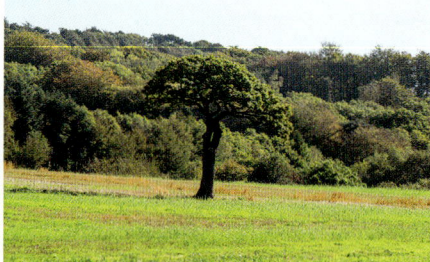

» LENS ISSUES

› Flare

Lens flare is usually seen when shooting towards the sun or other bright light sources. Caused by reflections within the lens, it may produce a string of colored blobs or a general veiling effect.

Advanced lens coatings help reduce flare, as does keeping lenses and filters clean. Even so, when the sun's directly in shot, some flare may be inescapable. You can sometimes mask the sun, perhaps behind a tree.

If the sun isn't actually in shot, you can shield the lens. A good lens hood is essential, but may need to be supplemented with a piece of card, a map, or your hand. This is easier when using a tripod; otherwise it requires assistance, or one-handed shooting. Check carefully to see if the flare has gone—and that the shading object hasn't crept into shot!

Lens hoods

A lens hood helps to exclude stray light which may degrade the image and cause flare. It can also shield the lens against knocks, rain, and other hazards. Most Nikkor lenses are supplied with a dedicated hood. Lens hoods are also available separately but Nikon's own tend to be disproportionately expensive; third-party offerings may be less than half the price. However, do check that the hood in question is compatible with the lens—try before you buy, taking test shots to check there's no vignetting (see page 197).

FLARE ⌄

The flare in the first shot (left) is pretty disastrous. In the second, with a very slight shift of position to mask the sun behind some foliage, there's no flare at all.
24mm, 1/60 sec., f/11, ISO 100, tripod.

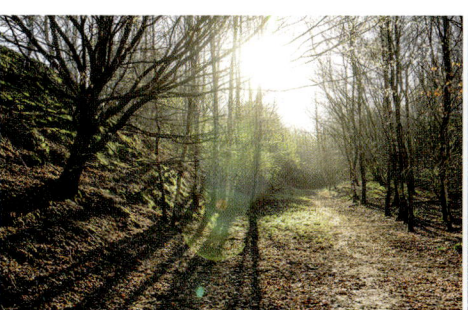
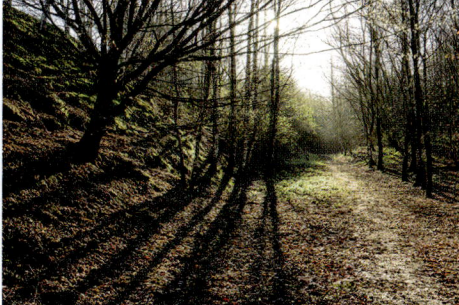

› Distortion

Distortion makes lines which are really straight appear curved in the image. Distortion is usually worst with zoom lenses, especially at the extremes of the zoom range. When straight lines bow outwards, it's called barrel distortion; when they bend inwards it's pincushion distortion. Distortion often goes unnoticed when shooting natural subjects with no straight lines, but can still rear its ugly head when level horizons appear in landscape or seascape images.

Distortion can be corrected using Auto Distortion Control in the Photo Shooting menu (for compatible lenses) or rectified later using Distortion Control in the Retouch menu or in post-processing. However, using all of these methods will crop the image.

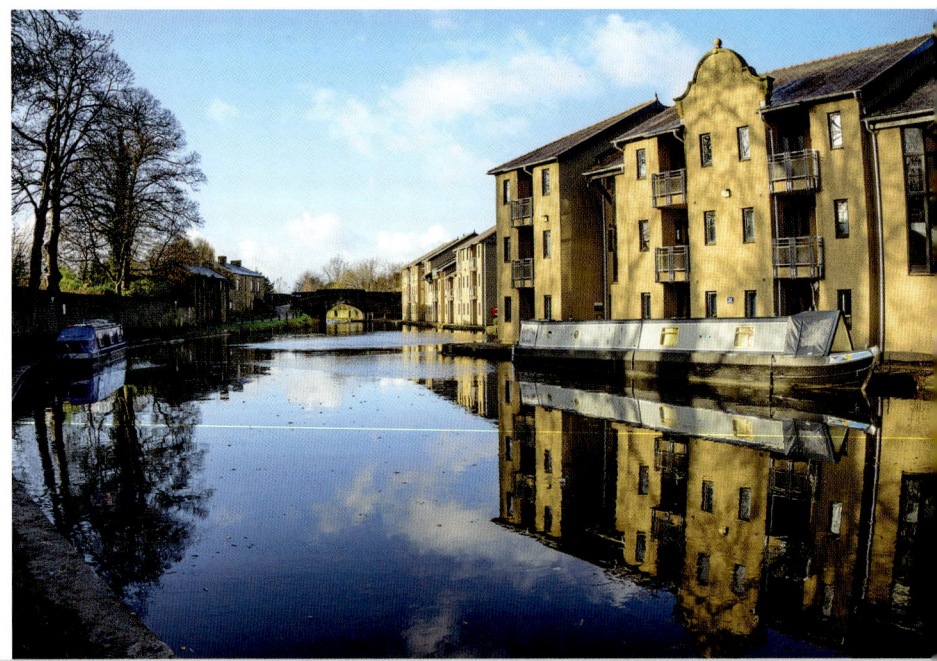

› Chromatic aberration

Chromatic aberration occurs when light of different colors is focused in slightly different places on the sensor, and appears as colored fringing when images are examined closely. The D750 has built-in correction for chromatic aberration during processing of JPEG images. Aberration can also be corrected in post-processing; with RAW images this is the only option.

› Vignetting

Vignetting is a darkening towards the corners of the image, most conspicuous in even-toned areas like clear skies. Many lenses show slight vignetting at maximum aperture, but it should reduce on stopping down. The D750 has built-in Vignette control (see page 104) for JPEG images. It can also be tackled in post-processing. Severe vignetting can arise if you use unsuitable lens hoods and filter holders, or "stack" multiple filters on the lens.

› Lens care

Lenses require special care. Glass elements and coatings are easily scratched and this will degrade your images. Remove dust and dirt with a blower. Fingerprints and other marks should only be tackled with a dedicated lens cleaner and optical grade cloth. Skylight or UV filters (page 212) can protect the lens, and lens caps should be replaced when the lens is not in use.

DISTORTION 	«
Barrel distortion (exaggerated in post-processing) is essentially undetectable in the curves and natural forms on the left side, but all too obvious in the buildings on the right.
24mm, 1/200 sec., f/11, ISO 400, tripod.

› Standard lenses

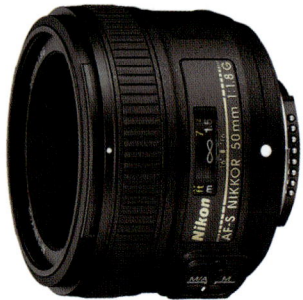

Traditionally, a 50mm lens was called standard, as its field of view was held to approximate that of the human eye. Standard lenses are typically light, simple, and have wide maximum apertures. Zoom lenses whose range includes the 50mm focal length are often referred to as "standard zooms".

Nikkor 50mm f/1.8   ⌃

STANDARD VIEW   ⌄
Standard lenses are generally held to give a "normal" or "natural" view.
55mm, 1/1000 sec., f/5, ISO 800.

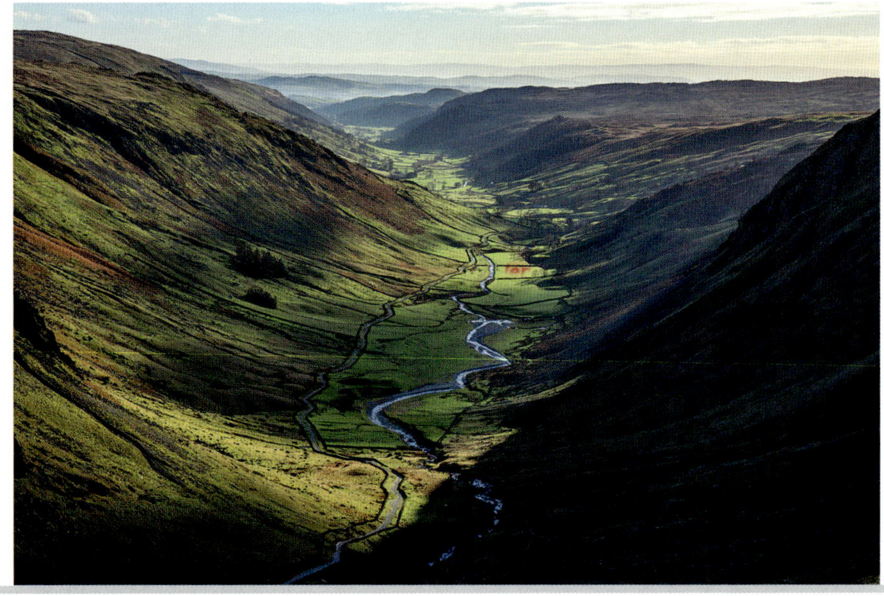

› Wide-angle lenses

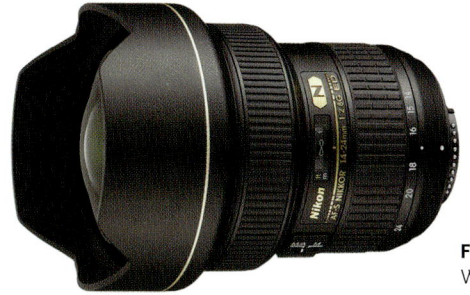

Nikkor 14–24mm f/2.8G ED AF–S ⌃

A wide-angle lens is really any lens wider than a standard lens—for the full-frame D750, this means any lens with a focal length shorter than 50mm. Wide-angle lenses are valuable for working close to subjects or bringing foregrounds into greater prominence. They lend themselves both to photographing expansive scenic views and to working in cramped spaces where you can't just step back to "get more in".

In the 35mm film era, anything wider than about 24mm was regarded as "super-wide". The advent of DX-format cameras has spurred the development of a new breed of lenses like Nikon's widely-praised 14–24mm f/2.8G ED AF–S, yet these come into their own even more with full-frame cameras like the D750. Sigma's 12–24mm F4.5–5.6 II DG HSM has even wider range and is less than half the price.

FOREGROUND ⌄
Wide-angle lenses can make the most of strong foregrounds.
14mm, 1/30 sec., f/16, ISO 100.

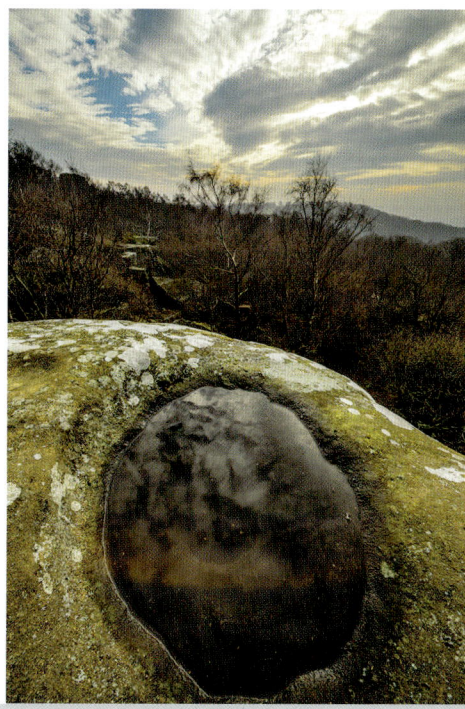

› Telephoto lenses

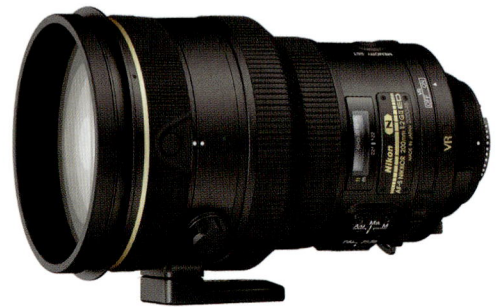

Nikkor 200mm f/2G ED–IF AF–S VRII ⌃

Telephoto lenses, often simply called long lenses, give a narrow angle of view. They are closely associated with wildlife and sports photography, but have many other uses, such as singling out small or distant elements in a landscape. Moderate telephoto lenses (traditionally 85–135mm) are favored for portrait photography, because the working distance gives a natural-looking result and is more comfortable for nervous subjects.

When using telephoto lenses, depth of field tends to be narrow. This is often welcome in portraiture, wildlife, and sport, as it concentrates attention on the subject by throwing backgrounds out of focus.

Longer lenses can be heavy, bulky, and hard to handhold comfortably. Their narrow view also magnifies any shake or wobble. High shutter speeds and/or tripods or other camera support are often

TELEPHOTO ⌄
Telephoto lenses give a closer view of shy subjects.
200mm, 1/500 sec., f/6.3, ISO 640.

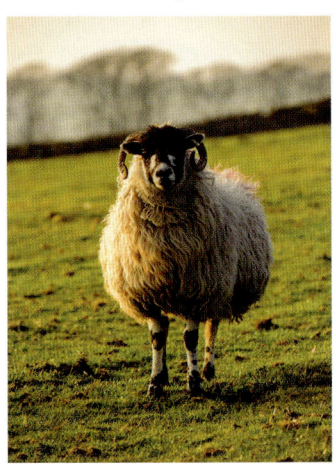

required. Nikon's Vibration Reduction (VR) technology also mitigates the effects of camera shake, but can slow down the maximum frame rate, which sports shooters in particular need to recognize.

> ### *Tip*
>
> *Switch VR OFF when using the camera on a tripod. Otherwise, it can add shake instead of removing it! (A few of the latest VR lenses have a "Tripod" setting—try that.)*

› Teleconverters

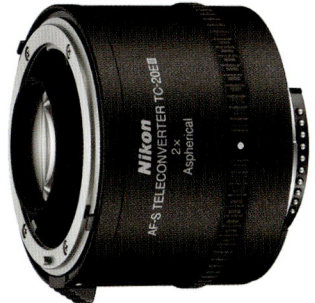

AF-S Teleconverter TC-20E III   ⌃

Teleconverters are supplementary units which fit between the main lens and the camera body, and magnify the focal length of the main lens. Nikon currently offers the TC-14E III (1.4x magnification), TC-17E II (1.7x), and TC-20E III (2x). The advantages are obvious, extending the focal length with minimal additional weight (the TC-14E III, for example, weighs just 200 grams).

However, teleconverters can degrade image quality. This can be particularly noticeable when shooting at maximum aperture. Results should improve when the lens is stopped down to f/8 or f/11; beyond this, sharpness may tail off again due to diffraction.

Converters also cause a loss of light. Fitting a 2x converter to an f/4 lens turns it into an effective f/8. The camera's autofocus may become sluggish or will only work with the central focus points.

Warning!

Some lenses are incompatible with teleconverters. Check carefully before buying or using one.

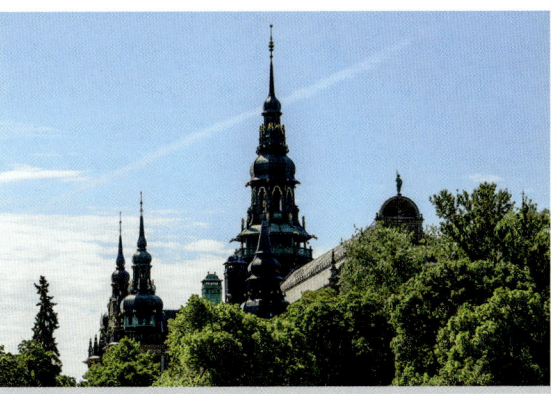

TELECONVERTERS   »
Teleconverters can extend the available focal length range when you are traveling light.
140mm, 1/400 sec., f/11, ISO 200.

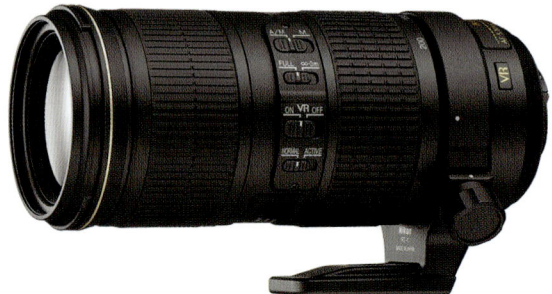

Nikkor 70-200mm f/4G ED AF-S VRIII ⌃

Zoom lenses have variable focal length, like the AF-S Nikkor 24–85mm f/3.5-4.5G ED VR, as opposed to prime lenses, which have a single fixed focal length.

A zoom lens can replace several prime lenses and is also able to cover the gaps in-between, scoring highly for weight, convenience, and economy. The flexible focal lengths of zoom lenses also allow precise framing.

In terms of sharpness and image contrast, there is now little to choose between a good zoom and a good prime lens. Distortion can still be an issue. Most zoom lenses will have a "sweet spot" somewhere in the zoom range where distortion is minimal, but may show discernible barrel distortion at wide settings and pincushion at the long end.

Cheaper or older zooms, and those with a very wide range (e.g. 18–200mm or 28–300mm) still tend to be optically compromised, and usually have a relatively small ("slow") maximum aperture. Besides, most such lenses are DX-only.

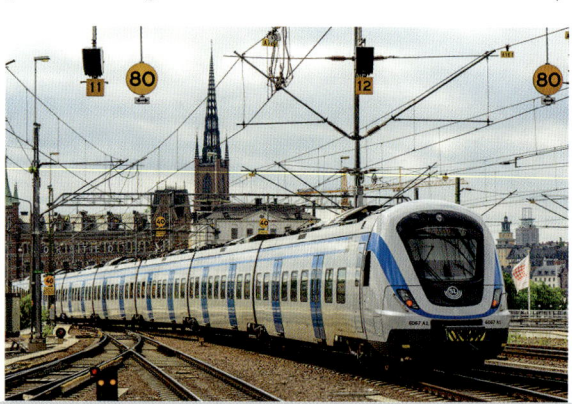

ZOOM »
Zoom lenses give you the flexibility to frame an image exactly as you want it.
98mm, 1/500 sec., f/8, ISO 200.

› Macro lenses

For specialist close-up work there is little to beat a true macro lens. For more on these see page 174.

› Perspective-control lenses

Perspective-control (also known as "tilt-and-shift") lenses give unique flexibility in viewing and controlling the image. Their most obvious application is in photographing architecture, when with a "normal" lens it often becomes necessary to tilt the camera upwards, resulting in converging verticals (buildings appear to lean back and/or to one side).

The shift function allows the camera-back to be kept vertical, which in turn means that vertical lines in the subject remain vertical in the image. Tilt movements also allow extra control over depth of field, whether to extend or to minimize it.

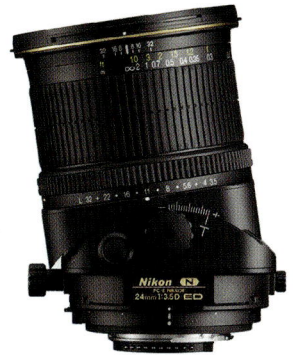

PC-E Nikkor 24mm f/3.5D ED　　　　 ⌃

The current Nikon range features three PC lenses, with focal lengths of 24mm, 45mm, and 85mm. The lenses retain many automatic functions, but they too require manual focusing.

CONVERGING VERTICALS　　　　 ⌄
The converging verticals aren't excessive (below left), but the image still looks a lot better when they are straightened out (right). 24mm, 1/60 sec., f/11, ISO 200.

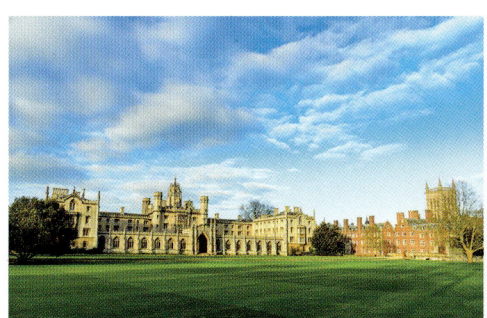

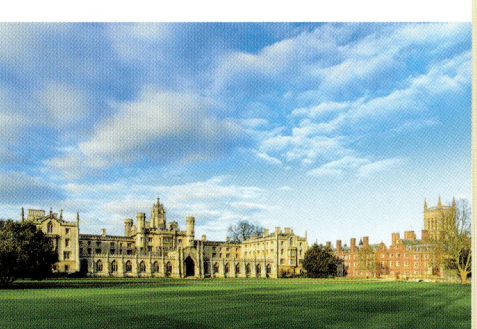

7 » NIKON LENS TECHNOLOGY

Many Nikkor lenses incorporate special features or materials, usually referred to by cryptic acronyms (as in the table on pages 206–209). Brief explanations of the main terms are given here.

Abbreviation	Term	Explanation
AF	Autofocus	Lens focuses automatically. The majority of current Nikkor lenses are AF but a substantial manual focus range remains.
CRC	Close-range Correction	Advanced lens design that improves picture quality at close focusing distances.
D	Distance information	D-type and G-type lenses communicate information to the camera about the distance at which they are focusing, supporting functions like 3D Matrix Metering.
DC	Defocus-image Control	Found in a few lenses aimed mostly at portrait photographers; allows control of aberrations and thereby the appearance of out-of-focus areas in the image.
DX	DX lens	Lenses specifically designed for DX-format digital cameras; will not give full-frame coverage on 35mm cameras or FX-format DSLRs like the D750.
E or PC-E	E-type lens	Lens without mechanical aperture linkage; aperture control is implemented electromagnetically within the lens. So far, only seen in PC-E perspective-control lenses, and a couple of long telephotos.

Abbreviation	Term	Explanation
ED	Extra-low Dispersion	ED glass minimizes chromatic aberration (the tendency for light of different colors to be focused at slightly different points).
G	G-type lens	Modern Nikkor lenses with no aperture ring; aperture must be set on the camera.
IF	Internal Focusing	Only internal elements of the lens move during focusing; the front element does not extend or rotate.
N	Nano Crystal Coat	Said to virtually eliminate internal reflections within lenses, guaranteeing minimal flare.
PC	Perspective Control	See page 203.
RF	Rear Focusing	Lens design where only the rearmost elements move during focusing; this makes AF operation faster.
SWM	Silent Wave Motor	Special in-lens motors which deliver very fast and very quiet autofocus operation.
VR	Vibration Reduction	System which compensates for camera shake. VR is said to allow handheld shooting up to three stops slower than would otherwise be possible (i.e. 1/15 instead of 1/125 sec.). New lenses now feature VRII, said to offer a gain of an extra stop over VR (1/8 instead of 1/125 sec.).

» NIKKOR LENS CHART

This table lists currently available Nikkor lenses. DX-series lenses, which do not cover the full sensor area of the D750, are listed last. The angle of view quoted for these lenses is the effective angle of view on the DX frame area—but be aware that some of these lenses actually cover a significantly wider area, as discussed on page 193.

AF PRIME LENSES

	Optical features/ notes	Angle of view on FX format	Minimum focus distance (m)	Filter size (mm)	Dimensions (diameter x length, mm)	Weight (g)
14mm f/2.8D ED AF	ED, RF	114	0.2	Rear	87 x 86.5	670
16mm f/2.8D A Fisheye	IF	180	0.25	Rear	63 x 57	290
20mm f/1.8G ED AF-S	ED, NC	94	0.2	77		355
20mm f/2.8D AF	CRC	94	0.25	62	69 x 42.5	270
24mm f/1.4G ED	ED, SWM, NC	84	0.25	77	83 x 88.5	620
24mm f/2.8D AF		84	0.3	52	64.5 x 46	270
28mm f/1.8G AF-S	NC, SWM	74	0.25	67	73 x 80.5	330
28mm f/2.8D AF		74	0.25	52	65 x 44.5	205
35mm f/2D AF		63	0.25	52	64.5 x 43.5	205
35mm f/1.8G AF-S	RF, SWM	63	0.25	58	72 x 71.5	305
35mm f/1.4G AF-S	NC, SWM	63	0.3	67	83 x 89.5	600
50mm f/1.8G AF-S	SWM	46	0.45	58	72 x 52.5	185
50mm f/1.8D AF		46	0.45	52	63 x 39	160
50mm f/1.4D AF		46	0.45	52	64.5 x 42.5	230
50mm f/1.4G AF-S	IF, SWM	46	0.45	58	73.5 x 54	280
58mm f/1.4G AF-S	NC, SWM	40.5	0.58	72	85 x 70	385
85mm f/1.4G AF	IF, SWM, NC	28.5	0.85	77	86.5 x 84	595
85mm f/1.8D AF	RF	28.5	0.85	62	71.5 x 58.5	380
85mm f/1.8G AF-S	IF, SWM	28.5	0.8	67	80 x 73	350
105mm f/2D AF DC	DC	23.3	0.9	72	79 x 111	640
135mm f/2D AF DC	DC	18	1.1	72	79 x 120	815
180mm f/2.8D ED-IF AF	ED, IF	13.6	1.5	72	78.5 x 144	760
200mm f/2G ED-IF AF-S VRII	ED, VRII, SWM	12.3	1.9	52	124 x 203	2900
300mm f/4D ED-IF AF-S	ED, IF	8.1	1.45	77	90 x 222.5	1440
300mm f/2.8G ED VRII AF-S	ED, VRII, NC, SWM	8.1	2.2	52	124 x 267.5	2900
400mm f/2.8G ED VR AF-S	ED, IF, VRII, NC	6.1	2.9	52	159.5 x 368	4620

AF PRIME LENSES

	Optical features/ notes	Angle of view on FX format	Minimum focus distance (m)	Filter size (mm)	Dimensions (diameter x length, mm)	Weight (g)
400mm f2.8E FL ED VR AF-S	ED, SPORT VR, NC, SWM	6.1	2.6	40.5 (internal)	159.5 x 358	3800
400mm f/2.8D ED-IF AF-S II	ED, SWM	6.1	3.8	52	160 x 352	4800
500mm f/4G ED VR AF-S	IF, ED, VRII, NC	5	4	52	139.5 x 391	3880
600mm f/4G ED VR AF-S	ED, IF, VRII, NC	4.1	5	52	166 x 445	5060
800mm f/5.6E FL ED VR AF-S	ED, NC, SWM, FL	3.1	5.9	52	160 x 461	4590

AF ZOOM LENSES

	Optical features/ notes	Angle of view on FX format	Minimum focus distance (m)	Filter size (mm)	Dimensions (diameter x length, mm)	Weight (g)
14–24mm f/2.8G ED AF-S	IF, ED, SWM, NC	114–84	0.28	None	98 x 131.5	970
16–35mm f/4G ED VR	NC, ED, VR	107–63	0.29	77	82.5 x 125	680
17–35mm f/2.8D ED-IF AF-S	IF, ED, SWM	104–63	0.28	77	82.5 x 106	745
18–35mm f/3.5-4.5G ED AF-S	ED, SWM	100–63	0.28	77	83 x 95	385
24–70mm f/2.8G ED AF-S	IF, ED, SWM, NC	84–34.3	0.38	77	83 x 133	900
24–85mm f/2.8-4D IF AF	IF	84–28.5	0.5	72	78.5 x 82.5	545
24–85mm f/3.5-4.5G ED VR AF-S	ED, VRII, SWM	84–28.5	0.38	72	78 x 82	465
24–120mm f/4G ED-IF AF-S VR	ED, SWM, NC, VRII	84–20.5	0.45	77	84 x 103.5	710
28–300mm f/3.5-5.6G ED VR	ED, SWM	75–8.1	0.5	77	83 x 114.5	800
70–200mm f/2.8G ED-IF AF-S VRII	ED, SWM, VRII	34.3–12.3	1.4	77	87 x 209	1540
70–200mm f/4G ED AF-S VRIII	ED, IF, SWM, NC, VRIII	34.3–12.3		67	78 x 178.5	850
70–300mm f/4.5-5.6G AF-S VR	ED, IF, SWM, VRII	34.3–8.1	1	67	80 x 143.5	745
80–400mm f/4.5-5.6D ED VR AF-S	ED, VR, NC	30.1–6.1	2.3	77	95.5 x 203	1570
200–400mm f/4G ED-IF AF-S VRII	ED, NC,VRII, SWM	12.3–6.1	2	52	124 x 365.5	3360

7

MACRO LENSES

	Optical features/ notes	Angle of view on FX format	Minimum focus distance (m)	Filter size (mm)	Dimensions (diameter x length, mm)	Weight (g)
60mm f/2.8G ED AF-S Micro	ED, SWM, NC	39.6	0.185	62	73 x 89	425
105mm f/2.8G AF-S VR Micro	ED, IF, VRII, NC, SWM	23.5	0.31	62	83 x 116	720
200mm f/4D ED-IF AF Micro	ED. CRC	12.3	0.5	62	76 x 104.5	1190

PERSPECTIVE CONTROL LENSE

	Optical features/ notes	Angle of view on FX format	Minimum focus distance (m)	Filter size (mm)	Dimensions (diameter x length, mm)	Weight (g)
24mm f/3.5D ED PC-E (manual focus)	ED, NC	84	77	None	82.5 x 108	730
45mm f/2.8D ED PC-E (manual focus)	ED, NC	51	77 x 94	77	83.5 x 112	780
85mm f/2.8D ED PC-E (manual focus)	ED, NC	28.4	77	77	82.7 x 107	650

DX LENSES (ANGLE OF VIEW ASSUMES DX CROP IN EFFECT)

	Optical features/ notes	Angle of view on FX format	Minimum focus distance (m)	Filter size (mm)	Dimensions (diameter x length, mm)	Weight (g)
10.5mm f/2.8G DX Fisheye	CRC	180	0.14	Rear	63 x 62.5	300
10-24mm f/3.5-4.5G ED AF-S DX	ED, IF, SWM	109-61	0.24	77	82.5 x 87	460
12-24mm f/4G ED-IF AF-S DX	SWM	99-61	0.3	77	82.5 x 90	485
16-85mm f/3.5-5.6G ED VR AF-S DX	VRII, SWM	83-18.5	0.38	67	72 x 85	485
17-55mm f/2.8G ED-IF AF-S DX	ED, IF, SWM	79-28.50	0.36	77	85.5 x 11.5	755
18-55mm f/3.5-5.6G VR II AF-S DX (Retractable)	VRII, SWM	76-28.5	0.28	52	66 x 59.5 (retracted)	195
18-55mm f/3.5-5.6G AF-S VR DX	VR, SWM	76-28.50	0.28	52	73 x 79.5	265
18-70mm f3.5-4.5G ED-IF AF-S DX	ED, SWM	76-22.50	0.38	67	73 x 75.5	420

DX LENSES (ANGLE OF VIEW ASSUMES DX CROP IN EFFECT)

	Optical features/ notes	Angle of view on FX format	Minimum focus distance (m)	Filter size (mm)	Dimensions (diameter x length, mm)	Weight (g)
18–105mm F/3.5–5.6G ED VR AF-S DX	ED, IF, VRII, NC, SWM	76–15.3	0.45	67	76 x 89	420
18–140mm F/3.5– 5.6G ED VR AF-S DX	ED, IF, VRII, SWM	76–11.5	0.45	67	78 x 97	490
18–200mm f/3.5–5.6G ED AF-S VRII DX	ED, SWM, VRII	76–8	0.5	72	77 x 96.5	560
18–300mm f/3.5–5.6G ED VR AF-S DX	ED, IF, SWM, VRII	76–5.3	0.45	77	83 x 120	830
35mm f/1.8G AF-S	SWM	44	0.3	52	70 x 52.5	210
40mm f/2.8G AF-S DX Micro Nikkor	SWM	38.5	0.163	52	68.5 x 64.5	235
55–200mm f/4–5.6 AF-S VR DX	ED, SWM, VR	28.5–8	1.1	52	73 x 99.5	335
55–200mm f/4–5.6G ED AF-S DX	ED, SWM	28.5–8	0.95	52	68 x 79	255
55–300mm f/4.5–5.6G ED VR	ED, SWM	28.5–5.2	1.4	58	76.5 x 123	530
85mm f/3.5G ED VR AF-S DX Micro Nikkor	ED, IF, SWM, VRII	18.5	0.28	52	73 x 98.5	355

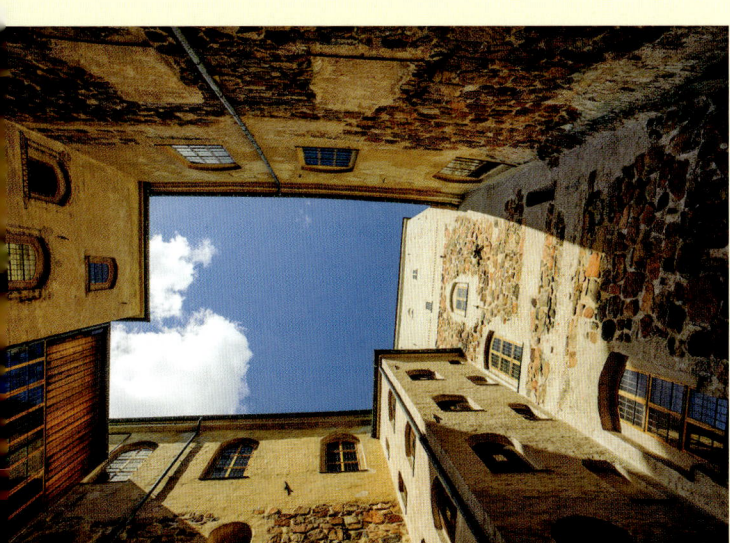

LOOKING UP «

Wide-angle lenses encourage us to explore unusual angles and different perspectives. *14mm, 1/100 sec., f/11, ISO 250.*

8 ACCESSORIES & CARE

Beyond lenses and flashguns, there are many other accessories which can extend the capabilities of the camera. Nikon's system is huge, and third-party suppliers offer even more options.

» ESSENTIALS

Nikon supplies several items with the camera. Most of these are essentials, for which it's well worth considering the value of spares (notably spare batteries) and upgrades (e.g. for the strap). Small items like the body cap (BF-1A or BF-1B) and hotshoe cover (BS-1) are easily misplaced but cheap to replace.

› EN-EL15 battery

While the camera's battery life is good, it can't hurt to keep a fully charged spare on hand—especially in cold conditions, when using the monitor extensively, or when shooting movies. Third-party batteries are cheaper but may have a slightly lower power rating.

› Strap

The supplied strap is nice if you want to advertise that you're using a Nikon D750, but it's not very comfortable when carrying the camera for long periods. The D750 is one of the lightest full-frame DSLRs available, but it's still a substantial camera. I use OpTech straps, which are far more comfortable. There are many alternative straps and other carrying systems.

POLAR EXPLORATION »
The same view, without (top) and with (below) a polarizing filter. With the filter, colors are richer and the distant landscape is clearer.
50mm, 1/15 and 1/60 sec., f/11, ISO 100, tripod.

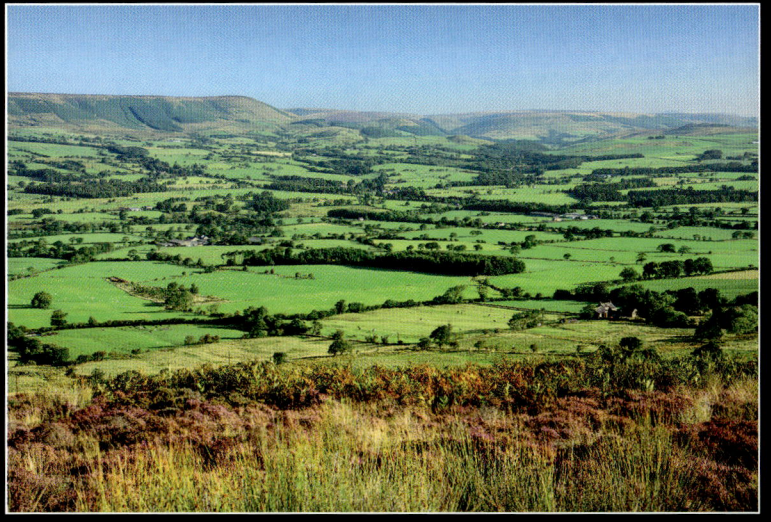

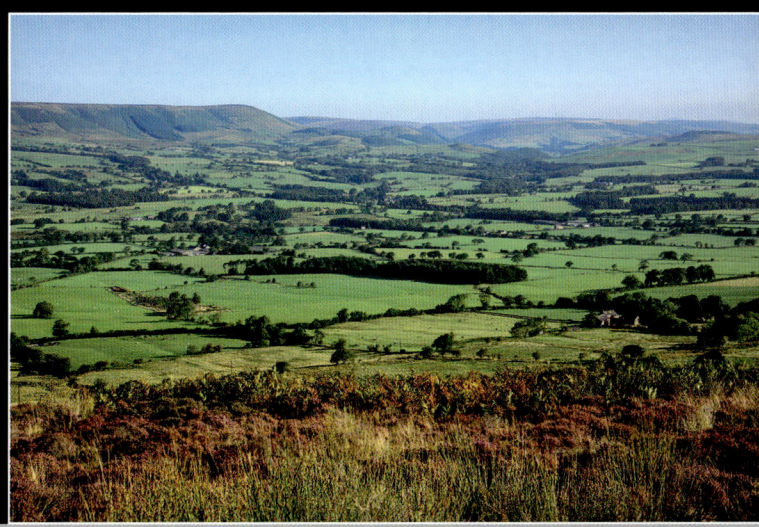

8 » FILTERS

Digital features such as variable white balance (page 62) have made many filters almost redundant. Soft-focus and starburst effects, among others, can be added in-camera via the Retouch menu (page 141)—although the starburst lacks finesse. A far wider range of effects is applicable in post-processing.

However, some filters still have value. Many people keep a UV or skylight filter on each lens to protect against knocks and scratches, although many working pros rely purely on lens hoods.

› Polarizing filters

The polarizing filter reduces reflections, cutting glare, intensifying colors, and restoring transparency to water and glass. It can also cut through atmospheric haze and enrich blue skies. Rotating the filter strengthens or weakens its effect, which is strongest when shooting at right angles to the sunlight. Be wary with wide-angle lenses as the effect can vary across the field of view. The effect is virtually impossible to reproduce in post-processing.

› Neutral density filters

Neutral density (ND) filters reduce the amount of light reaching the lens, without changing its color. Plain ND filters allow you to set slower shutter speeds and/or wider apertures. A classic use is shooting waterfalls, to allow a long shutter speed to create a silky blur.

Graduated ND filters have been widely used in landscape photography to compensate for wide differences in brightness between sky and land. However, the straight-line transition can be unpleasantly obvious, especially against irregular skylines. The immense dynamic range of cameras like the D750 reduces the need for them.

» OPTIONAL ACCESSORIES

Like other camera-makers, Nikon is often criticized over the price of its accessories. Third-party alternatives may be much cheaper, but take care to source reputable, fully compatible products.

› Multi-Power Battery Pack MB-D16

The MB-D16 provides extra power; it can be loaded with a second EN-EL15 battery or with AA cells. It also provides an extra shutter-release button, command dials, multi-selector, and **AE-L/AF-L** button. Expect makers like Hähnel to offer alternatives for around half the price.

› AC Adapter EH-5/EH-5a/EH-5b

Power the camera directly from the AC mains, allowing uninterrupted shooting in long sessions. A power connector will also be required.

› Wireless remote control ML-L3

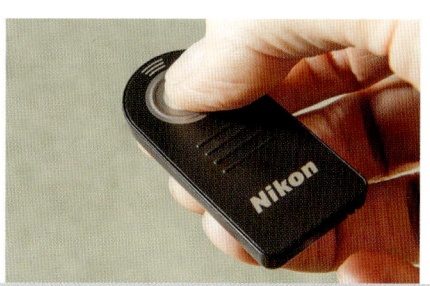

This inexpensive little unit allows you to trigger the camera from up to 16ft (5m) away. Units like Nikon's WR-1 or Hähnel's Giga T Pro II allow fuller control of the camera.

› GP-1 and GP-1A GPS units

Dedicated Global Positioning System devices (see page 230).

› Diopter adjustment

If the viewfinder's built in dioptric adjustment (page 22) is insufficient, Nikon produces viewfinder lenses between −3 and +2m^{-1}.

› Remote cords

Nikon's 39in.- (1m-) long MC-DC2 remote cord allows shutter release without touching the camera.

› Screen shades

Camera LCD screens can be impossible to see properly in bright sunlight. The viewfinder is better for shooting in bright light, but you still need the screen for Live View, movie shooting, and image review. The best known maker of accessory screen shades is Hoodman.

8 » CAMERA SUPPORT

› Tripods

VR lenses, and the D750's image quality at high ISO settings, make handholding fully viable for many shots. Still, dynamic range is best at low ISO ratings, and some shots will always require a solid support. Tripods are essential for serious movie shooting, too (see page 185).

Titanium and carbon fiber combine low weight and good rigidity. They aren't cheap but a good tripod is an investment which should last for many years.

› Monopods

Monopods are light, easy to carry, and quick to set up. They are favored by sports and some wildlife photographers, who often need to react quickly while using hefty long telephoto lenses.

› Other camera support

There are many other proprietary products and improvized alternatives. It's hard to beat the humble beanbag, which can easily be homemade.

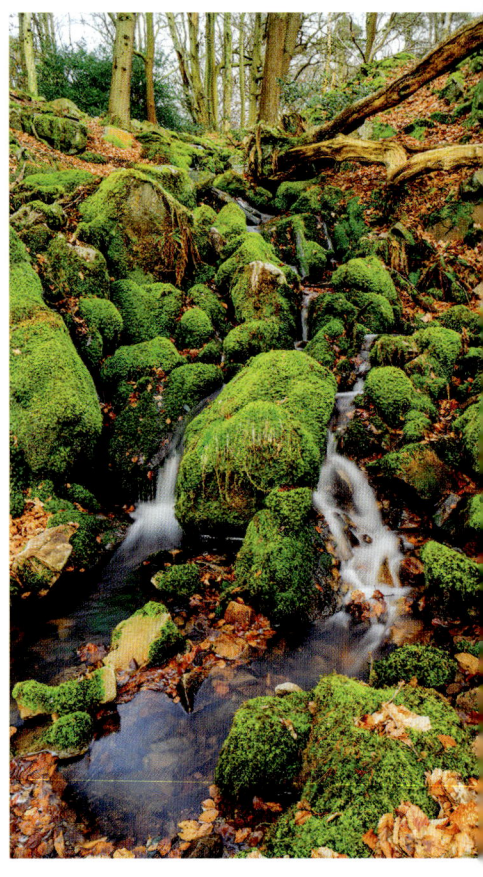

TRIPOD ⌃
Tripods are ideal for a wide variety of subjects, and are essential for longer exposures.
24mm, 2.5 sec., f/16, ISO 100, tripod.

» CAMERA CASES

A case is arguably essential for outdoor use. A simple drop-in pouch, worn on a waist-belt, is the most practical option. Makers include Think Tank Photo, Camera Care Systems, and LowePro. To carry a larger system, a backpack-type bag is kindest on your spine.

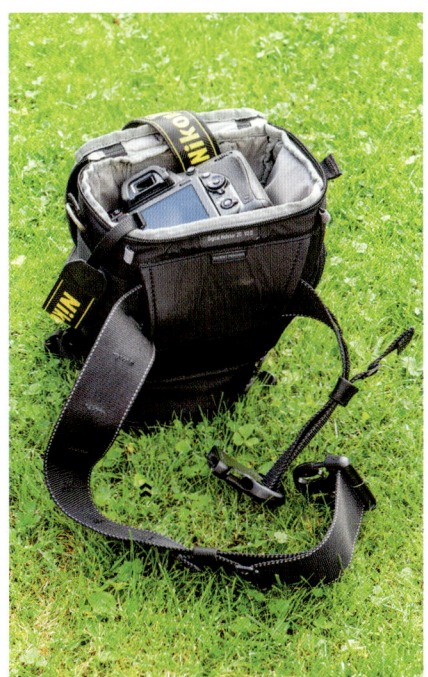

POUCH ⌃
A padded pouch (this one's by Think Tank Photo) combines good protection and easy access.

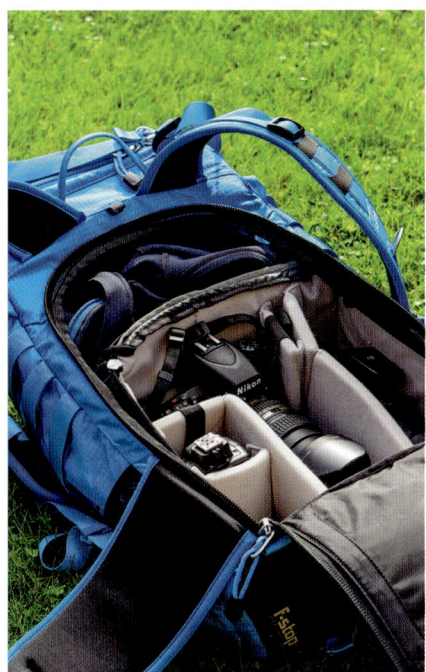

BACKPACK ⌃
Backpacks (this is an f-stop) are essential for carrying more gear and are best for the spine.

8

» STORING IMAGES

› Memory cards

The D750 stores images on Secure Digital (SD) cards, including SDHC and SDXC. Large-capacity cards with fast write speeds are recommended, and it's often advisable to carry spares.

Memory card performance is measured in various ways. Read speed applies mostly when transferring files to a computer. Write speed is what counts for in-camera performance, especially when shooting long continuous bursts or video. Cards of Class 6 or better are recommended for video and are equally good for stills.

› Backing up on the move

Memory cards rarely fail but it's always worth backing up valuable images as soon as possible. You can back up in-camera to Slot 2 (see page 103). On longer trips without regular computer access, you can use a mobile device for further backup. Dedicated photo storage devices are becoming rare, supplanted by laptops, smartphones, and tablets.

BACKING UP WHILE AWAY »
Backing up assumes even greater importance on trips far away from home.
50mm, 1/100 sec., f/11, ISO 250.

› Card care

If you lose or damage a memory card before downloading or backing up, your images are lost too. Blank cards are cheap but cards full of images are irreplaceable. SD cards are robust but it's still wise to treat them with care. Keep them in their original plastic cases, or something more substantial, and avoid exposure to extremes of temperature, direct sunlight, liquids, and strong electromagnetic fields. (Modern airport X-ray machines aren't harmful to cameras or memory cards.)

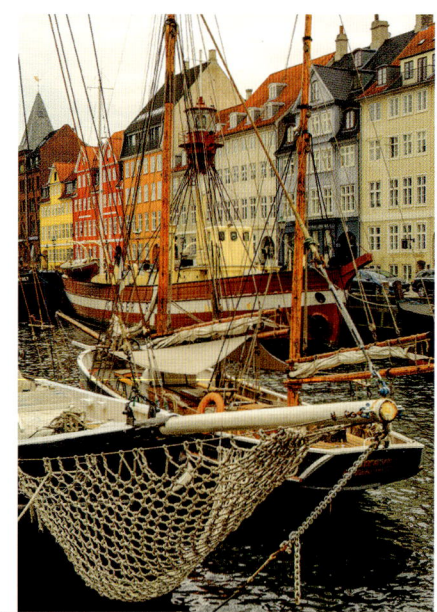

» CAMERA CARE

The D750 is a rugged camera, but still full of complex and potentially delicate electronic and optical technology. A few simple and common-sense precautions should help it keep functioning perfectly for many years.

› Basic care

The camera body can be cleaned by removing dust and dirt with a blower, then wiping with a soft, dry cloth. After exposure to salt spray, wipe off carefully with a cloth dampened with clean fresh water (ideally distilled water), then dry thoroughly.

If the rear screen needs cleaning, use a blower as above, then wipe the surface with a soft cloth or a swab designed for the purpose. Do not apply pressure and never use household cleaning fluids.

Warning!

*The Nikon manual (page 447) implies that the reflex mirror can be cleaned with a cloth and lens-cleaning fluid. This is dangerously misleading: **never touch the reflex mirror** in any way. It is extremely delicate. Remove dust from the mirror with gentle use of an air blower, and nothing else. The advice about using a cloth and fluid is only applicable to lenses (see page 197).*

› Cleaning the sensor

Strictly speaking, it's not the sensor itself but its protective low-pass filter that concerns us. Dust on this will appear as dark spots in your images.

Prevention (page 219) is better than cure but—unless you never change lenses—some dust will eventually get in. Fortunately, the D750 has a self-cleaning facility. This can be activated manually at any time or set to operate automatically when the camera is switched on and/or off: select options via **Clean Image Sensor** in the Setup menu.

Occasionally, stubborn spots may remain, making it necessary to clean the

SENSOR CLEANING   ❯❯
Cleaning the sensor requires confidence—and great care! Heavy-handed manual cleaning or the use of inappropriate products could void your warranty.

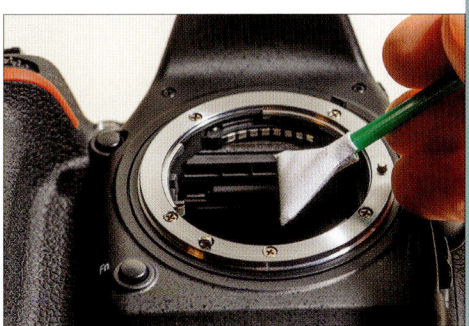

filter manually. Do this somewhere clean, draught-free, and well lit.

Ensure the battery is fully charged, or use a mains adapter. Remove the lens, switch the camera on, and select **Lock mirror up for cleaning** from the Setup menu (page 131). Press the shutter release to lock up the mirror. First, attempt to remove dust using a hand blower (**do not use** compressed air or any other aerosol). If this appears ineffective, consider using a dedicated cleaning swab, carefully following its instructions. **Do not** use other brushes or cloths and **never** touch the filter with your finger. When finished, turn the camera off and the mirror will reset.

> ### Tip
>
> *Spots on images can be removed in post-processing. In Nikon Capture NX-D this process can be automated using a Dust-off reference image (see page 131). Spot-removal can be applied across batches of images in Adobe Lightroom (page 229).*

ICE-SCAPE »
Winter conditions offer wonderful photographic opportunities but cameras may need a little extra care to protect them.
80mm, 1/30 sec., f/16, ISO 200, tripod.

› Cold

Nikon specify an operating temperature range of 32–104°F (0–40°C). When temperatures fall further, you can still use the camera, but aim to keep it within the specified range as far as possible. Keeping the camera in an insulated case or under your outer clothing between shots will help keep it warmer than the surroundings. If it does become chilled, battery life can be severely reduced (always carry a spare!). In extreme cold, the displays may become erratic or disappear, and ultimately the camera may cease to function. If allowed to warm up gently, no permanent harm should result.

› Heat and humidity

Extremes of heat and humidity (Nikon stipulate over 85%) can be even more problematic, and carry more risk of long-

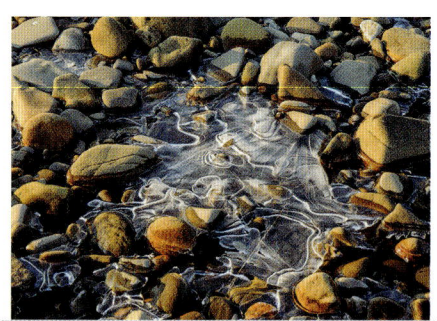

term damage. Rapid transfers from cool environments to hot and humid ones (air-conditioned hotel to sultry streets) can cause internal condensation. When anticipating such transitions, pack the camera and lens(es) in airtight containers with sachets of silica gel to absorb moisture. Allow equipment to reach ambient temperature before unpacking.

› Water

The D750 is reasonably weatherproof, so can be used with confidence in light rain. Keep exposure to a necessary minimum, and wipe regularly with a microfiber cloth (always handy to deal with accidental splashes). Ensure all access covers on the camera are closed, avoid using the built-in flash, and keep the hotshoe cover in place.

Take extra care around salt water. If contact does occur, clean carefully and immediately with a cloth lightly dampened with fresh, preferably distilled, water.

Ideally, protect the camera with a waterproof cover. A simple plastic bag will provide rudimentary protection, but purpose-made rain-guards give better protection and access to controls. Aquapac's reasonably priced DSLR case is a very snug fit for the D750, but can be used with a slimline lens.

› Dust

To minimize spots on images or the need for sensor cleaning (page 217), try to avoid dust entering the camera. Above all, take care when changing lenses. Aim the camera downward and stand with your back to the wind. In really bad conditions (such as sandstorms!) it's best not to change lenses at all, and better still to protect the camera with a waterproof, and therefore also dust-proof, case. Dust on the outside of the camera is relatively easy to remove; ideally, use a hand-operated or compressed air blower. Do this before changing lenses, memory cards, or batteries, keeping all covers closed until the camera is clean.

IN THE RAIN ❯❯
When people need waterproofs, your cameras may need them too.
100mm, 1/400 sec., f/2.8, ISO 400.

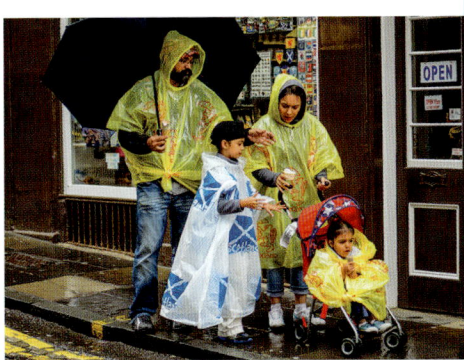

9 CONNECTION

Connecting to external devices enables you to store, organize, view and print your images. The Nikon D750 is designed to facilitate these operations, and a couple of useful cables are included with the camera.

» CONNECTING TO A COMPUTER

Connecting to a Mac or PC allows you to store, organize, and backup your images. It also helps you exploit the full power of the D750, including the ability to optimize image quality from RAW files.

› Computer requirements

The large file sizes produced by the D750 are demanding on processor speed, hard disk capacity, and memory (RAM), for which 4GB is a suggested baseline. Fortunately, for most systems adding extra RAM is relatively easy and inexpensive. Extra hard disk space can also be helpful, as the system will slow significantly when the hard disk becomes close to capacity. Photos eat up hard drive space and videos even more so.

The D750 supports USB3 for connecting the camera; this is backwards-compatible with USB2 but transfer speeds over USB2 will be slower. You can also use a card-reader (see page 222). A CD drive is no longer essential, as the supplied software can also be downloaded from

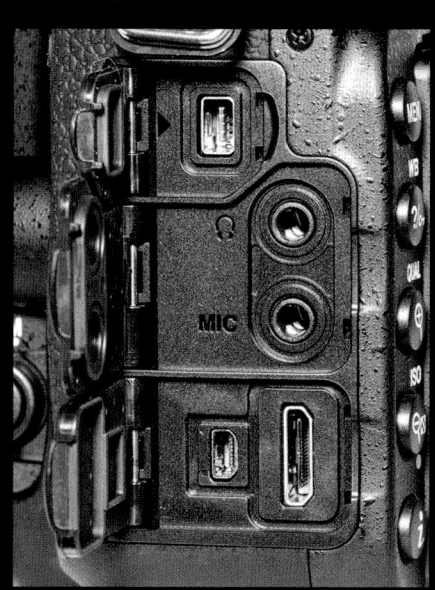

CONNECTING THE CAMERA ≈
Connection ports on the left side of the D750.

Nikon web sites. Of course, there are many alternative apps available for handling your images and video, as we'll see on pages 227–229.

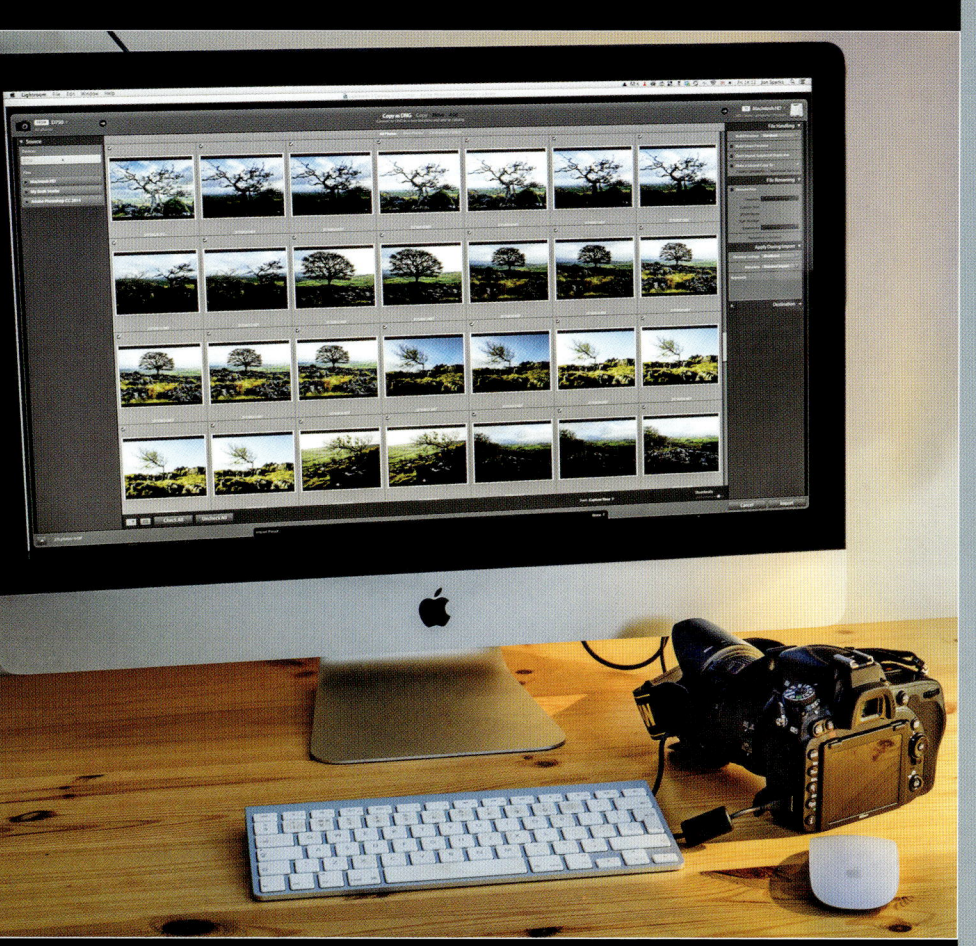

GETTING CONNECTED   ⌃
A D750 connected to a computer.

› Importing photos

The supplied USB cable allows direct connection to a computer, but when simply transferring photos and/or video, it's more convenient to use a card-reader. Many modern computers have built-in SD card slots.

The exact procedure for transferring images depends on the software you are using. Nikon Transfer, supplied along with View NX2, is simple to use and facilitates backup of photos during import, but if you're using an app like iPhoto or Lightroom (see page 229) to manage your photos, it makes sense to use this for import too.

Whatever software you use, there are several issues to consider, including whether to backup automatically on import. You also need to decide where on your hard drive(s) photos should be stored.

You may also wish to rename files as they are imported. With apps like Lightroom you can also apply keywords during import.

› Backing up

Without a backup, an image exists only as data on the camera's memory card (both cards, if you use Slot 2 for **Backup**—see page 103). When you transfer images to the computer and format the card(s) for reuse, those images again exist in just one location—the computer's hard drive. Any mishap to that hard drive—whether fire, theft, or hardware failure—could lose you thousands of irreplaceable images.

You can back up photos during import, but this means backing up duplicates, rejects, and other duds too, and you may well prefer to back up after weeding these

PLUGGED IN ⋁
Built-in SD card slot on a modern iMac.

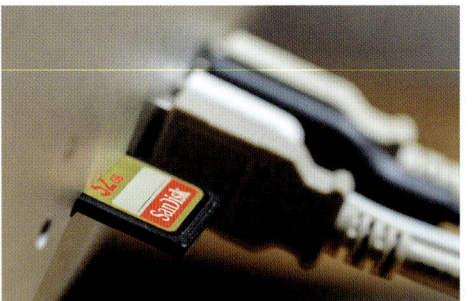

BACKING UP ⋁
Apple's Time Machine maintains file backups automatically.

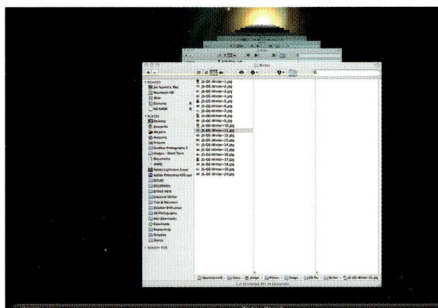

out in the initial edit. The simplest form of backup is to a second hard drive—the "gold standard" requires multiple drives, one always kept off-site.

Online backup is also an option, but free services offer limited space. Flickr now gives you an impressive 1TB, but commentators have questioned how secure it is against both data loss and image theft. Paid services give higher levels of security and Google Drive and Dropbox Pro have made them much more affordable.

CALIBRATING
Screen calibration in progress with a Datacolor Spyder4Express.

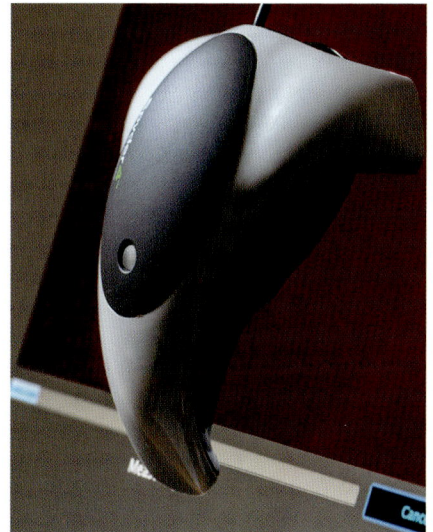

› Color calibration

A major headache for digital camera users is that images look one way on the camera monitor, different on your computer screen, different on a friend's screen, and different again when printed. To achieve consistency across different devices, it's vital above all that your main computer screen is correctly set up and calibrated. This appears time-consuming but ultimately saves much time and frustration.

Detailed advice is beyond the scope of this book but try searching System Help for "monitor calibration". There's more detail in the *Digital SLR Handbook* (from this author and publisher) and there's some useful advice at *www.cambridgeincolor. com/color-management-printing.htm*.

Onboard WiFi

The D750 is the first full-frame Nikon DSLR with onboard WiFi. This is welcome, but its capabilities are strictly limited. It will only connect to mobile devices (iOS or Android), not laptop or desktop computers. Wirelessly transferring images to a computer is easy with an Eye-Fi card but it's irritating that the onboard WiFi doesn't support it.

Further, Nikon's claim that you can "control the camera remotely" is wildly optimistic; you can set focus and trigger the shutter, but can't change any other settings. Finally, the WiFi doesn't work with movies.

Still, Nikon's Wireless Mobile Utility is very simple to set up (especially on iOS devices) and to use. The app allows you to view and transfer photos already on the camera, and to take new shots. However, because you can't change camera settings within the app, you need to ensure beforehand that all settings, including Live View focusing options (page 81) are as you want them.

In ⌖ Wide-area AF or ⌖ Normal-area AF, you can focus by tapping the subject on the device screen. You can't zoom in (as you can on the camera) for a precise focus check. However, the preview on an iPad or other tablet is significantly larger than the camera's screen, especially in landscape orientation.

ON THE MOVE «
Taking photos with Nikon Wireless Mobile Utility.

WATCH THE BIRDIE »
Remote shooting minimizes disturbance to shy subjects.
150mm, 1/250 sec., f/11, ISO 200.

Tethered shooting

Tethered shooting allows you to operate the D750 from an external device, and to transfer images directly. Nikon's Wireless Mobile Utility (above) is a rudimentary example. Other packages, like Nikon Camera Control Pro 2 (optional purchase) go much further.

Camera Control Pro 2 allows full control of the camera from a Mac or PC, integrating Live View for real-time viewing. However it requires either a physical (USB) connection or a very expensive network adapter kit (Nikon UT-1WK)—you can't use onboard WiFi. Lightroom, and several other apps also support tethered shooting via USB.

A more affordable solution for wireless shooting is the CamRanger, which supports Live View and control of all the main camera settings. It can link to iOS and Android devices as well as Mac and PC computers. It requires a short USB link to the camera but can connect wirelessly to the controlling device over a range of around 160ft (50m). It creates its own network so it can be used anywhere.

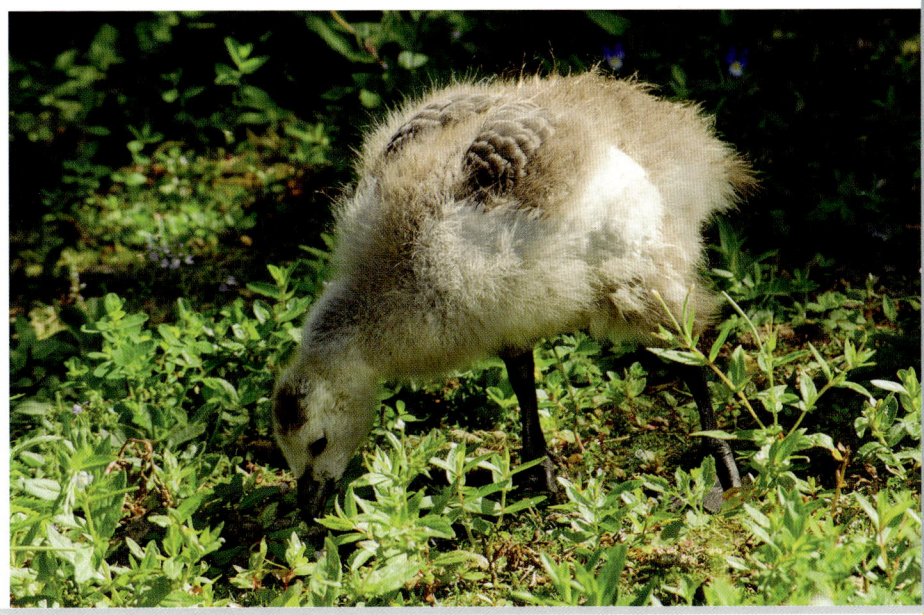

» SOFTWARE AND IMAGE PROCESSING

Most of us want to do more with our images than simply store them. Backing up, printing, organizing, and making our photographs look their best all require the right software.

Software choice depends partly on how you shoot. If you always shoot JPEG images, you may feel little need to tinker with them later, so organizing and cataloging will be your main priorities. If you shoot RAW files, on the other hand, image processing is essential—and gives you great freedom to adjust tone, color, and so on, to your liking.

› Nikon software

The D750 is bundled with Nikon View NX2 software. This includes the aforementioned Nikon Transfer. Nikon View NX2 itself covers several important processes: you can view and browse images, save them in other formats, and print. However, editing and enhancing images (including RAW files) is very slow, compared to iPhoto or Lightroom. View NX2 also doesn't support organizing and cataloging.

NIKON CAPTURE NX-D

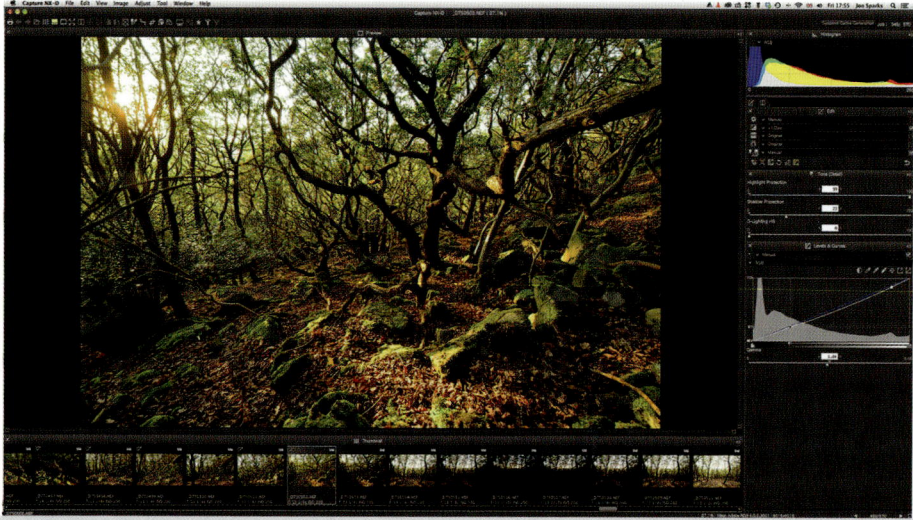

› Nikon Capture NX-D

Nikon Capture NX-D has recently supplanted Capture NX2. Some changes are welcome, including the price (it's free). It's more intuitive and seems faster. Editing is now non-destructive, and batch processing has been improved. However, many advanced tools have been removed from the program, and it is still no help with organizing and cataloging images.

› Third-party software

The undisputed market leader is Adobe Photoshop. Adobe has recently changed to a subscription model under the Creative Cloud label, which means that the software is continuously updated—but it will stop working if you don't keep up the subscription payments.

Photoshop's feature set is vast, and many users' needs are amply covered by the more affordable Photoshop Elements. It has sophisticated editing features, including the ability to open RAW files from the D750. Its Organizer module

ADOBE PHOTOSHOP CC　　　　　　　　❯❯

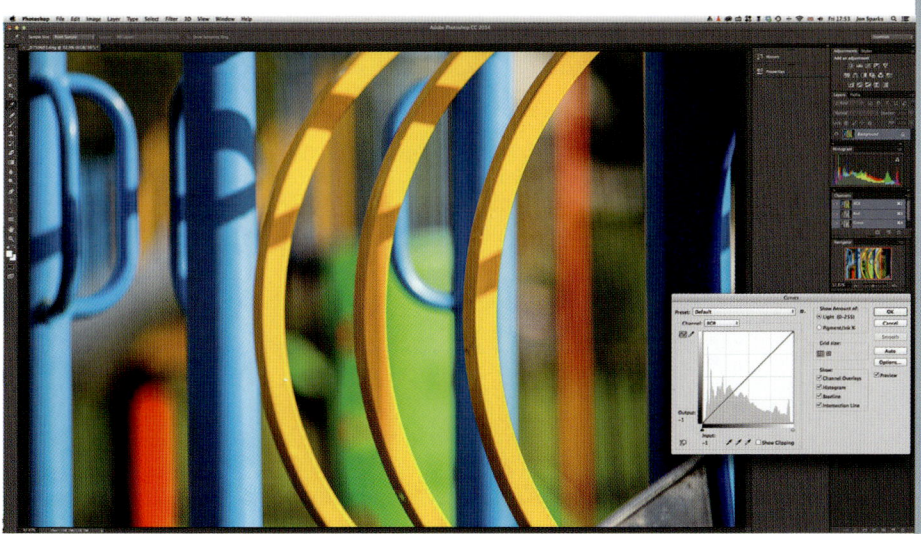

9

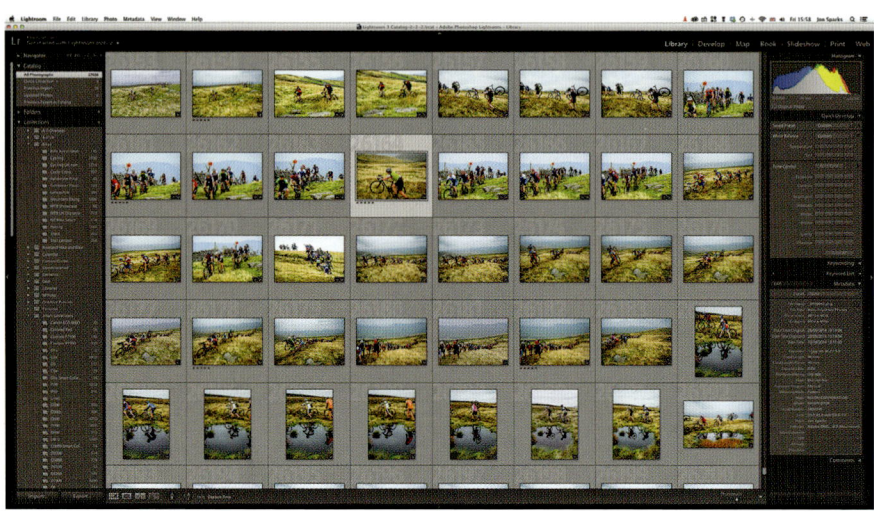

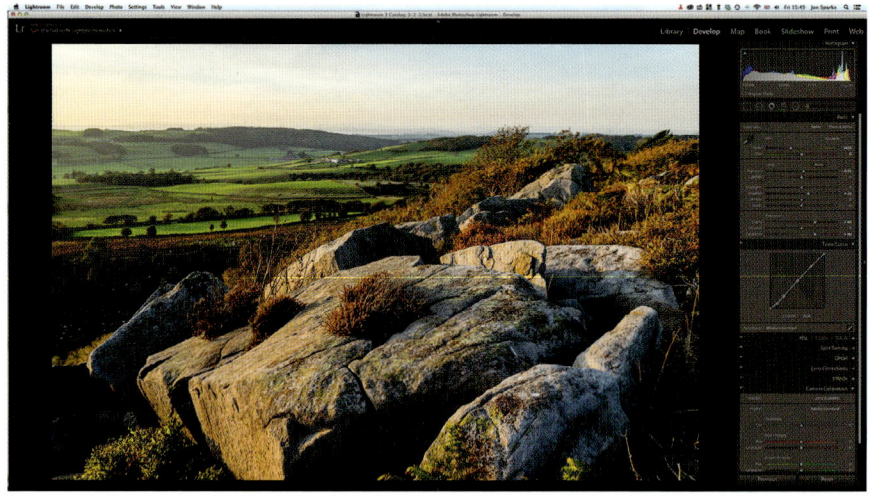

allows you to "tag" photos, assign them to "Albums", or add keywords. Elements is not part of Creative Cloud—you pay once for a perpetual licence to use the software, in the familiar way.

Many Mac users have been happy with the free iPhoto, which also unifies organizing and editing. However, Apple has announced that iPhoto (and Aperture) are being discontinued in favor of a single Photos app. It's not yet clear whether this will offer advanced features; comparisons with the existing Photos app for iOS

devices are not particularly encouraging. Complete integration of organizing and editing was pioneered by Apple's Aperture (Mac only) and Adobe Lightroom (Mac and PC). The imminent demise of Aperture leaves Lightroom in a near-monopoly position, although this may be challenged by Corel's AfterShot Pro.

Highly recommended, especially if you shoot RAW, Lightroom offers powerful organizing and cataloging, integrated with advanced image editing for seamless workflow. Editing is "non-destructive": all your edit settings—such as color balance, exposure, and cropping—are recorded alongside the original RAW (or DNG) file. TIFF or JPEG versions, embodying all your edits, can be exported when needed. A Creative Cloud photography subscription includes both Photoshop and Lightroom.

IN THE LIBRARY »
Adobe Lightroom's Library module.

RAW PROCESSING »
Adobe Lightroom's Develop module offers a very wide spectrum of RAW adjustments.

9 » GPS

Nikon's GP-1 or GP-1a GPS (Global Positioning System) units mount in the hotshoe or clip to the camera strap. They link to the camera's accessory terminal using a supplied cable. Certain other third-party GPS units can also be connected.

GPS units add information on latitude, longitude, altitude, heading, and time to image metadata. This is displayed as an extra page of photo info on playback and can be read by many imaging apps.

When the camera is connected to, and receiving data from, the GPS, **GPS** shows in the information display. If this flashes, the GPS is searching for a signal, and no data is recorded.

Set GPS options via **Location data** in the Setup menu as follows.

Standby timer

Disable stops the meters turning off and returning the camera to standby. This should ensure a stable connection to the GPS satellites. If you select **Enable**, the meters will turn off after 1 minute, saving battery power. However, next time you take a picture, the GPS receiver may not have time to get a fix, in which case no location data will be recorded.

Position

Displays the current information as reported by the GPS device.

Set clock from satelite

The GPS network embodies extremely accurate timing. Setting **Enable** should keep your camera clock bang on.

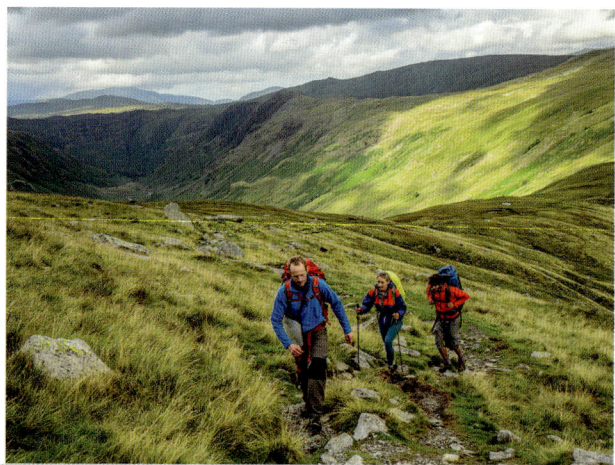

REFLECTION　》
In remote areas, the ability of a GPS unit to record locations precisely must be balanced against the extra drain on battery life.
28mm, 1/60 sec., f/11, ISO 400.

LOCATION, LOCATION　《
GPS information allows you to see exactly where your photographs were taken.
44mm, 1/400 sec., f/7.1, ISO 200.

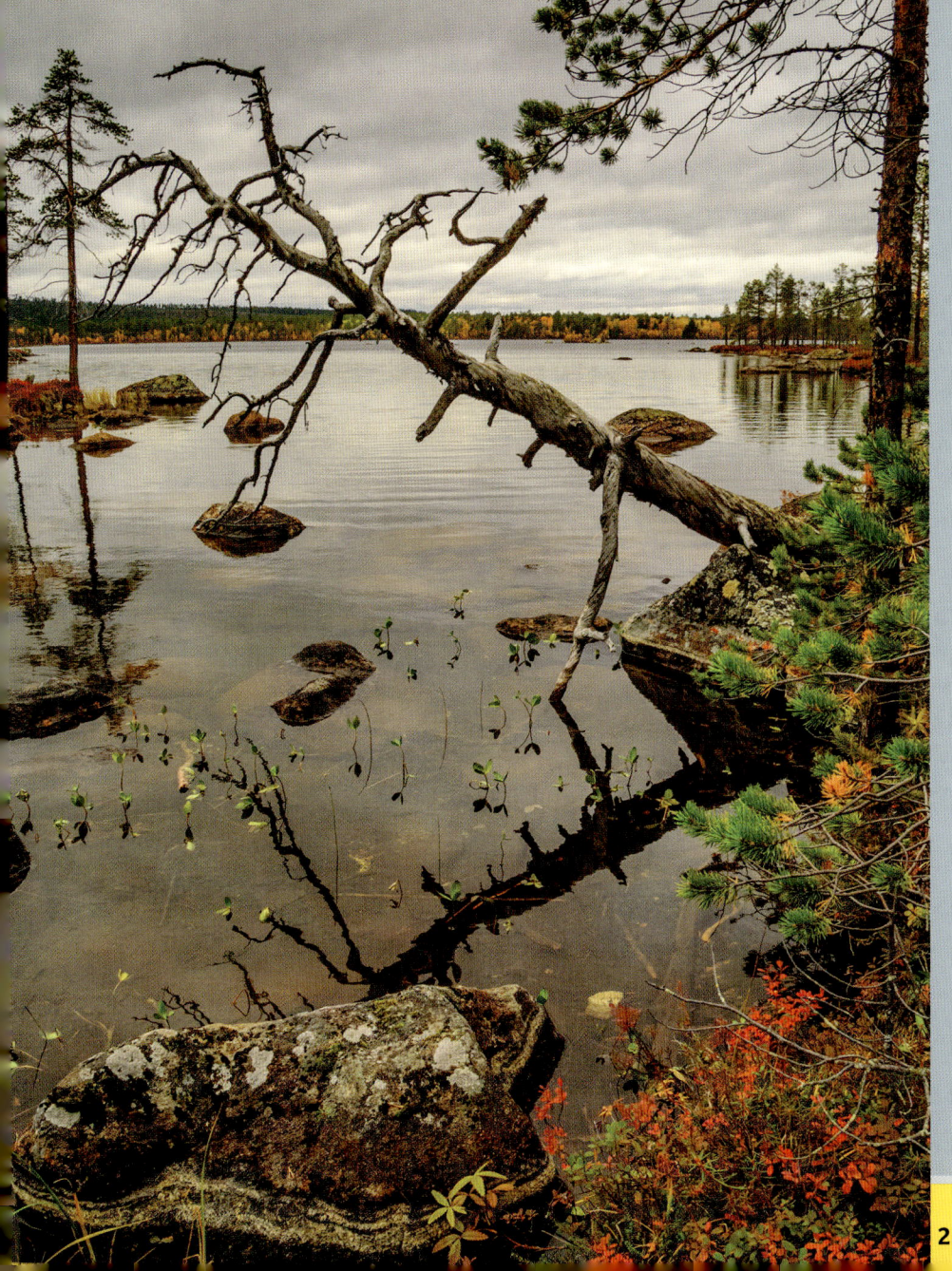

» CONNECTING TO A PRINTER

For maximum flexibility and control when printing, transfer photographs to a computer first. The procedure for printing will then depend on your operating system, imaging software, and the printer you are using. It's now also easy to print from iOS or Android devices.

At times you may still need to print directly from the camera or memory card. The memory card can be inserted into a compatible printer or taken to a photo printing store outlet. Alternatively, the camera can be connected to any printer that supports the PictBridge standard. Only JPEG files can be printed in this way. To print from RAW files, create JPEG copies first (see page 74).

When you connect directly to a compatible printer using the supplied USB cable and turn the camera on, the camera back displays a welcome screen, followed by a PictBridge playback display. You can choose between **Print pictures one at a time** or **Print multiple pictures**.

To print a single picture, select it in the usual way (page 85), then press (OK). This reveals a menu of printing options, including **Page size**, **No of copies** (1–99), **Border**, **Time stamp**, and **Crop**. Setting Crop options is similar to using Trim in the Retouch menu (page 139). Having set options, select **Start printing** and press (OK).

Print multiple pictures allows you to select pictures manually. Hold Q▦ and use ▲/▼ to set the number of copies. You can also create an **Index Print** of all JPEG images (up to a maximum of 256) on the memory card. **Select date** prints one copy of each picture taken on selected date(s). **Print (DPOF)** prints images already selected using **DPOF Print order (DPOF)** in the Playback menu (see page 101).

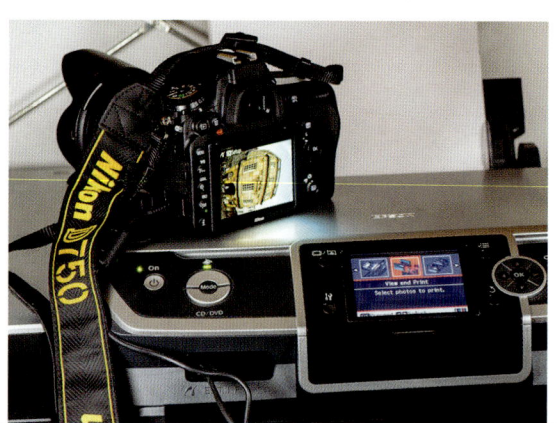

CONNECTING TO A PRINTER   «

» CONNECTING TO A TV

You can play photos and movie clips through an HDMI (High Definition Multimedia Interface) TV or set-top box.

1) Check settings via **HDMI** in the Setup menu (see page 136).

2) Turn the camera off (always do this before connecting or disconnecting the cable).

3) Open the HDMI cover on the left-hand side of the camera and insert the cable into the slot. Connect the other end to the TV.

4) Tune the TV to an HDMI channel.

5) Turn the camera on and press ▶. Images remain visible on the camera monitor as well as on the TV and you navigate using the multi-selector in the usual way. You can use **Slide show** (Playback menu, see page 101) to automate playback.

> **Note:**
> A mains adapter is recommended for lengthy playback sessions. No harm should result if the camera's battery expires during playback, but it is annoying.

SHARING MEMORIES ⌄
Connection to a TV makes it easy to share your pictures and movies with family and friends.
50mm, 1/100 sec., f/11, ISO 200.

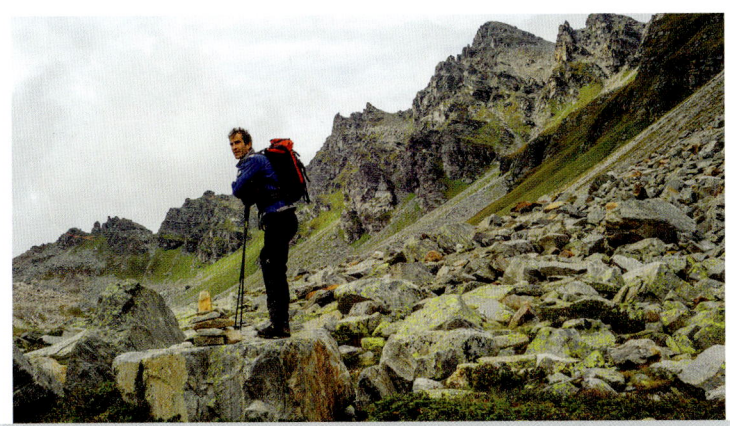

» GLOSSARY

8-bit, 14-bit, 16-bit *See Bit depth.*

Aperture The lens opening which admits light. Relative aperture sizes are expressed in f-number (*see f-number*).

Artifact Occurs when data or data produced by the sensor is interpreted incorrectly, resulting in visible flaws in the image.

Bit depth The amount of information recorded for each color channel. 8-bit, for example, means that the data distinguishes 2^8 or 256 levels of brightness for each channel. 16-bit images recognize over 65,000 levels per channel, which allows greater freedom in editing. The D750 records RAW images in 12- or 14-bit depth and they are converted to 16-bit on import to the computer.

Bracketing Taking a number of otherwise identical shots in which just one parameter (e.g. exposure) is varied.

Buffer On-board memory that holds images until they can be written to the memory card.

Burst A number of frames shot in quick succession; the maximum burst size is limited by buffer capacity.

CCD (charge-coupled device) A type of image sensor used in many digital cameras.

Channel The D750, like other digital devices, records data for three separate color channels (*see RGB*).

Clipping Complete loss of detail in highlight or shadow areas of the image (sometimes both), leaving them as blank white or black.

CMOS (Complementary Metal Oxide Semiconductor) A type of image sensor used in many digital cameras, including the D750.

Color temperature The color of light, expressed in degrees Kelvin (K). Confusingly, "cool" (bluer) light has a higher color temperature than "warm" (red) light.

CPU (Central Processing Unit) A small computer in the camera (also found in many lenses) that controls most or all of the unit's functions.

Crop factor *See Focal length multiplication factor.*

Diopter Unit expressing the power of a lens.

dpi (dots per inch) A measure of resolution—should strictly be applied only to printers (*see ppi*).

Dynamic range The range of brightness from shadows to highlights within which the camera can record detail.

Exposure Used in several senses. For instance, "an exposure" is virtually synonymous with "an image" or "a photo': to make an exposure = to take a picture. Exposure also refers to the amount of light hitting the image sensor, and to systems of measuring this. *See also Overexposure, Underexposure.*

EV (Exposure Value) A standardized unit of exposure. 1 Ev is equivalent to 1 "stop" in traditional photographic parlance.

Extension rings/Extension tubes Hollow tubes which fit between the camera tube and lens, used to allow greater magnifications.

f-number Lens aperture expressed as a fraction of focal length; f/2 is a wide aperture and f/16 is narrow.

Fast Lens with a wide maximum aperture, e.g. f1.8; f/4 is relatively fast for long telephotos.

Fill-in flash Flash used in combination with daylight. Used with naturally backlit or harshly side-lit subjects to prevent dark shadows.

Filter A piece of glass or plastic placed in front of, within, or behind the lens to modify light.

Firmware Software which controls the camera. Upgrades are issued by Nikon from time to time and can be transfered to the camera via a memory card.

Focal length The distance (in mm) from the optical center of a lens to the point at which light is focused.

Focal length multiplication factor In DX-crop mode, the image area is smaller than a 35mm film frame, so the effective focal length of all lenses is multiplied by a factor of 1.5.

fps (frames per second) The number of exposures (photographs) that can be taken in a second. The D750's maximum rate is 5–7fps (depending on Image size and power source).

Highlights The brightest areas of the scene and/or the image.

Histogram A graph representing the distribution of tones in an image, ranging from pure black to pure white.

ISO (International Standards Organisation) ISO ratings express film speed and the sensitivity of digital sensors is quoted as ISO-equivalent.

JPEG (from Joint Photographic Experts Group) A compressed image file standard. High levels of JPEG compression can reduce files to about 5% of their original size, but not without some loss of quality.

LCD Liquid Crystal Display Flat screen, like the D750's rear monitor.

Macro A term used to describe close focusing and close-focusing ability of a lens. A true macro lens has a reproduction ratio of 1:1 or better.

Megapixel See Pixel.

Memory card A removable storage device for digital cameras.

Noise Image interference manifested as random variations in pixel brightness and/or color.

Overexposure When too much light reaches the sensor, resulting in a too-bright image, often with clipped highlights.

Pixel (picture element) The individual colored dots (usually square) which make up a digital image. One million pixels = 1 megapixel.

Post-processing Adjustment to images on computer after shooting. Can cover anything from minor tweaks of brightness or color to extensive editing.

Prime lens Lens with a single fixed focal length, e.g. 50mm.

ppi (pixels per inch) Should be applied to digital files rather than the commonly used dpi.

Reproduction ratio The ratio between the real size of an object and the size of its image on the sensor.

Resolution The number of pixels for a given dimension, for example, 300 pixels per inch. Resolution is often confused with *image size*. The native size of an image from the D750 is 6016 x 4016 pixels; this could make a large but coarse print at 100dpi or a smaller but finer one at 300dpi.

RGB (red, green, blue) Digital devices, including the D750, record color in terms of brightness levels of the three primary colors.

Sensor The light-sensitive chip at the heart of every digital camera.

Shutter The mechanism that controls the amount of light reaching the sensor by opening and closing to expose the sensor when the shutter-release button is pushed.

Speedlight Nikon's range of dedicated external flashguns.

Spot metering A metering system which takes its reading from the light reflected by a small portion of the scene.

Telephoto lens A lens with a long focal length and a narrow angle of view.

TIFF (Tagged Image File Format) A universal file format supported by virtually all image-editing applications.

TTL (through the lens) The viewing and metering of SLR cameras, including the D750.

Underexposure When insufficient light reaches the sensor, resulting in a too-dark image, often with clipped shadows.

USB (Universal Serial Bus) A data transfer standard, used to connect to a computer.

Viewfinder An optical system used for framing the image. On an SLR camera, such as the D750, it shows the view as seen through the lens.

White balance A function which compensates for different color temperatures so that images may be recorded with correct color balance.

Wideangle lens A lens with a short focal length and a wide angle of view.

Zoom A lens with variable focal length, giving a range of viewing angles. To *zoom in* is to change focal length to give a narrower view, and to *zoom out* is the converse. *Optical zoom* refers to the genuine zoom ability of a lens; *digital zoom* is the cropping of part of an image to produce an illusion of the same effect.

» USEFUL WEB SITES

NIKON-RELATED SITES

Nikon Worldwide
Home page for the Nikon Corporation
www.nikon.com

Nikon UK
Home page for Nikon UK
www.nikon.co.uk

Nikon USA
Home page for Nikon USA
www.nikonusa.com

Nikon User Support
European Technical Support Gateway
www.europe-nikon.com

Nikon Historical Society
Worldwide site for study of Nikon products
www.nikonhs.org

Grays of Westminster
Revered Nikon-only London dealer
www.graysofwestminster.co.uk

GENERAL SITES

Digital Photography Review
Independent news and reviews
www.dpreview.com

Thom Hogan
Real-world reviews and advice
www.bythom.com/nikon.htm

Jon Sparks
Landscape and outdoor pursuits photography
www.jon-sparks.co.uk

EQUIPMENT

Adobe
Photoshop, Photoshop Elements, Lightroom
www.adobe.com/uk

Aquapac
Waterproof cases
www.aquapac.net

f-stop
Backpacks and accessories
http://fstopgear.com

Sigma
Independent lenses and flash units
www.sigma-imaging-uk.com

CamRanger
Remote camera control
http://camranger.com

PHOTOGRAPHY PUBLICATIONS

Photography books
Ammonite Press
www.ammonitepress.com

***Black & White Photography* magazine,
Outdoor Photography magazine**
www.thegmcgroup.com